MW00436661

# I Believe in Miracles

*Do You?*

## Paula Weidenkopf Welsh

ISBN 978-1-0980-5980-4 (paperback)
ISBN 978-1-0980-5981-1 (hardcover)
ISBN 978-1-0980-5982-8 (digital)

Copyright © 2020 by Paula Weidenkopf Welsh

All rights reserved. No part of this publication may be reproduced, distributed, or transmitted in any form or by any means, including photocopying, recording, or other electronic or mechanical methods without the prior written permission of the publisher. For permission requests, solicit the publisher via the address below.

Christian Faith Publishing, Inc.
832 Park Avenue
Meadville, PA 16335
www.christianfaithpublishing.com

Printed in the United States of America

To my children, Grace, Mitchell, Chandler and Genevieve. Dream as big as you can. Always be aware of God's blessings and miracles He has already bestowed upon you. Remember God lives in our hearts and souls. Always remain faithful, hopeful and grateful.

# Acknowledgments

My sister Karen for all the endless conversations about my book. You took so much time out of your life to edit and research the authors of my favorite quotes. Little did I know, my lack of forethought gave you something to do in your spare time, haha. I wish I could say I learned from my mistakes, but my phone is filled again with quotes that I jot down in a hurry!

My sister Ruth your visit couldn't have come at a better time for many reasons. Thank you for helping me implement all of Kim's suggestions. Your eagerness and tireless spirit was contagious and exactly what I needed to make all the changes happen.

Tracy, for opening up your home to Karen and I, we were able to stay in a cozy home those first couple of nights in Fresno. I know Karen and I looked forward to your almost daily visits to the hospital. Your presence seemed to lighten the mood, change the subject, and bring comfort to us. I will always hold a special place in my heart for you.

Pat, I am eternally grateful for the gifts you gave me. The first one were the keys to your condo. I had a quaint place to retreat to, and it housed so many family and friends that traveled to see me. The second gift was encouragement. From very early on, you believed my journaling was book worthy. Thank you!

Katie, for reading my manuscript and giving me such good advice. And little did you know that dropping by Jeannie Gaffigans, *When Life Gives You Pears*, that Sunday evening because she reminded you of me, started a fire under my you-know-what!

Susie, taking on the task of transcribing our speeches. You so graciously volunteered to help and it came at a time when I was wondering how to conquer that daunting task.

Thank you from the bottom of my heart.

Susan, you have cheered me on from the minute I mentioned I wanted to write a book. I have appreciated all of your encouragement and am eternally grateful for your friendship. Also, thanks for volunteering your hubby, Jim.

Jim, for your descriptions and explanation of the Coso energy plant. I know you worked hard and took time out of your life for me. Thank you for putting up with my critiquing and getting all the particulars to read the way I wanted.

Jamie, my first friend I made when I moved to Big Bear in eighth grade. You willingly volunteered to edit my book too. Your support, ideas, and love of my manuscript and God was the incentive I needed to keep pressing on.

Theresa, for taking time out of your life for me and my memoir. Your monthly visits were so fulfilling and the motivation I needed to keep persevering. Our common love for God and our Catholic faith made our visits even more rewarding. I am eternally grateful for your guidance and friendship.

Kim—thanks for pulling more reflections out of my brain. Your inspiring suggestions helped me put the finishing touches on my labor of love. I now have the love and support of a lifelong friend sprinkled through my memoir.

Donna and Judie—letting Karen's little punk–a#& sister tag along all these years. Your friendship, prayers, and support have meant the world to me. All the laughter and tears have been the best therapy.

To all those that signed the CaringBridge Guestbook—I wish I could have kept all the entries, but unfortunately, the book would have been a thousand pages.

It was not easy deciding on which ones would stay but please know you and your thoughtful words are not forgotten.

Last but not least, I want to thank my family and friends for their prayers and support they showed to me during a trying time. God has continued to show me countless miracles. Life is still full of surprises, but with all of your unending love, I am able to conquer whatever may come my way.

My main goal, hope, or inspiration for writing this book was so that when you are faced with your own challenges, whatever they may be, you will turn to prayer; and if you still feel overwhelmed, you will reach out to family and friends for more prayer. As you can see by all my acknowledgements I always have had a faith-filled village supporting me. As far as I know, I don't believe anyone has overdosed on prayer.

> *Prayer is not one occupation among many,*
> *but is at the center of our life in Christ. It*
> *turns our attention away from ourselves and*
> *directs it to the Lord. Prayer fills the mind with*
> *truth and gives hope to the heart. Without a*
> *deep experience of prayer, growth in the moral*
> *life will be shallow. (Pope John Paul II)*
> —Johnnette Benkovic, *Experience*
> *Grace in Abundance*

# My Decision to Share

Before my husband, Mark's, accident, if anyone would have told me I would be writing a book in my forties, I would've said they were crazy. I don't even like to read that much. But here I am, about to pour out my life on these pages because life can take you by surprise, change in an instant, and take you on a journey that you never could've imagined.

So to give you an idea where and how this story began and all started, I had my good friend Jim write up a few pages about Coso Operating Plant. Then with the help of my friend Katie, it was pared down so that it didn't sound too scientificky (that's a word, right?). This journey of miracles all started approximately fifty miles north and west of Ridgecrest, California in Hell's Kitchen—what they call the site where Mark was burned. It is where the Navy drilled the first Coso geothermal test well.[1] That should tell you something about geothermal energy and the surrounding areas where it is produced. Coso, like most of California, is a seismically active area. The tectonic plates on either side of the San Andreas fault slide in opposite directions. This forms a strike-slip fault. Movement along this type of fault causes the rock on either side to bunch up in places and thin out in others. Think of putting your hands next to each other on a tablecloth and sliding one toward you and the other away. Pull on it hard enough and the seams will even start to separate, creating weak spots. In regions like Coso, where the surface has been stretched and fractured, molten rock (magma) from the interior of the earth can rise closer to the surface.

---

[1.] *Land Use History of Coso Hot Springs* ( Inyo County, California, Naval Weapons Center Administrative Publication 200, 1979), 233.

Look up Coso Hot Springs in an app where you can view satellite photos (Google Earth is a good one). Keep it zoomed out so that Little Lake (on Highway 395) is on the southern edge and Haiwee is on the northern edge. You won't see any towns or cities. Coso Junction is the biggest development in the area and it's just a gas station and some mobile homes. But you will see some round features that are small volcanoes and lava flows from the big volcanoes. These were all recently active (geologically speaking), around two to four million years ago, and again possibly forty thousand years ago. The lava that was hot enough to liquefy is now cold. But just below the surface, it's another story.

Coso is in a rough volcanic mountainous area within a Navy base where things are blown up nearly every day. You're not going to see anything that indicates people are around until you zoom into the geothermal plant (A search for "geothermal near Coso, California" will get you there). Then you'll see the network of roads that follow these pipelines from the production wells to the power plants and then to the injection wells. Most of the workers drive at least an hour from Ridgecrest just to get there. Then they spend their twelve-hour shift working next to all that explosive power contained by a complex system of pipes and valves. Any weakness will be found by the hot pressurized water. It could quickly blow open a hole, which is easily noticed, the line shut down, and repaired. Or it could slowly drip, softening and heating the ground around it without changing its appearance. This was the type of leak Mark found May 30th, 2009 during his lonely rounds on the pipeline roads. He found it when the solid ground he was walking on turned to scalding mud in one step and he dropped in up to his chest.

In September 2012, I was asked to speak at Coso's third annual safety conference that was to take place on January 2013, in Las Vegas. They wanted me to talk about how a tragedy that was accidental affected my family. I agreed because life had come full circle, and I felt there would be meaning and purpose to my story.

Over the course of a few weeks, while I was preparing my speech, I was having an out-of-body experience. I knew I wanted to speak, needed to speak, but I was worried that my story would not flow. English composition is not my strong suit. I worried it would be disjointed and I would sound like an idiot. I started feeling like I was going to break out in hives. I got a huge cold sore on my lip. It didn't help that Mark was baffled at my nervousness. He kept asking me, "What's your problem?" He told me it was my story and I could not go wrong in telling it. I wasn't making it up. There was no right or wrong way in telling it. I prayed a lot during that time. I was feeling pretty calm on the day we traveled to Las Vegas. I fine-tuned some areas in my speech.

But on Wednesday, my nerves were shot again. When I walked into the conference room, there was no podium. I wanted to die. I really thought I would be able to hide behind something so that if I fidgeted, no one would notice.

The men at the conference later told me I did not sound nervous. Little did I know that my friend Susan's fifth grade class was praying the rosary for me at the exact time of my speech. When I listened to my recorded speech later, I did not sound nervous.

While I was preparing to write my speech, I researched some books to help me prepare; and what I noticed, there was a common thread. Many of the books said the same thing. I soon realized it would be okay if I was to say something that has been said before. Hearing about miracles, faith-filled experiences, and words of encouragement gave more meaning to my faith.

I wanted to talk about faith, family, and, most importantly, miracles. My story needed to be told. I thought that even if I got one person to think about safety differently, it would be worth it. It wasn't about Mark's employer but about the people we might touch with our story.

I found myself standing in a ballroom in Las Vegas, at the annual safety convention kick-off, in front of about fifty people from Coso and Terra Gen, the company that owned Coso at the time.

*Paula's Speech*

So I did a dry run with my speech on Monday with my girlfriends. I've been so nervous about doing this. I've never done anything like this before. Mark kept asking, "What's the big deal? You talk all the time!" But I think it's a little different.

I want to thank you for allowing us to share our experience. I want to tell you a bit about myself. I'm the youngest of seven. My parents were married for 53 years before my dad died in 2010. My mom and dad lived at our house for 42 days; my children got to live with their grandpa for 42 days. Little did we know, a year later, he would die. So, I'm eternally grateful to them. I'm a cradle Catholic. I'm involved in our local parish at Saint Ann's in Ridgecrest, California where I went to school. Mark and I were married there almost 21 years ago. We have four children. Grace, she's 19; Mitchell, 16; Chandler, 14; and our youngest Genevieve is 5. The three oldest have gone kindergarten through 8th grade at St. Ann's. Our youngest will start kindergarten there in August. I worked there for the last five years and off-and-on. To say Saint Ann's is our extended family, would be putting it lightly. It is where I have met so many of my faith-filled friends.

When Mark was burned on that morning, our priest requested prayers for him during the 5:30 p.m. Mass that night, and so the many chains of prayers began. So, for me, preparing for this speech got me thinking about that tragic day, now almost four years ago. I decided I needed to reread my Caring Bridge journal website and all the uplifting posts. I was a little apprehensive to read my posts. I had not looked in the journal for more than three years. I was a little worried about the feelings it would stir up inside—and it did stir them up. Some tears were shed but that was soon followed by laughter.

Most of you might not know that even though what happened to Mark shook me up, my faith was still intact—and so was my silly and sarcastic personality and sometimes very warped sense of humor. So, I had heard about this Caring Bridge website earlier in the year, and when all the phone calls started coming in that Saturday evening, I thought that I needed a better means of communication. Caring Bridge was set up the next day. For a moment, I thought I shouldn't share. It would be sad, it would be overwhelming for me to write it, and then overwhelming for people to read it. Boy, am I glad that thought did not last long. I did not realize that journaling would be so therapeutic for me. Reading the responses of prayers and comforting words would give me the strength and courage to go to the hospital every day and cheer Mark on. I felt so connected. Even though I was away from family and friends, I definitely was not going through this alone. Over a thousand entries were made during that time. I am eternally grateful for each and every one. To give you an idea of my state of mind, I will read my very first entry just 36 hours after Mark was burned and the aftermath of outpouring love that followed after my first entry…

May 31ˢᵗ, 2009

We are grateful for so many things. This website, critical care nurses and doctors C-crew and all of the Coso family—my family and friends near and far. Here it goes. At approximately 4:58 a.m., Saturday May 30ᵗʰ Mark was checking a large sump near an area known as East Flank. A leak had sprung. The ground looked stable but as Mark got closer he fell into a hole filled with 140 degree brine. By the grace of God he was able to lift himself out. He called April at the control room—his radio still working despite being submerged. Another miracle—he ran 100 feet to the shower. Friend and coworker Israel was the first to respond. He transported him to the control room to meet the ambulance. Mark was coherent the whole time. Mercy Air flew him from Coso Junction to Fresno Community Trauma Burn Center at 6:20 a.m.. April called me at 5:45 a.m.—what a call to receive and even a lot to process. The first time I was able to talk to Mark was around 8:30 a.m.. He told me he was fine and not to worry, that everything was going to be okay. I did not believe a word of it. Shortly after that he went into a five-hour surgery. Dr. Dominic and Dr. Bhakta cleaned up the wounds and began a tedious task of allografting. That's attaching strips of cadaver tissue with staples and the strips were like 2 inches by 4 inches and they started at his chest and upper arms all the way down to his feet. It was like a patchwork quilt. They had to put 8 staples in each little piece of tissue. Meanwhile my sister Karen and I were driving to Fresno. It was taking forever to get there. We arrived at 1 p.m. and went straight to the burn center. Mark's nurse explained what was going on, then we waited until 2 p.m. to speak to the doctors. I was finally able to see Mark at 4 p.m.. He was trying to sit up and was a little confused. The emergency response training in him was making him recreate the accident. "I'm trying to orient myself, I'm trying to orient myself." His pain level was at a four. I had to tell him gently that he didn't have to be in pain and that the medicine was there to help him get to a zero. He has continued to stay ahead of his pain and is being a great patient. He is peaceful and blurts out things when we think he is not listening. My siblings, Karen, Ann, and Vince, brother-in-law, Doug, had been with me the whole time. Nobody ever prepares you for this. The texts, the emails, and messages are very comforting for me. Everybody is rooting for him. When I walked in this morning he was sitting up and eating breakfast with his hands. It is very important he eats a lot of protein because of a hyper metabolism from the burn wound. He also has a feeding tube for giving him proteins and vitamins along with an IV of Vitamin C concentrate. It is necessary for the collagen formation and tissue repair. He also has an IV of fluids to help with dehydration and swelling. We pray that his body does not reject the tissue. The swelling and dehydration is controlled and the lungs stay clear. We are beyond blessed with the supportive network. We feel the love and prayers. Please keep them coming! Paula and family

**Two hours later—8 p.m. Okay, I forgot one minor detail. He is burned over 73% of his body with second degree burns. No 3$^{rd}$ degree burns at this time. His toes and the pads of his feet were spared, so he will be able to tip toe back to recovery. Another miracle. Bye for now kiss kiss love love (KKLL), Paula**

When I was journaling on Caring Bridge I had no idea the impact of my words until I was home and friends and family told me they looked forward to my daily entries. People couldn't wait to read about Mark's recovery process and what I was going to say.

Even though it has been at the back of my mind to tell my story, I would just daydream about it, visualize it but never took any action to put pen to paper. I didn't think my story was interesting enough to tell.

I want people around the world to see the humanity, kindness, and love that was shown to us. I often wonder where I would be without friends, family, and genuine companionship. I don't think I would be here writing, a few years later.

This has been a journey that has made me reflect on my marriage, children, family, friends, faith, and the true meaning of the word, "*miracle.*"

While I was preparing to write this book, I started reading *52 Mondays* to motivate me and lead me down the right path. I wanted my book to be able to relate to faith, marriage, friendship, and hard times.

I talked a lot about writing the book but didn't get started until late April 2013. I originally gave myself a timeframe of a year. I had the idea that at my weekly adoration hour at the chapel I would read my daily entries and responses then reflect and journal my thoughts and ideas from each of those entries (made four years earlier) and how they relate to and affect me today.

So as I started reading my very first entry (and the guest entries) I started to cry. The love that was poured out to us in such comforting words was very overwhelming. We were blessed by phone calls, cards, emails, etc. I want everyone to know what a huge impact it made in our lives by those who reached out to us while we were bearing our cross.

I had friends at my house by 7:00 a.m. on the day he was burned, helping me pack, helping me figure out where my children would go and basically keeping me calm as I was preparing for my four hour trip. Some were telling me how courageous I was. I sure didn't feel that way but it was comforting that they saw me that way.

So many miracles were already happening it was hard to keep track of them all. Keys to a condo, just 20 minutes away from the hospital; world-renowned doctor who specialized in treating burns; God knew what He was doing when Mark was being flown to Fresno. All this talk of bravery and courage was starting to make sense when you think of all the friends and family and strangers that were taking time out of their day to pray for us. Who wouldn't feel like they could conquer anything?

So many of my friends, family and, most importantly the Holy Spirit have cheered me on. I didn't want to let anyone of them down, which led me to get started. So, let's see where the Holy Spirit takes my thoughts.

Many friends volunteered to read the first rough draft of my book and make corrections. Others have volunteered to go with me on my book signing tour! My friends knew I would need an accountant and stylist so they were eager to see my book come to fruition.

I do believe that talking about a goal to those you love and trust can boost your motivation. Although I am sure some were sick of me talking about it and wanted me to just get it finished. But everyone has negative voices in their heads that keep them from achieving personal goals and dreams. I had to ignore mine several times and re-boot my energy and keep on writing.

The daily journaling started as a means of communication for loved ones near and far. I had no idea the joy it would bring to look at the guest book each day. I loved hearing how my children were doing, (Genevieve was only 1 ½ at the time); how the world was doing; what Mark's co-workers were up to. We didn't pick this tragedy but we were getting prayed for across the world, with well-wishes, outpouring love, and uplifting words of encouragement. Many guest entries were inspiring to others and many thanked me for all my posts.

After I posted my first entry on the Caring Bridge website, the following guest entries flooded the portal which spurred me on to keep journaling about Mark's journey and recovery:

Dear Paula, Mark & family,

Just a note to say how sorry we are to hear about Mark's accident—it is just unbelievable!! You are all in our thoughts & prayers—hope you have a quick recovery & do not have too much pain. Know that we love you & if there is anything we can do, please let us know. I am in touch with your Mom, so have been updated. Take care & God Bless you all! Love & Hugs, Dorothy & Tom

Dear Mark, Paula and Kids,

Just wanted to send my prayers your way. I feel like I know you all so well, as Amy always keeps me up to date on what is happening with her family. I know that God will help you all through this difficult time. Remember He never gives us more then we can handle! Keep the faith and your chin up. You will get through this and come out even stronger than before.

Sending Hugs your way. Love, Jo Elaine

Dear Daddy

sdfjkewruiopwerwe9+rewrfsfhewrdslasfbn-vbnmxcvnmvcxmndsfhreuyqrtewyreytreytgdhfg gfhsdgfhjsdgfsdhfgdhgsdjfgsdfhgsdhfd

Love
Your loving Daughter
Genevieve

Dear Dad,

I hope you make through this. I will always be there for you. All my friends and family will be there. Your a great warrior. I hope you heal soon.

Love, your caring son Mitchell

Mark & Paula & kids, of course,

Dorothy called about 5 p.m. tonight with the news of Mark's major body burn. I am so glad that you contacted us through CaringBridge.

I don't know much about the details, but I do know that it is important to keep ahead of the pain—with whatever it takes.

Courage to you, Paula—you are a courageous person. I'm hoping that better days lie ahead this week.

Teresa K

Mark, Paula, Grace, Mitchell, Chandler and Genevieve,

You have the entire Hogan family praying for you—and that is a lot of people! I am anxious to get home and see you all. I will fly out first thing in the morning and get to Inyokern by noon.

We pray for healing and manageable pain— no infection and protein campaign working. You are in our thoughts always and we will begin to now ask for special graces from Saint John— thanks to the Nazecks.

Bless you all—with all our love, Mike, Ruth, Kelsey, Torrey and Michaela

Mark, Paula, Grace, Mitch, Chandler, and Genevieve

We can't believe what you're going through and are thinking about you constantly. We're glad to hear things are going as well as they can be, so far. Please let us know if we can do anything.

With love, Wendy, Craig, Otto, and Kaysa

The Bolasky Family is still praying for all the Welshs. I'm grateful he is eating and allowing meds to help ease the pain. YOU GO, MARK. LOVE< KISSES< PRAYERS Claire B and Family

Uncle Mark,

You are such an amazing fighter! You and Aunt Paula are in our prayers. We pray for your strength and courage to both overcome this. We love you both and miss you terribly. Much Love, Ben, Erin, Charlie and Ella

Mark, you are in my prayers. You are one of the strongest dudes I know.

Stay strong, Tad

My dear friends Paula and Mark,

As I sit here and reflect on what is going on with you right now I can't help but look back at how we have talked about how strong our faith is and that gives me great comfort to know that our loving God is watching over you Mark, and comforting your wife and kids. We will keep you and your family in our prayers; and know that you will come out of this healthy and stronger than ever. Please let me know if there is anything that I can do for you. I am just a phone call away. Con mucho Amor Love always, Sara

P.S. Con mucho amor means with much love in Spanish :)

Best wishes to you, Mark and your family. You are a warrior of a man! We miss you here at work, and all hope for your speedy recovery.

Best wishes, Elvis.

Hi Mark and Paula,

We are all anxious to watch God at work as He tenderly cares for all of you. We are praying and asking God for a full recovery. We are also ready and able to care for your family here in Ridgecrest…!

Sending you love, Hope, Russ and Katy

Paula & Mark,

You've been in our prayers pretty much constantly since we heard the news yesterday morning. May God give you strength & peace & comfort as you take each day on this difficult road.

*"Do not fear what may happen tomorrow; the same loving Father who cares for you today, will care for you tomorrow and every day. Either He will shield you from suffering or He will give you unfailing strength to bear it. Be at peace, then, and put aside all anxious thoughts and imaginings."—St. Francis de Sales*

I looked up who the patron saint of burn victims is and it is the apostle, St. John. He's the apostle who stood with Mary at the foot of the cross when Jesus died. Tradition has it that he was condemned to death in the year 95 and was thrown into a cauldron of boiling oil but he came out of it unharmed, so the Roman emperor ended up banishing him instead. His feast day is May 6. Keep your chin up—you will get through this.

With much love, Katie N

P.S. If there's anything at all that we can do, just say the word.

Sitting Bear & squaw (Paula),

You guys are constantly in our thoughts & prayers. All the Indian Guides have been contacted & are thinking of you as well. All the not-so-Little-anymore Braves know what a strong Big Brave you are and know that the Great Spirit will pull you through this. When it's all said & done, this will be quite a tale for the Tally Keeper to end our journal with. Your friend, Running Wolf, Mark N

Dear Mark and Paula,

We send you our prayers and love. Know that you have the prayers of so many people who love and care for you. We are here for you for anything you need! God will take care of you both. Lots of love, Jim, Susan and Sam

Dear Mark, Paula, & Family,

May God keep you in the palm of His Hand as your family travels through this. Our prayers are with you. We think of you often. Let us know how we can help here on the home front. Blessings, Vic & Susie

Mark,

God bless you and your strength. What an inspiration you have been to everyone. We are thinking and praying for you continuously. I believe deeply in my heart that you will make a full recovery. Jessica colored a picture for you today and constantly asks about you. Keep up your strong, stubborn, and incredible strength! No doubt, someday, your story will help someone else all the way if it hasn't already. Infinite blessings to you, Paula, and my nieces and nephews. Sheri

Just found your site from the Wojos. Praying for Mark and Family. What a blessing that there were no third degree burn issues. God is awesome. Praying for a healthy recovery and peace for the family. God bless. Dawn

Paula & Mark,
Our heartfelt prayers are with you and your family as you go through this difficult time. We know that God is the ultimate healer and He has Mark in His care. We pray for a speedy and complete healing for Mark and for comfort for Paula and your children. May God's peace be with all of you at this time. Jim, Terry, & Brittany

From the bottom of my heart I just want you and your family to know we are here for you. You and your family are and will stay in our thoughts and prayers to see you through this most difficult time. God Bless you always and safe travel to your visitors. With all our love. Ann and Karl and family

We are praying for you, Mark. We have confidence that your strength, humor, beautiful family and good friends will pull you through this difficult time. Sophia and Lucas ask about you frequently. Much love, Clara, Greg, Sophia & Lucas

Paula, Mark, Grace, Mitchell, Chandler and Genevieve,

Our family is praying for you all. We pray that Mark makes a complete recovery and that his fluid levels are maintained; that he manages his pain, and that his healing is complication-free. We are just a 45-minute drive away, so please don't hesitate to call on us when you need anything. With love and prayers, Kirsten, Marcel, Kate, Charlotte, Natalie, Lon and Luc

**Hello again. I just have to tell you that when Mark's night nurse saw him at 7:00 p.m. tonight she said "Is that my 73% guy in there? You look great! This is unbelievable!" I love her. She is vivacious and loud like me, yippee! She is so impressed with Mark's recovery. His swelling is down, his eyes are not bulging. She said this is incredulous. She has not seen this in the nine years she has been there. I started to cry and Vince consoled me. God is miraculous. The physical therapist will be there tomorrow to get him walking, this is also unheard of with a 73% burn. My brother Vince will be there with them, getting the scoop and being supportive. This could be very painful for Mark, so I am very grateful for Vince to be in there with him. Mark's boss Chris visited today and got Mark talking. I so appreciate visitors. Mark is awake, then asleep, but amazingly alert and listening to conversations. He keeps eavesdropping. I read the guestbook out loud all the time and I make Karen cry.**

**Good times! I think the vino is working and I should go to bed. I will write more tomorrow. KKLL. Paula**

Saint Ann Perpetual Adoration Chapel-. Parish members spend time in prayer and adoration around the clock (24hrs a day, 7 days a week.) It has been active for over 20 years.

*Reflection*

*I believe a power bigger than me guided me to share my story. I can't explain the force I felt to share Mark's journey. Once I started I couldn't stop. I look back at some of my entries and know that God had His hands guiding mine.*

# Finding Comfort and Strength in Others

June 1, 2009

Hello. This morning Mark started off with clear lab reports. The therapist got the orders to start on Mark early afternoon. My brother Vince was by his side for the duration. Thank God for him, I am not ready for that. Adam, the therapist had Mark turning hands, bending elbows, and raising arms up to shoulders. This is to help the muscles from getting atrophied and helps stretch the skin. Forgive me if I am not using the correct lingo. They got Mark out of bed and into a chair. This is quite painful but Vince said Mark was a trooper. When all was over, it was a task to get him back into the bed. Mark got some good drugs after and has been sleepy ever since. I am wondering when I get the good stuff. My pain is at a 25. I know God is with him every step of the way. Thanks for all the love and prayers sent up to Fresno. I feel them constantly. Visitors are welcome so feel free to come. It is so comforting reading the guestbook too. They okayed me to bring in copies of the guestbook, so I will read each and every one to Mark tomorrow. Vince traveled home tonight and my sis-

**ter Ruth arrived safely shortly after he left. My sister Amy comes tomorrow, and Mark's folks arrive from Iowa early evening and my brother David arrives on Friday. I love my family and am truly grateful for their strength to hold me up right now. My folks continue to care for my children who will see their father on Sunday. God bless our support team. Love to all, Paula**

Hello, I just wanted to let you know you have many people praying for you ALL that you do not even know. My name is Toby. Also, Tom (another contractor in town) is my father-in-law. My mother-in-law called me yesterday, and I received an email today from another friend requesting prayers for you all. One of the AMAZING benefits of a small town, is everyone knows someone...prayer requests FLY at lightning speed! I pray you feel the peace that can only come through Him at this time, for Mark's continued miraculous healing; for a family bond that will only grow stronger during such a difficult time. Above all, His will be done...because God's plan, as we know, is much bigger than ours!

Your Sister In Christ, Toby

Dear Paula,

Hang in there. Sometimes when times are most difficult we realize newfound strengths in ourselves. Mark is lucky to have you by his side and I know that he is fighting very hard. Know that you are both in my thoughts. I wish you the strength to persevere during this difficult time and to find peace of mind. Take care, Julie

Dear Mark, Paula and kids,

I am so happy that you are progressing, Mark. I want you to know that our crew is praying for you. I know that God was and is with you. He will see you and your family through this. My family and I pray for your recovery and for Paula's strength daily. Your name has been added to our church prayer chain. Paula, thank you for doing this posting of Mark's condition. We are all real concerned here at work. If we can help, please let us know. God Bless you. Jason

Paula,

Many years have separated us…and I have never met Mark and your family, but know that you are in my prayers during this difficult time. I am getting updates via Amy, and hoping for a speedy recovery for Mark! You are in my thoughts and my whole family (and I have a lot of little ones now that are praying for you nightly :))

Stay strong, and know that you have a prayer chain going in Arizona!

Hang in there! One thing I always think about in the hardest of times…it gives you the opportunity to reflect on how great your life is! Take care of yourself and your family!

Michele

Mark and Paula,

We want you to know that we have been praying since we heard the news on Saturday afternoon. You are both strong people and we know this will make you even stronger. I just read your latest post, Paula, and we are so excited that Mark is doing so well. The prayers are still coming your way! I had the beautiful picture you sent at Easter with me so I shared your family picture with my friends at school. They are praying for you and your family. Please know that we are here for you and we look forward to hearing all the updates. We love you! Stay strong, Mark! You'll have to be even stronger Paula…I've known you for a long time and I know you can do it! Love, Lisa and James

Hi Mark, Paula,

Hoping improvement keeps happening. Have added your name/cause to prayer lists at national shrines I am visiting. So far this includes Our Lady of the Snows, Shrine of the Miraculous Medal, and Our Lady of Sorrows. These are in Illinois and Missouri, where I am at tonight. I had a long talk with a Fr. Clarance Zackman at the Our Lady of the Snows shrine. He is 88 and has been associated with it since the beginning in WW2. He was telling me of the history of miracles that he had seen, and was happy to include you in his prayers. Hope to hear good news soon. Jim

Dear Mark and Paula,

Amy just called and told me what has happened. I've read some of the guestbook comments and from the sound of it, Mark, you are one strong and determined kind of guy. So I am sure you will take these great qualities and use them to get yourself and your beautiful family through this. Paula I sense you are a stable and strong woman, (and that sweet little girl I remember from a lot of years ago grown to an amazing woman). I know you will take care of Mark and your family to see that they will all stay strong. I will make my prayers heard! Much love to all of you. God Bless. Edie

Hello,

My name is Kelly and I am a friend of Lisa's. Please know that a family in Huntington Beach is praying for your speedy and complete recovery and also for peace for your family as well. It is my prayer that not only will you fully and quickly recover, but that through this situation, God's name would be glorified and that you would be a miraculous testimony to everyone you encounter about the power of prayer and the awesomeness of our God! Kelly

Mark,

So good to hear that you are progressing so well. I know that you have it in you to overcome your challenges. And of course you can draw on your faith, family, and friends in the measures you require.

Our thoughts and prayers are with you, Paula, and your family. Looking forward to see-ing you in top shape soon Big Guy!! Alan

Mark, Paula, and family,

Just heard the news. We can tell from your other guestbook entries that you have many wonderful friends and family to support you all through this challenge. Although it is hard for us to be upbeat at this moment due to our concern, we know Mark is a fighter (he's the toughest son-of-a-[GUN] I've ever known!), so we already know the cards are stacked in his favor.

Our prayers are with Mark and all of you. We are ready to help in any way we can!

We love you guys! Bruce, Susan, Brett and Derrick

Mark and Paula...Tony is having me type this in his words...

Everybody that knows Mark knows there is nobody more stubborn or stronger than Mark. This is a minor step that won't take him down; he will overcome this as he has everything else.

Paula stay strong as I know Mark will. Our thoughts and prayers are with you both.

Love, Tony & Karen

Hello daddy it is Chandler and Grace. We hope you get better soon. We miss you very much and will see you this weekend.

love, Chandler and Grace

Mark, Tad here just thinking of you. Hope you are doing well today. I better get back to work. Peace. Tad

Hi Paula and Mark,

Our prayers are with you in wishing you a speedy recovery. As you continue to progress, please know that all the healing prayers we can muster will be sent your way!

Paula, I'll keep in touch with Missy for HEART/Scrip program issues and I'll be glad to help wherever needed over the coming weeks.

Peace be with you! I'm a phone call away and will do whatever I can to help. Take care, Dan & Joyce

Mark and Paula,

The power of first grade prayer is with you! All of the first graders went to the Grotto this morning and we prayed a decade of the rosary for Mark. Paula, you get any "left-over prayers" that Mark does not need, but he comes first :) We love you and you are all in ongoing prayerful thoughts throughout the day. Chris

Paula:

We're so pleased to see that Mark's recovery is going so well, and hope it continues on the same path. We know you have an awesome support group of family and friends that will see you through this—count us in! You're in our thoughts and prayers.

God has certainly already blessed you in so many ways in this situation—I'm sure he'll see you through to the end. Love, Dave & Julie

Dear Paula and Mark and the rest of the family,

Our thoughts and prayers are with you. Reading Paula's entries shows how great God is as there are truly miracles that occurred when Mark fell.

Hank says "When the hospital food starts to taste good Mark has stayed too long.

We love you. Linda

Mark, Paula and family,

You are very loved and supported. When the days ahead bring new challenges, they will also bring a full measure of faith, comfort, and resources. You are never alone. Praying for the best. Pat B

Hi Paula & Mark—I just read your latest updates—incredible!!!! You both have to be the strongest people I know—God is good!! I have been thinking about you all day—Tom & I may come up to Fresno on Saturday—we don't want to be in the way, though so you can let us know. Know that we are praying for you 24-7. Stay strong Mark & you too Paula. Hugs to you both—Love, Dorothy & Tom

Paula and Mark,

We heard of Mark's accident through our extended connections to our Ridgecrest and St. Ann's family of friends. Please know that Pete, Loren, Josh, Patrick, Sam, John and Brian are praying for Mark's speedy recovery! In particular, we are praying that Mark will not experience any more pain and that Paula and Mark and your family receives great strength and grace to get through this tough time. With warm regards... Pete and Loren

Hey Mark, Paula, Karen & Vince,

Please know everything is running like a tight run ship here at the Welsh compound! GiGi is running the halls like a mad woman and Grammy did have to get her from under her chair in her room! HA! We are all praying for everyone and holding you close in spirit and heart.

Mom is only busting out the scotch after everyone is asleep. See you tomorrow and take good care...KKLL, Amy

Paula and Mark,

What a blessing to hear of Mark's progress today. God will use this to the glory of His name! Amen! Prayers are abundant as is evident by the messages left by so many family members and friends. We will continue to pray for healing, for comfort, and to thank God for His gifts, especially those He has given to you today. God bless, Terry

Paula...Kim and I are thinking of the "Big Lug" and you constantly! Please know we will do anything to help you and yours...including the weather forecast (our joke). Let us know if you need anything.

Mark...hang tough as you always do! I guess I'll have to give Jimbo the ass whoopins while you're gone. Love you guys, Greg and Kim.

Paula, Mark and Family,

With the patron saint for burns being Saint John, how can we go wrong as we know another Saint John who is up there rooting for you. Paula, take care of yourself. Mark, you are a strong guy, we know you can recover quickly. Prayers always. Margie and Walt

Mark, Paula, and family,

You have all been in my prayers the minute I heard. Okay...now you know with our family, news travels at the speed of light, so my prayers were being lifted up...let's see...early afternoon on Saturday. God is so amazing and his healing touch has already been placed on Mark...as is evident by his incredible and miraculous progress so far. I have extended your CaringBridge site to all my prayer warriors so Mark will be covered in prayer. Love to all...XOXO, your cuz Lisa W dear welshes,

i am praying for you all and for a speedy recovery.

Pat N

Mark,

It is so great to hear that you are doing so well. But, there is a whole network of people thinking about you, pulling for you, and praying for you. I spent the first hour of my day today fielding questions on your progress. It was cool though, to be able to pass on your blindingly bright outlook. Any who, take care and I will see you soon. And don't pay any attention to Mike. You will be getting more shit when you get back. Keep on Truckin' Bro. All the best to your family, Dave

Mark and Paula,

You've been in our thoughts and prayers since we got the news. And from looking at the guestbook there's been a lot of people thinking about you and praying for you and it's working!! So we'll continue to pray you all the way home! And...I would like to second Genevieve's comment because I couldn't find a better way to say it...

sdfjkewruiopwerwe9+rewrfsfhewrdslasfbn-vbnmxcvnmvcxmndsfhreuyqrtewyreytreytgdhfg gfhsdgfhjsdgfsdhfgdhgsdjfgsdfhgsdhfd

BF...Please behave and remember to use your hospital voice. And if you need anything just let us know. Love Ya, Danielle

Mark,

Keep up the fantastic work. When my friends hear what happened to you they are utterly amazed when I tell them how well you are doing. Not even the pastor at our church could believe it. All of my recovery friends are using your story as a way to keep them focused and moving in a positive spiritual direction.

My thoughts are with you. I am sure you will face this next step of getting up and walking with as much determination and courage as you have with everything else. I continue to pray for you and your family. Paula has done a tremendous job of keeping us updated. God bless her. We will be in Ridgecrest to see you on June 18th. Love, Sheri

Hey Mark, so glad to hear your great progress. We all sure miss you around here. Weird not to talk to you every day at turnover. Couldn't you have found a better way to get out of work? You're a tough son of a gun—hopefully tough enough to endure all the guff we throw at you while we have the advantage. Stay strong buddy—talk to you soon—Mike

Dear Paula, Mark and family!

Just found out about this cool website—modern tech at its best! Walking already—my, you guys definitely have the power of prayer and faith! It sounds like you have the best docs too! Wishing for a very speedy recovery—all of our thoughts and prayers are with you.

Paula—if you need us to run up more supplies, clothes, toothpaste, vino…:) let us know. Take care. We love you, Teresa & Rodger

Dear Mark & Paula,

Just a quick note to say hello and I am still praying for you both. I am working and showing half my class this web site. They all wish you well!!! YOU GO MARK!

P.S. Easy on the vino. Wait for me. Love and Prayers Claire B

Dear Mark and Paula

Just wanted to let you know that we're praying for you. You're such a wonderful, strong family with great faith. I know if anyone can get through this, you can, Mark!

Your progress so far has been amazing! Stay strong and we'll keep those prayers coming.

Paula…you helped me so much when Dad died. Just remember the VINO and GIGGLES help! Love you both…Connie

Dear Paula and Mark…all of you are in my prayers…just got updated from Ann (I guess her foot will have to take 2nd place now!)

Going by to see your Mom and Dad today… as with everyone, I can't believe this happened… words with God later on why He is picking on the W family!!!! On my way to get Hannah as Montessori is only going to work until 11:30 all week…I'll offer it up for Mark! In my thoughts and prayers…hang in there, Mark…sounds as if you and God are amazing the Drs!!!! Love from Char and Mr. Nobody

Hey Mark, Paula, and family

Just would like to give you and everyone best wishes and tell you that the fire dept. guys are sending you and the family the best... I'll check back in on ya later. Monty (O.C.F.D.)

Uncle Mark,

It is so great to hear how well you are doing! We are amazed at your strength and courage during all of this. It is such great news that you will be up and walking. We continue to pray for your strength!

Aunt Paula,

Hang in there! I'm so glad you have the family there with you. There is nothing like family and friends at a time like this! We are truly blessed to have such an amazing family. We love you both. Ben, Erin, Charles and Ella

Dear Mark and Paula,

We continue to keep you and your family in our prayers (a rosary a day for you!) and are thankful you are in good hands. Should we send Paula her sheet music from choir so that she can sing to Mark on his way through a speedy and complete recovery? Gino would probably approve of this message. Take care, Fred, Kathy, Amanda and Jackie

Hi Mark, glad to hear things are looking better. We will be missing you around here. I know it will be awhile but we are waiting for you to get back up here. Paula started the jokes about the cadaver skin and we had a little bit of fun with as you can imagine. Send more later, keeps you spirits up, not those spirits, Paula... Lynn

Hello, Mark and Paula

I am so happy that you are coming right along. It's amazing what prayer can do and as I have seen, you have an army praying for your speedy recovery. Sit back and see our Precious Lord at work. Our prayers will continue. Paula, stay strong and know that I have your back. Call me if I can do anything for you. LUV YA, SARA

Hey Mark and Paula

So glad to read that Mark is doing so well. We all know you have it in you. We wouldn't expect any less. Paula is your wife!!!! She won't let you slough off. We will continue to pray for a speedy recovery and that you all get home soon. Love to Karen too. KKLL

Leslie and Family

Hi, Mark and Paula,

Wow! What good news! You two are so brave. Third grade is praying for you and the nurses and doctors, too. God knew what He was doing when He sent you to Fresno. Guess that I should get back to teaching. Love, Susan

P.S. Fr. Paul again asked us all to pray for your family at Mass this morning.

Hi Mark and Paula,

Mark, glad to hear you are doing so well. That walk today will be a piece of cake. Before you know it you'll be sprinting down those hallways. Say hi to Vince for me. Ask him if he remembers that special Birthday Surprise that Amy and I gave him one year…lol

Paula you are the Rock of your family now, at least temporarily, you will be fine. Keep drinking more "Vino"... :-) Keeping you in my prayers, Jo

Hey, Mark,

Really sorry to hear of your accident. What a bi***. Here's hoping for the very best outcome for you and your family. That would be to get back to normal in the shortest time possible. Good thoughts and vibes coming your way. Jeannie (former water truck driver at Coso)

Dear Paula and Mark,

First, thank you so much for using CaringBridge! It was so comforting to read your words, Paula, and know that we can send our love to both of you by this means.

Scott called us the moment he heard the news and has passed info on as quickly as he received it. I don't think our family has communicated like this in years! And all because we have a common love for you and your entire family.

We hold you close in thought and prayer and will stay close to the website for updates. We love you. Pat and Joe

Sending Blessings today for Mark as he takes that 1st move out of bed today...your story is SO AMAZING already...we are praying for you every step of the way!

You have so many people sending 'good vibes' adding their strength to yours, be assured that you are going to continue at a [fast] pace for an Incredible Recovery.

Also know that we are glad to have the girls here with us each night to try and re-energize.

Keep your chin up today, Paula & Karen. Our
Prayers & Love, Tracy~Louis~Jared & Audra

Dear Mark and Paula,

Our thoughts are with you and hope the
rehab will go smoothly. You're in luck, because
I'm the hospital wound nurse. When you get
ready to come back to Ridgecrest I will help! I
have taken (ABLS) Advanced Burn Life Support
at Sherman Oaks Burn Center, and have training
at Lake Arrowhead for a 60% burn patient. So
keep this offer in mind when you guys head back
to Bedrock (Ridgecrest) if you have any needs
please let us know. Mark and Pam

That is amazing that you're going to try
to walk already, Mark. It's so great to hear that
you're recovering so well. Thanks for the updates,
Paula!—Wendy

Paula & Mark,

I got tears in my eyes reading your latest
post, but I'm not surprised. I think I was expecting a miracle, just as everyone else here is. You're
one tough broad with one tougher hubby. :) You
guys have never been far from our thoughts this
past weekend. Our prayers are still going on for
you and your family. Missy & Vic

Mark,

Your Father and I have been blessed in life
with three wonderful children. You are a blessing Mark and we are so sorry that you are going
through this. You have always been strong, independent and very courageous. I know these qualities will help you through this time of healing.

We are so thankful that you are in a Care Center that can provide the care and treatment you need right now. God has blessed you with Paula, Grace, Mitchell, Chandler, and Genevieve, and their love will pull you through this. We love you and will see you soon. Love, Mom and Dad Welsh

Mark and Family,

Mark, you are full of amazing strength! God is good! Keep up the awesome recovery so that you can give all those beautiful children of yours a big squeeze from me. Know that we are praying for all of you daily. We are sending our love your way. We miss all of you. Emily, Lou, Samantha and Li Mei

Mark,

I just read Paula's latest entry and I am actually not surprised by how well you are doing. You are one of the most stubborn men I have ever met, LOL and, in addition, whatever you try to do you stick to it until you do it the best way, as you are doing right now with your healing. We all miss you here at work, and don't think or worry about anything other than getting yourself better so you can come back and deal with all of your other kids up here at work. I hope your physical therapy goes well today. Stay strong Mark.

Paula, you stay strong too hon; he is doing so great, call me if you need anything at all.

Thinking of you guys, April

Hello again. I am back at the Linney's now with my nightly vino. Thank you, Tracy. They finally hooked up the phone tonight and Mark spoke with Grace, Mitchell, Chandler and my mom and dad. He heard about Chandler's field trip to Bishop, Mitchell's day; and how Grace starts her finals tomorrow, plus gets her license @ 3:30pm, God willing.

My mom told him to get better and get back to his four children. She had to have a scotch every night but he told her he didn't understand, he doesn't need a drink when he cares for them. He is amazing and hopefully will get dressings changed in the next day or two. He has his femoral line out and they are pricking his ear for his blood checks, mucho progresso! (how's my Spanish, Sara?) They have even lowered his pain meds. I am heading to bed early tonight so thanks again! I will take all you nurses up on your offers when we get home. KKLL, Paula

P.S. Please set your CaringBridge accounts to Pacific Time, it always defaults to Central time. Thanks.

*Reflection*

*By now, we already had some visitors. They were changing the subject, taking my mind off the obvious. I had always had no problem visiting people in the hospital, but it took on a whole new meaning that people were traveling four hours to visit us. Visitors did impact my attitude and gave me strength beyond any other form. Jesus is amazing, and He uses the Holy Spirit to guide the faithful to support and love another through difficult times. Never underestimate the impact you will have by visiting, calling, reaching out to someone in the hospital, or visiting the caregiver.*

In pain, failure and brokenness, God does his finest work in the lives of people.
—Gordon MacDonald, *Rebuilding Your Broken World*

# Therapy Through Releasing Emotion

June 2, 2009

Hello. Mark had physical therapy again and walked 2 laps today! He said he is doing 3 tomorrow! He sat in a chair for 4 hours. Sitting up is so good for him, stretches the muscles and skin. We are continually blessed with miracles. Loved all the cards from the St. Ann's students. We had some good laughs and, some little child said "So sorry you fell in a sink hole." Thanks for the care package, Elaine. I guess I will be seeing the captain tonight! (Morgan that is). KKLL, Paula

Hello, I am catching up on my journaling withdrawals. They have taken him off his pain drip and will put the medicine in his IV as needed. He will have to get to know himself. Pray he is a fast learner. Feeding tube is out! Another miracle! They have never seen a patient start back to eating so well. My meat and potatoes guy is surprising them. We had a little bath, (head only) but have to hurry; with no skin he gets the shakes real bad. I am quick, though, I am used to bathing Genevieve at warp speed. His folks are visiting him right

**now. They arrived from Iowa last night. I am thankful for the break! Mark, Katie, Gordy (bro-in-law), and Dave and Mike from work should be here soon! I am getting my second wind. The nurse also reminded him that now he will be awake more. He might start to think about life, worries, bills, kids, Paula's shopping habits, etc. and they have a pill for that so he will have to speak up if he feels anxious. I wonder if they can give me one? KKLL, Paula**

Mark/Paula—
May the force be with you!
may the germs ignore you,
may the doctors do right by you
may thy vino do its job,
may Paula keep her chin up
(and voice down),
may the love notes never stop,
may the time fly by,
may Mark enjoy chauffeuring by Grace,
may the love we all feel shine through to you,
may Pat's scotch bottle last
may we all see you soon.
Love-prayers-drinks-smiles from our family to yours xxoo Rose and gang

Dear Mark: I heard you are pushing yourself! Slow down, I know your super loving family inspires you to get home fast but don't overdo it. You know I am pulling for you but you don't know how much. (I only feel .04% of your pain. 10 when the kids are home.) Tell Paula to pace herself too. LOVE AND MANY PRAYERS. you go mark!!!!!! Claire, John, Veronica, Serena, Steven and John G, Allie Jo!!!

Mark & Paula,

Glad to hear you're doing better. Had a glass (okay 2) of wine tonight in your honor. The kids are remembering you all in their prayers and we are too. Missy

Yeah Mark! I'm so glad things are going better for you. You are my new hero. We are praying for you every day and we are so sorry you have to go through this. Sista Paula, we are praying for you too. Hang in there Sis, I know it must suck. Be strong and keep your sense of humor. That will keep you both going. You are an amazing woman and if you need anything please holler. Love ya tons, Sista Sue and Dichard

Hey Mark, Paula & family,

Just wanted to let you guys know we are all thinking about you down here in Santa Clarita. When we were in Ridgecrest the weekend before last (when Mark was off) we were planning to call and ask if we could stop by, but we ran out of time. We hope to come by and bother you all soon!

All this talk of drinking Scotch. Too bad *I* don't drink Scotch. Well, off to the liquor cabinet and, eenee meenee mine-ee mo, ah, that'll work! :) Get well soon, Dude! Bruce & family

We are sooo sorry to hear about your unfortunate event. But, sooo happy to hear the recovery is going great!!! We wish with all our soul for godspeed. Prayers & Blessings,

Scott, Leanna, Alexis, Hannah & Kirstyn

Hi Paula and Mark,

We are feeling so positive about your progress. What an incredible amount of miracles have been put into play to create this outcome. Keep on striving to be the remarkable team that we know you are. Love and prayers from all of us. Marg, Walt, Scott, Jeff, Stacey, Jessica, Bill and THE grandkids

Hi Mark and Paula, We are so proud of you Mark—just wow—very glad to hear how well you are doing!! We have much prayers and thoughts for you—love to you and Paula.

Love Don-nah

Hi Mark and Paula—this site is great. I just dropped in to say Hi—that was 30 minutes ago. Doesn't surprise me there are so many notes to you. You were one of the first new hires right after I came to Coso—in all those years I don't think I ever heard you complain—you were always positive and smiling. With that attitude nothing can get you down—after all you've overcome all those clowns up on the hill. (They are pretty funny). Compared to dealing with the pain and grief they dish out dealing with this should be a piece of cake for you. It is clear your family and friends have been a strong support system for you and God has you in his hands. Stay strong and keep smiling. Anyway I can help let me know. Diana

Dear Paula and Mark,

We're all praying for a quick recovery. Jamie is especially worried about Chandler's dad, and has added a 'God Bless Chandler's dad' line to her nightly prayers, right after 'God Bless my two alive fish and my four fish who passed away'. Mark, you need to get back on your feet quickly, and take Chandler to the bowling alley for some practice. Jamie claims she beat him today (with a 94) during the kindergartener's bowling trip with their prayer pals. Love, Nicki

Dear Paula and Family,

We just heard about Mark's accident. We're all so very sorry and will be praying for ALL of you! Loved the picture you sent at Easter! Glenda and Steve

Dear dad

it's your son again. i hope you recover fast. everyone in the school are praying

love
your loving son
Mitchell

Mark and Paula,

Jeff and I are sooooo happy to hear you are recovering quickly. You would not believe the amount of people that are praying for you and your family. Please let us know if there is anything we can do to help you...mow the lawn, watch the kids, etc...I promise I won't drink Scotch while I'm watching them. LOL. :0) May our loving God bless you and your family. Jeff and Lisa

Hi Paula and Mark,

I was so sorry to hear about the accident! Amy e-mailed me to keep the prayers going...we are all praying for a quick and complete recovery! May God be with you all!

Take care, Erin

Just wanted to send a quick note to let you know that you are in our thoughts and prayers. Sounds like the recovery is coming along quite well—we will continue to pray that Mark makes a speedy recovery and can get home to the family soon. Love from, Marty and Maria

P.S.—Cassie saw your kids at McDonald's recently and couldn't believe those were the "little kids" she used to babysit!

Mark,

I was excited to hear about your progress and how amazingly you keep moving forward. I continue to pray for you and your family every day. I hope that you keep sprinting forward at the lightning speed that you have been.

Jessica says to you, "I love you." In fact, we all love you. Sheri

Mark,

I'm glad to hear that you're doing OK. It does not surprise me that this is not going to keep you down. If anyone I know has the will to bounce back quickly, it would be you. From the amount of postings here, you've got a lot of friends and family by your side.

Get well and I'll be thinking about you. Mark (the other Mark)

Paulina~

Just want you to know that you, Mark and the kids are in our thoughts and prayers every single day. I'm so glad to hear the recovery is going so well. Take care and stay strong.

Love, Shelbie

Hey Mark and Paula,

Sounds like things are moving along well. It is so amazing how this all works. It is so up lifting to read all the love and support. I saw Grace at school and she was all excited about getting her license...She is an amazing young lady!!! I know how proud you both are of her. I have some shirts to drop off to the boys. That will give them something fun to go through. Wish I could be there with you and Karen. I don't get why Mark doesn't need drinks...Love to you all. Can't wait to see Mark at home again. We have some camping to do this summer! KKLL, Leslie

Mark,

It sounds like you're really kicking this in the butt man, just remember that work starts again on the 6th...Be well, be strong. Our prayers are with you and your family. Travis, Grace, Patience, Presley, Maverick

Uncle Mark,

Every time I check the page I am blown away with all the love and support! You and Paula have so many amazing friends! And of course the family isn't so bad either :-). I love you and wish I could be there. I'm not sure I would be much help with a 4-year old who asks 100 questions or a 2-year old who is totally feeling her oats! I'm sure they both would keep you amused. Keep up all the hard work! I hope your days get easier. I love you and miss you. Hang in there! Erin

Hi Paula & Mark,

We just found out what happened from Edie. We are also praying for a full recovery. We read some of your progress so far—you are indeed remarkable! Love, Carol & Aunt Virginia

Hola! Mi Amigos Mark and Paula, I couldn't wait to come home and check in on Mark's progress. And to no surprise he is right on track. Mark I have to ask you a big favor PLEASE hurry up and come home, because soon we are going to be visiting Paula at rehab with all the wine she is drinking. Amiga, your Spanish is mucho muy bueno. Con Mucho Amor Tu Amiga, Sara. We are coming to see you soon.

Hey Welsh Family, and Weidenkopfs too...

This is adopto-sissy here, Mark we are praying for your speedy recovery, and Paula for your continued strengths...Keep up the great work and keep us informed on what's up with all that you have to go through...Mark I guess you will not need a spray tan after all of this huh?? Just get some darker skin sewed on instead!

We love ya like a fat kid likes Chocolate Cake!!

Keep on keeping on...We are all praying for you guys and family in T town and will continue to lift you up for strength and continued recovery.

Love u guys and your Amer TOO...Hugs, Jill

Hi Paula and Mark,

My prayers and love continues to grow with each minute. I am so blessed to have you both as dear friends and also be family. I am amazed at Mark's strength and courage as well as yours. Miss you and I will see you this weekend.

Spent time with kids and Mom and Dad yesterday. They are all doing great and I was Genevieve's new best friend. Of course I spoiled them.

Hello to my sissies! May the strength and courage continue with you as you have been a huge support to all! Love to you all! Sending big hugs and kisses to you all.

Many blessings and prayers to you. Love, Ann and Jerry (Doug)

Hi, Paula & Mark,

I think I'm getting this website figured out. I talked with Katie today and she said she was going to visit Wednesday. She told me how you have found the miracles and blessings even in this bad situation. There is a reason you are surrounded with people who care and love you and that is because you have shown love and care to them. God Bless you, Mark and the whole family. I'll get an update from Katie Thursday. Love, Gene & Elaine. You and Mark are my heroes!

Mark & Paula:

-Hi, you don't know me; I was Amy's supervisor while she was at Colombo Construction. I was very sorry to hear about the accident at work, and your entire family is in my thoughts and prayers, plus the prayers of all the prayer warriors at my church. Hang in there and may God give you comfort and peace as well as a speedy recovery. Priscilla

Mark and family,

We are all thinking of you daily and pray for your speedy recovery. Thank you for this website to keep us updated as to your progress and to stay in touch with you.

The prayer chains are getting stronger for you and your family. God Bless you all, Colleen

Paula and Mark,

Hi, I am Clara-Leigh; a friend of Kirsten's from way…don't want to say how many years… back!!! She called me on Saturday and we were all in the truck returning from a fundraising rodeo where our girls competed, and we all just began praying. We are thrilled to read of the miracles, the top-notch medical care you are receiving, and the amazing strength you all have!!!! I am also praying for continued progress, strength, rest, and that you guys are close enough to wine country out there that you don't run out…HA!!!! Paula, I always LOVE any friends of Kirsten's!!!! We'll have to cross paths in person someday and share some laughs!!! She is certainly one of the greatest blessings in my life!! Please hug her for me!!!

Mark, please behave yourself and don't get behind the pain!! You are an inspiration and a fighter for sure. We will continue to pray not only for you, but for your children, as I know it is very difficult for a daddy to be involuntarily separated from his beautiful children. We are thankful you created this so we can check in on you. May you continue to experience God's love, healing and comfort. Much love, Clara

I'm going to get in trouble for keeping on checking this at work but I want to help get the count up for Mitchell. We saw Ann at Burroughs last night & she said he's keeping track of how many people are posting! I think I'm like #299 in the last couple days. You all are very loved by so many people. Hopefully all that love is lifting you up in this difficult time.

Hang in there…although you may not want to be, you are all an incredible inspiration.

Love, Katie N.


Hang in there, Paula (and Karen too)! You are both keeping up your sense of humor and supporting each other so well, what an inspiration you strong sisters are…Thank you for sharing it with me. It honors me to be involved, no matter what the task may be.

My love to you and yours, Tracy


Hey Mark & Paula,

Well good to hear you're getting better this fast. Now I have been dared so here we go…

"It rubs its lotion on its skin, or else it gets the hose again."

Buffalo Bill

Our version:

"It rubs the lotion on its skin or else it falls in the hole again."

With your temporary skin going on we just can't help ourselves,

Dead man walking…

Are you comfortable in your own skin or someone else's??

Need to get some dark skin so you can finally get a tan. Gonna go for now, Smile. Lynn

Hi guys,

Looks like the highways and byways between here and Fresno are going to get a good work out as the visitors come to see the Miracle for themselves!! I don't know how you read all this everyday—I'm a mess reading all the wonderful messages! For once, Genevieve liked me more than Russ when I visited yesterday!! It helped she was mad at your dad for taking all the kids to school, so I guess I went up a few notches!!! GOOD LUCK TO GRACE TODAY!!!!! KKLL, Hopie

Paula,

Sounds like you are learning a new language—the language of medicine!

You are doing the best thing for Mark by being there; it's huge for Mark, but huge as well for the hospital staff. Keep moving forward, it sounds like Mark sure is! Teresa K

Mark and Paula

Please know that we are thinking of you and expect continued good news. High hopes and best wishes. Mike

Hi Paula and Mark…and family!

I am soooooo sorry to hear this story! It makes you realize how something can change your course in an instant. I want to send big hugs your way…I will keep posted via the Caring Bridge and will be thinking and praying for his continued recovery!

BIG BIG HUGS!!!!! Love, Sandy and Family!!

Hi Paula and Mark, Take care of yourselves. You are both missed in Ridgecrest and we all want you back soon. I hope you can feel all the prayers coming your way. Chuck and I are at Lake Tahoe for a while but I am keeping up on your progress. Paula, good wine can't be beat. Carol

Mark,

Way to go! You are courageous! Know that our prayers are coming your way. God is good to let us all have such a wonderful way to share our support with you. Thanks to Paula and CaringBridge.

Paula,

I wish I was there to share in the vino. You were always there for me! Maybe, when you all decide to vacay in TN next year. The door is always open! Love you both, Emily

Hey Mark,

I'm thrilled to hear you are doing so well. I triple checked my midnight paperwork tonight and it made me think of you. :) Keep up the great recovery. April

*Reflection*

*As I reread my post, so many miracles had already happened. I also see how therapeutic the journaling was for me. The thoughts and prayers that were being sent to us was overwhelming. Through writing, I was able to release the emotions that threatened my sanity, and in doing so was able to find the courage and strength from others' responses. I was able to make it through another day.*

# Too Tired

June 3, 2009

Hello Again. It is morning. I was too dang tired to write or have a glass a wine last night, but do not worry I will be off the wagon tonight. My sissies have my back. Ok this will be a long one. Yesterday morning I brought the guest book entries and only got through the 5th one before it was too much for him. Toby you broke my big tough guy. Thank you from the bottom of my heart. He needed to let it out. I told him so many people love us and it is what is sustaining us. Anyways, on to the medical stuff. Ace is his physical therapist and will be with him for the duration. We know we will be traveling here a lot over the next few months, but God is good, a friend of ours has a condo in Kingsburg, quaint little town for my in-laws and myself to retreat to right now and as long as we need it. Thanks Pat! It is the haven I need right now. Mark got his Foley catheter out so he was grateful. He did exercises again and walked 50 ft. He was very tired and took a long nap and geared up for his dressing change. I was a big girl and stayed for that, even though I wanted to run screaming. His wounds are something else to look at, but he is not rejecting any of the tissue so another miracle (how many is that now?) He is tan now in some places. He was exhausted after that and did not eat dinner. My specific prayer today is that he keeps staying ahead of the pain. He has NEVER been a patient so it is hard for him to bark orders-comes naturally to me. (Opposites attract). Also, he promised to drink 3 Ensures a day and the feeding tube (that has been bothering the back of his throat) will be out today, so he's happy to choke down the Ensures.

He has a new nurse, Sandy. Love her, very silly! Not sad to see Connie go, she was messy and I was constantly picking up her trash. She made me nervous (Molly Shannon nervous)! We are out of our private room now that we had for 3 days even though we were only to have it for 24 hours, we just played stupid. So now we have been moved to the main hospital waiting room, God Help Us! Hey Ann I am eating my own words, "God gives us many distractions!" I think I have rambled enough and please know I check my emails and the guest book all the time, it helps so much. Love to all, Paula

Hey Mark,

I know you're still in a lot of pain, but it must feel pretty good to be up and walking cuz I know you have a hard time sitting still, lol. I'm glad to hear you are still progressing well. I will be coming to visit you on Sunday! So Paula I will call you when we are close. Oh and Paula say hello to the Captain for me! I may pay him a visit tomorrow :). Love ya Mark and I will see you Sunday. Thinking of you often, April

Hi Mark, Paula, Grace, Mitchell, Chandler, and Genevieve,

My sister told me what happened and gave me this website (which you are doing an awesome job with Paula!). I couldn't believe my ears when I heard what happened, but just reading how well you are doing Mark is amazing! I'm constantly thinking about your whole family and just know you have MANY people praying for all of you! Sounds like you are blowing all those expectations out of the water... Keep it up! I truly believe everything happens for a reason, and I know you will all come back even stronger! Good luck and hang in there! Cali

Hi Mark (and Paula),

So sorry to hear of your accident, but glad to hear how many miracles you are having. We are praying for the miracles to continue and for a quick recovery. If there is anything we can help with, let us know. Jamie

YOU GO MARK! I am so happy for you. Finally a good reason to bark orders at Paula. Don't hold back! She shouldn't be left with that Pirate (Morgan) bad news. May you have the strength to go one day at a time. LOVE N PRAYERS Claire B.—96 hours or so,

Mark & Paula,

wow! This is an amazing website. Can't keep my eyes dry while reading it. I was at the Grotto yesterday and the 1st grade class came and said a decade on the rosary for you, Mark. Couldn't keep my eyes dry there either. Can't imagine the pain you are in and your strength of will to progress like this leaves me speechless, (though my fingers don't seem to have a problem typing). Know that we pray continually for God's help in your recovery and that He is there for you, Paula, and your family. Now I'll go have my glass and think of all of you!

Oh—Tom said to quit playing in the mud. Rob said to get well and that he's praying for you. Big K & H, Michelle

Hi again…

This really is an amazing way to keep your network of friends and family informed. Your long update was touching. I can only begin to imagine the road you both are traveling. I wanted to check in to make sure Sandy is living up to the name…usually they are fiery and fun folks, eh??!!…hopefully she is bringing another ray of sunshine into your path!!!!

Be careful to pace your progress…both of you! Hope you enjoyed your visit with Captain Morgan, Paula!!!! Many hugs again!!!!! Thinking of you often!!!! Sandy L.

Hey Mark,

I've been getting verbal updates from Chris on your condition, but this website with Paula's updates and notes from your family, extended family, and friends is fantastic. All this support is such an encouraging example of the positive influence You and Paula have on your family, community, and fellow co-workers, although I have to admit you may want to keep your eye on a few of those fellow co-workers. They are a tough crowd based on some of the comments I've read.

Melba and I have You, Paula, and all your family in our prayers and thoughts each day as You recover. Cheers and Hope to See You on Friday, Dick

Paula and Mark,

Chuck, Kate and I continue to think about you and pray for your speedy recovery. Mark, Kate wanted me to tell "Genevieve's Daddy to get better soon so you can go home and play with Genevieve." That's a 3 year olds inspiration for you. Take care of yourselves.

Love, Kim

Dear Mark, Paula and Family,

After reading all on this web site I can't stop crying. It took me a while to figure it all out. I have been getting up dates from Dena. Didn't want to even bother MOM and DAD. Paula your update is wonderful!!!! Jon and my thoughts and our prayers are with you all day long. You all are soooooo brave!!! I just can't imagine. It sounds like something you would read in a book!! Our HEARTS and PRAYERS to all of the WELSH Family. Jon and Joann (Grandma and Grandpa L)

Hi Paula and Mark,

Greetings and well wishes from this side of the country. We are praying for you both: For Mark, that he may recover as much as possible, and for Paula, that you can hang in there through it all. It is great to have such a wonderful support system and so many people that love you. We are too far away to offer more than prayers at this time, but if you need a place to go after all is over, just give us a call! Love, Loren, Peter, Josh, Patrick, Sam, John and Brian.

Hey, Paula and Mark,

Perhaps Mark's recovery will be enhanced by everyone having a little bit more of the recuperative spirits! I'll get on it right away. Hey, it's already noon, maybe time to start.

I am glad I do not have to drink Ensure! The flavors get old real soon—ask for some other products that the hospital has on hand. It all depends on what Mark likes—but he should try everything they've got—which means Paula gets to ask! Hospitals generally have pretty good high calorie shakes, too, which do just as much good as Ensure. Bottoms up! Teresa K

I was shocked and sadden to hear about the accident. Working with you all those years I know how strong you are physically and mentally and that you will pull through this. I just hope you don't give the doctors and nurses too much trouble. Our thoughts and prayers are with you. The team here at Beowawe are all pulling for you. Andrew

Thank you Paula for the lively update. (I can tell that you've got that 2nd wind by your tone of voice...or written word, rather) but be careful not to overdo it. It's a bit of a marathon you are running, and even though Mark is AMAZING the heck out of you & everyone else, he will need you strong in these days ahead.

Good Job on the 3 Ensures yesterday Mark!! Bet you are thrilled to get rid of that tube. Each little milestone gets you closer to that full recovery day. Praying for you & yours, Tracy

Good news today. God Bless. Edith

Mark, when I heard of the accident, I was waiting for a call to come drug test you. When that call didn't come, I knew it was serious. I'm so glad to hear you are beating the odds and showing the medical staff what healing can be done with determination, prayers, support, friends, and a great wife. Keep fighting and working hard. We'll do the praying. (And Paula can do the drinking!) Janis

Hello to the Welsh Family!!!
Just want you all to know that we are thinking about you and praying for a fast recovery!! Sounds like you guys have an awesome team of people helping every step of the way. If there is anything that we can do for you here at home let us know. Michelle

Mark,
I am so sorry to hear about your accident! The kids and I will be praying for you and your family. If anyone can get through this it is YOU! It won't keep you down for long. Keep fighting!! I hope you are up and about real soon. Take Care Mark! Nolyne

Good morning! and thanks for the updates and this site to keep us all informed on what's going on!! Glad that you are doing so well…but Pace yourself…it will take a while to stretch and grow into your new skin. Paula having a drink for you both…teehee…and keeping you all in our prayers. God will give you strength and heal Marks wounds…We love you. Jill

Mark,

I was very sorry to hear about your accident. The stories of your bravery and fortitude do not surprise me at all. You have always been a strong and determined man. Dawn and I have been reading Paula's updates and we are sending our thoughts and prayers to you all. Take your time and do not rush to get back into the game. Paula, make sure all those dealing with Mark know how stubborn and determined he can be. Take care my friend!

Snowy

Mark and Paula,

Mark I am glad to hear you are making a quick recovery. My thoughts are with you and your family. I know you will recover fully and quickly since you never let anything get the best of you. Let me know if there is anything I can do to assist you or your family.

Kevin

Dear Mark, Paula and Family,

At Mass Sunday Father asked us to pray for you, Mark, as you had been in an accident. I prayed very hard, but prayed even harder after talking to Anna, who informed me of what had happened. I wanted so much to reach out to you and your family in some way. So, I pray along with all your dear friends and family. What a powerful website this is! God bless all of you. Sally

Good Evening, Cheers! I am having my skinny pirate as I write. yummo! I was a big girl today and asked for what I needed and borrowed my good friends car (thanks Marcel and Kirsten) so I could drive myself to my new home in Kingsburg (20 minutes). I rocked out to top 20, Lady Gaga, Poker Face and all the good dance tunes. I had to laugh. I do not think I have ever had a poker face. Ok enough about me. Mark did well today and enjoyed all the visitors and it was a nice break for me. Mark was so sweet yesterday and told me I could go shop if I needed to. It wasn't all about him, 1% was about me and 99% was about him. I am still moved by all the entries and love to hear what people have to say. My sisters set me up with a temporary desk/office so I can read the guest book all day long. I look very important at this county hospital. In about week or so he will have surgery to take out all the staples that hold on all the skin grafts. They will begin to slough off 10–14 days after they have been put on. Mark has been craving water, which he cannot have, it has 0 calories. He has never liked drinking water so all the visitors and I decided today it must be his new skin. Miracles are happening right before my eyes thanks to the power of prayer. Love to all, good night and I will journal more tomorrow. Paula.

*Reflection*

*Fatigue had set in. Anyone that has had to be a caregiver and advocate for a loved one in the hospital knows that you sometimes have to fight the urge not to crawl back in bed or get in your car and head north! The long road to recovery is the same you-know-what different day. It is exhausting both mentally and physically.*

# The Power of Prayer

June 4, 2009

Good morning, Mark is already starting out the day kind of tired, so pray for some energy. He has a new nurse today, Tim. He is talking sports to Mark and Mark is listening. He asked Mark if he ever played football so that helped Mark kind of perk up. He will have to sit up two times today and continue to push himself. I can still only handle the room for about 1–2 hours at a time, please pray for my strength. I cranked the music coming here this morning and Poker Face was on again, it's my new fave! Karen and Gordy headed back to Ridgecrest, as they gear up for Neal's graduation! I am sorry I will miss Neal and all our friends' children graduating Fri. eve.

To: Neal, Brennan, Lauren, Todd, Molly, Keith and many more. I would have been storming the football fields with your parents after graduation for hugs. They all love you so much that they have brought you up with faith because we all know we CANNOT survive this earth without it. Have a great time at safe grad! KKLL Paula

P.S. A skinny pirate is Cap'n and Diet coke:)

Mark the laps you are doing must be hard. But I have some valves that I can't open. So the crew needs you back at work ASAP!!!!! Stay strong Mark I know you will. Tad

Hey guys my time was wrong. It is now 10:42 and I am still thinking about you!!!!! I'll call Friday for a quick debriefing. I am keeping a running list. love and Prayer. again YOU GO MARK. Claire B.

Dear Mark and Nurse Paula,
I know I shouldn't be writing so late at night I probably won't make sense but then again I don't make sense normally. Mark, I wish I could take this all away. I wish I could say something to make you feel better but I can't so know each day, once an hour I pray you feel the power of love. YOU GO MARK!!! You too Paula pissant, Claire B

Paula,
All this talk about vino and Capt Morgan, while those of us slaving away at Safe Grad (all night), get none at all? Maybe we'll have to come visit when it's all over :)
You will be missed at the grad festivities. It sounds like Mark is still making some great strides in his recovery. We don't know Mark well, but from what you've said about his will to get through this, it's obvious he's an amazing man. We'll keep the prayers coming. Love, Julie and Dave

Mark,

Glad to hear you are doing so well, however, it doesn't surprise me. Our thoughts and prayers are with you and your family. Tony and Karen

P.S. As soon as you can handle it I would like to come see you.

Paula and Mark,

Paula you made me cry!!!! We are going to miss you both sooo much Friday night and Saturday too. Thanks for the message of encouragement to our kids. I stopped by to see your mom and dad yesterday. The boys liked the shirts from Dylan. You and Mark should be so proud of your kids. Looks like they are all doing well. Even Miss G reached for me.!!! She seemed happy. I know she misses you both so much. Mark hang in there I know you miss those kids. They are a big part of your life. We all wait for your arrival home. KKLL. Leslie

Paula and Mark

Just wanted you to know that I am checking in daily on Mark's progress. I am always happy to hear how well he is doing. You are in my prayers. Carmel (Amy's friend in Bakersfield)

Dear Mark,

I just want you to know how you are in our prayers each and every day. We are so proud of you.

Dear Paula,

Quit taking about alcohol so much…you are making me thirsty! Love, Ann

Dear Paula, Mark & Family,

We want you to know that you are in our prayers as you take this journey toward Mark's recovery. Mark is blessed to have such wonderful family and friends. Our thoughts are with you. If you need anything, you know where we are! We'll be checking in to keep updated on Mark's progress. Stay strong. Love, Mike, Diana and Family

Hello Mark and Paula!

Paula it is so encouraging to read your daily entries. You have been gifted with a great sense of humor! It sounds like Mark is continuing to live up to his reputation of being able to defy all odds. It is also comforting to know that he has such a devoted wife, family and friends around him. I see that you are both in need of some prayer for strength. Here is a verse out of Philippians 4:13 "I can do all things through Christ who strengthens me". This passage has had a significant impact on my life…as it causes me to remember that I can't do anything in my life worthwhile without "Him". When the chips are down, He is always there for me. Just remember, the Lord is near. Because He is near, we need not be anxious for anything. Because he is near, we have a peace within. A deep abiding peace that surpasses all understanding. And because the Lord is near, our hearts, minds and bodies can be renewed and restored. Mark, it is evident that you are loved and respected by many…please just take this time to recover and heal your body; everyone else will take care of the small stuff! Coso misses you! P.S. Paula, try that pirate with some margarita mix…makes a good Mai Tai. :0) Lisa H

Hi Paula and Mark,

Heard there was more "boy time" yesterday with Mark and Gordy to visit. Mark was probably relieved to not have as many women around mothering the living daylights out of him, huh? The Prize Patrol is moving ahead...next year you're on!!! We sure miss you and know it must be rough missing being home. Grace had a big 'ol bag (I mean fashionable purse) today to carry her new driver's license in...plus she said she really likes being in the car by herself! I'm here for ya, babe!! I was on the phone with your mom, and Katy was on the phone with Gracie the day she got her license, getting all the details. Only we didn't know each other was getting the same news at the same time! Only in Ridgecrest, right? Make sure Mark doesn't have to settle for the diet Italian dressing!!!! KKLL Hope

Dear Mark and Paula,

You and your family are in our prayers. God is Great!!! He is looking out for you all and I know everything will be fine. I just wish I was there with you. Please let me know if you need anything. I can always drive up to Ridgecrest and help out with the kids. Fresno isn't that far also. I can always drive up there in a flash Paula if you need me! Stay strong and keep the faith. God is with you every step of the way. We Love You, Tonia, Robert, & kids

Uncle Mark,

Sounds like you had a very busy day yesterday with all your visitors! I'm sure it will take you a day or two to catch up! Don't let it get you down! You have made such tremendous strides already, don't let today get the best of ya. We are thinking about you! Love you lots. Ben Erin Charles and Ella

Dear Paula and Mark.

It is quite clear that you all have no lack of family, friends, love and prayers on your side. We are right along with them in all the above mentioned. I am sure that with Gods helping hand and Marks stamina, he will have a speedy recovery. Our Love and Prayers, Bud and Connie

Hola! Mark and Paula,

Spanish word of the day, "Saludos" (means greetings, good health). I see you are improving right along, and amazing everyone with your strength. I will continue giving you Spanish lessons, and by the time you recover you will be bilingual. Sara

Mark,

It is great to read about your amazing progress and it was really nice to talk to you, Paula, the other day and get more details. Please know we're thinking about you guys all the time.

We are changing Craig's ticket to Vegas (previously planned trip for his friend's surprise 40th birthday party) so he can make it to visit you for a couple of days after. It sounds like you'll probably be home by then and he'd love to see you and help out with anything. Of course, the kids and I would love to see you guys, too, but we'll do that after some time passes so the kids won't be a threat and things are more settled for you. You let us know whenever that may be.

We love you guys and wish we were closer. Paula, please feel free to call and chat even if it's in the middle of the night and you can't sleep. I will get up and drink vino with you. Oh, and who sings "Poker Face"? I'm not up on the current dance tunes, I don't think. Wendy

Paula,

I was shocked to hear about Mark. Take care of him and yourself. Lisa and I will be praying for all of you. God Bless, Charlie L.

Mark & Paula

We continue to lift you up in prayer, knowing God is there with you every step of the way. With your family there and a caring community here, the prayer chain continues to grow. After reading your journal, Paula, it is assuring to know that you both are feeling all our prayers. GOD is good! I love that we can check in daily on Mark's progress and not have to call Vince for an update. You will continue to be in our prayers. May God's Miracles continue to flow your way! Bill & Patti

Mark and Paula,

It was so nice to see you both yesterday, and to meet all of your peeps. They are very swell people and I can see one of the big reasons why you both are doing so well. And, judging by the amount and content of your "Guestbook", y'all have quite an awesome supporting cast. I know that I do not have to say keep up the good work. We already know. May God bless you and yours, Dave

Good evening! Well it is a glass of vino tonight, the Captain and coke made me wirey, maybe I will start drinking those in the morning, juuuust kidding, people! Mark was tired today because he has a bacterial infection on his lower back. He gave the infection to himself, it is not the allograft. It is a contained area so we pray it does not spread. He had a hard time eating breakfast and did not eat lunch. Had some of his Jamba Juice and drank his Mtn Dew. Mark's folks, Ruth and I ate at Applebee's and brought Mark back a steak and potatoes but after 3 bites he could not eat anymore. We finally figured out he is nauseated. He had never felt that way before. Remember, I carried the four children. He will have to ask for medicine, I cannot make it all better and it is killing me. He will continue to have fevers at night and chills during the day. He shakes uncontrollably and it is a sight to see. His body is trying to regulate due to the burn. Ace, his physical therapist, talked to me today and told me there are always setbacks. It is one long rollercoaster ride. Mark loves rollercoasters so I will remind him of that in the morning. But in the end Mark pushed himself after his bandages were changed at 2 pm and then he walked four laps. I am still overwhelmed by the entries, they mean so much. I read them over and over and over again when I have my moments of fatigue, despair and anxiety. I love you all! KKLL, Paula

*Reflection*

All of our family and friends read my journal, cheered us on when we didn't feel like we had any more energy. Friends and relatives of our friends and relatives were praying for us, complete strangers were writing such encouraging words. From very early on we felt loved and through this love we were reminded of the power of prayer. It is what sustained us during his hospital stay and recovery.

When all you see is your pain
you lose sight of Me.
—*The Shack*

# Setback

June 5, 2009

Good afternoon, Just a quick update on Mark. He is feeling worse than yesterday. He hasn't eaten since yesterday morning. He has had a couple Ensures but no solid food. He has also had the hiccups since 9 am. The team has assessed him and has given him some Thorazine to stop them so he will eat again. They are going to change the bandage on his lower back again and watch his temperature. He has not talked much either. I know I sound like Debbie Downer but the nurses and doctors say he had so many good days this was bound to happen. The good news is that Monsignor Cleary came for a visit this morning. He was priest at St. Ann's for many years and also married us 17 yrs ago. He found work for Mark around the church when Mark was out of work. He has always thought Mark was a good guy and what was he doing with me! In fact, when he came in the room he said this could not have happened to a better guy. He then wanted to know if the crazy mexican (Israel) had anything to do with Mark's accident. Now let me explain Monsignors relationship with Israel's family so no one takes offense to his comment. They were the groundskeepers for

**Saint Anns for many years and Monsignor was very close to them and spent a lot of time and especially holidays them...He will visit Mark in a few days. It was comforting to see him. So we need to pray for Mark to get his appetite back and for the hiccups to go away and no infection occurs. They will run tests in the a.m. and compare. I will write more later when my sense of humor comes back. KKLL Paula**

Dear Paula & Mark, please don't let the more 'tired' and 'less momentous step' days get you down.

After a big day, like you had yesterday, Mark may need to rest & store up energy to surge ahead again.

You are still so far ahead of even the most positive recovery speed that your medical staff had predicted...keep hanging in there.

Maybe just take a nap, & then you can gear up for some more of your Miraculous Moments...I'm Praying for you!!! Tracy

Paula, Mark and Family,

Our thoughts and prayers are with you. You are all so brave! Thank goodness for the support of a large wonderful family and many friends. I wish that we lived closer so we could have been with you but I guarantee you we are there in spirit. What the heck is a skinny pirate? Please let me know if there is ever anything we can do. Love, Malana

Dear Paula & Mark—Hope you had a good night, Mark—you are one amazing guy!! We are so happy that things are going so well & we are praying every day & night that you continue to make such good progress. If anyone did not believe in miracles before, they sure must now!! Take care of yourself, Paula—Mark will need you so you must remain strong. This Website is wonderful—it is great to get all your news. Good luck with the walking today—take care & God Bless! Love & Hugs, Dorothy & Tom

Hi Paula, I can just see you working at the hospital with your computer. Yeah, people will think you are V.I.P. importante. Why can't Mark have water? What is a skinny pirate? Love, Elaine

Hey Mark,

I was in a state of shock when I heard what happened to you, but I am not surprised at all at your tenacious attitude and recovery. This website is a blessing in disguise, able to check on your condition and be updated on the changes as they are written has set a lot of people's mind at ease. Mine included. Keep being yourself and you will be out of there in no time, no doubt about that. Anything you or your family need is just a phone call away. Take care and God bless, Jeff

Mark,

I am thrilled that you continue to make progress. I hope that you feel a tremendous sense of accomplishment at your success. You cut the tree down one swing at a time. Don't underestimate yourself. You are facing the most physical challenge there is according to what I've heard from others. Mom and Dad say you look great. God bless you, your recovery and your family. Sheri

Hi Mark and Paula,

Just a note to let you know even off shift we will be thinking of you. I usually try to forget all about work when I'm off. Sounds like cricket won't let me be the only jokester. Got to remember the old line that laughter can be the best medicine.

Stay strong and you all will get through this together and with all the of the support you are getting we know you will. Lynn, Sherri and family...

Hi Mark,

Like everyone else, I check daily for updates on your healing, and am so happy to hear that it is going well.

Paula, I don't think I ever got to meet you, but you have such strength, I am impressed.

Maybe when Mark gets home, I can come visit. Jeannie

Good morning Paula and Mark,

I'm sure, like many, the first thing I do in the morning is get on line to see if there is a message from you. My heart leaps when I see CaringBridge and I can't wait to read your journal entry. We know you are hanging in there as you both still have your sense of humor. Mark, I hope you can have some water soon. Keep slurping that Ensure and they'll give in sooner or later. We keep you close all day in thought and prayer. Thanks for letting us be a part of the Welsh Team! Love, Pat and Joe

Many prayers are coming from out in the Southeast!!!! All us are cheering for you, Mark!!!!

Funniest if hearing my 6 year old, Ainslee, pray for you since she doesn't use her r's correctly, so you are "Mock." I still tend to think God knows who she's praying for!!!

Hang in there and keep fighting!!! Don't make us come out there out of the swamp with our cheerleading gear on!!!

Thanks for the posts and we look for things to take another turn for the awesome soon!!

In Christ, Clara and family

Paula,

We just got back from graduation...absolutely the coldest one I've been to in the last ten years of going. Froze our a###S off.

I'm so sorry to read that the last couple of days have been bad. As you said, it's like a roller coaster ride (but without the fun).

But I'm glad that Msgr. Cleary came by... he can brighten any day. He's one of those people that can tell you to go to hell and make you look forward to the trip...not that he'd ever actually tell you that, of course!!

We are praying for you. Praying that Mark's infection clears up, the nausea goes away and that he continues to heal. Hang in there. Love, Katie and Mark N

Dear Paula,

I'm sorry to hear that Friday has not been good. DON'T GIVE UP. I know how hard it is from my own experience. Now is when it is the toughest because you are so tired yourself. We pray for Mark but also for you dear girl. Take care of yourself for Mark's sake. Carol

Mark & Paula,

All of our thoughts and prayers are with you both. As you know all of Ridgecrest is praying for you. Sharon and I will be through Fresno on Thursday, I'll call your mom first to see if it's a good time to stop and if there's anything you need brought up.

Keep up your spirits and remember Paula always look up. Lewie & Mary

I am home now and wishing I was there as if somehow I could project healing. Know the comforting waves of prayer as you take this journey. Kiss Mark's forehead for me tonight and tell him I didn't want to wake him up to say goodbye as he was sleeping deeply...love, Ruth

Hi Mark,

You and your family are in my prayers, I pray and hope that you recover quickly and [will] be back to your good ol' self. We miss ya at work already. Rich

I guess there is no easy way to get this done is there? Things are hard right now and my heart is with you Mark. There will be two steps forward and one step back quite a few times as you heal. Don't let it get you down too far. There is always a hand up somewhere in the next moment. You just have to be there to grab it when it shows up. God Bless you Mark. Edith

Paula,

Greetings from the East coast (except Pete, who is on the West coast right now). We are all thinking of you and praying for Mark. Hang in there and remember that life is a roller coaster ride. Things may seem down today, but will go up again tomorrow. Give his body a chance to "catch up".

Thanks for keeping us all up to date on the website. It gives everyone a chance to let you know how much we care! Pete and Loren

Hi Mark and Paula...

I have been reading your updates daily and have continued my praying for you both.

Paula, I know how emotionally and physically draining this is for you, and Mark. Hang in there and stay strong. You're stronger than you will ever know. I learned so much from being with Dad all of that time. Wish there was a way I could help out. If you think of anything, please let me know. Mark is bound to have some days that are rougher than others, but he is so strong and will get through this. One day, hour, minute at a time.

Mom went home this week and it's awfully quiet! My Siamese twin!!

Having a glass of vino and wishing you & I were on the patio, having a glass giggling like school girls!!!

When you see Monsignor again, please tell him I said hello and that he meant the world to Dad. Love you guys!!!! Connie

Mark & Paula,

Hang tight...I was worried we might have a few of these days...and here they are. All it says to me is we just need to continue to pray our a****s (remember Mitch's paper I had to proofread as I was having a skinny pirate. LOL!) off for both of you…we will be bringing your muffins to you soon…I am on the countdown! They are the best perk up that any doctor could ever prescribe :) Everyone loves you and it appears the thoughts and prayers are spread across the US tenfold.

I can't wait to get there…it will be quite the roadtrip with lots of scooby snacks and singing! Chandler and I sang some Little Big Town at the top of our lungs on the way to Wal Mart…it was hilarious!

I love that Monsignor came…he is a great comfort all the time. Much Love and Prayers Always…Amy

Paula and family my thoughts and prayers are with you all. I contacted Neil, who is now a pastor and they are praying for Mark. I will keep checking this site for updates. I love you much. Willie

Hola! Mi amigos, Welsh,

Sorry that Mark is not doing that great today. That just means that we will be praying that much harder tonight. Mark you can feel however you want, because I'm sure your lovely wife has had an off date in your 17 years of wedded bliss. Paula I met your parents yesterday and Baby G was putting on a show for me she was adorable. Tequila (Mexican word of the day) Self-explanatory. My kind of vino. xoxo amor y besos Sara

Hi P & M,

Tell Mark that Walt had hiccups for a while after his surgery—they finally left and we never missed them. My heart goes out to Mark as I know how depressing a sudden illness can be. It WILL get better. Take a day at a time, that is all any of us can do. God must be wondering about us Ridgecrest folks bombarding him with prayers. Paula take care of yourself—you are the rock at least for now. Love you both. Margie

Hi Uncle Mark…

We see you have lots of love and support!! That's so awesome! We sure do love you and think about you and pray for you daily! Glad you've had lots of company!! Praise God for the wonderful miracles he is performing on you. What an amazing God we have! We hope to make it up soon and bug you!! Looking forward to reading about more great progress!! I'm sure all the nurses love having you. Not that often they have such a nice guy to take care of!! :) Blessings, Justin, LaRay, Matt & Lukerduke

Uncle Mark,

It is no fun not feeling well. I hope you start feeling better soon. You need to eat those calories!! You don't need to be worried about your figure right now:-) I hope you got rid of the hiccups and I hear you had a wonderful visitor in Monsignor today. He is a good guy to have on your side! I love you and am praying for you. Love, Erin

Gary and I just returned from Sansum Clinic and the first place I went to was this website to see how you, Mark, were doing. How grand to have so many thinking and praying for you! Your faith and your courage are a real inspiration to all of us. Yours is a very special family.

It was great hearing about Msgr. Cleary's visit. So glad he could be there. Sally and Gary

Paula,

Jay and I are thinking of you and pulling for a speedy recovery. Nancy

Hey sista,

This website is so great! Thanks for keeping us informed. I'm thinking and praying for you guys every day. Hang in there. Remember life is good and so is God. I wish we could come visit, but we are leaving for Montana on Friday. SCHOOLS OUT, thank God again. It has been a rough year. I'm happy you have so much support. Please let me know if there is anything I can do. I haven't heard from Amy, so I assume they have everything handled. We will miss you on Leslie's birthday. It won't be the same without you. We will have a toast to you and Mark. Give him my love and tell him to enjoy the successes and to try and ignore the set backs. Love you too sista! Sista Sue

Hi Paula & Mark,

Weather is weird in Ridgecrest today. Glad to see you and the Captain are getting along. We're off to Cayucos for the weekend and will think of you often, as we imbibe some vino with some old friends. We will make a toast to you and keep you in our prayers. Stay strong…Love, Susie & Vic

Good Morning Paula and Mark,

I pray this new day brings more strength and courage to you both. Every day is new and sometimes just a half a day works too! Love to you both. See you soon!

The kids are awesome! I visit with them in the evenings! Genevieve let Grandpa hold her for her night time bottle last night! Grandpa was on the bad list due to he was the one left home when kids and grandma went off to school!

Grace was thrilled that there was no more studying to be done! Yahoo!

Mitchell had a good time at his lock-in and had his hair perfect for the event! LOL!

Chandler had spent some time with his friend Christopher and then some more lovin' with Genevieve!

All in all it was peaceful and all looking forward to the graduation ceremonies tonight!

You are in our thoughts and prayers always. Love you, Ann and Jerry (Doug)

Good Morning Paula. It is Friday morning. Are your kids out of school now? I am sorry to hear of the trials of Thursday. I can't imagine what it is like to watch your beloved husband suffer. I feel awful that this has happened to you two. Did your daughter pass her driver's test? Tonight is Burroughs graduation and of course it is a windy day here. I hope today will be a better roller coaster ride. I can't believe the Capt'n made you jittery. Maybe you should have a little one in the morning to start you off. Be thinking and praying for you both today. Love Elaine & Gene

Dear Mark & Paula–

Continued prayers from our family to you & yours! Thank you for the updates, it helps to know what specifics we can add to our prayers, (like healing thoughts for that pesky infection spot).

Carpe Diem

...but remember it's a marathon, not a sprint.

...so pat yourself on the back whether it's baby steps or giant leaps, today. Louis, Tracy, Jared & Audra

Hi Mark,

Keep strong! We are asking God daily to get you through this. You have a wonderful loving wife and family by your side. Paula, hang in there. You are Mark's right and left side right now. When Mark is all better I'm sure he will treat you to a nice vacation with a spa. Although I am sure you would be satisfied by just having your husband healthy and back home. Wishing all the best to you and your family, Colleen

So sorry to hear about your accident, Mary phoned me on Saturday and told me about it. I know you will recover swiftly as you have almost all of Ridgecrest praying for you and we all know there is power in prayer. Mary and I will be coming through Fresno on Thursday if you need anything let us know and we can bring it up. We already have the wine packed for you Paula... Prayers for you both...Sharon

After playing phone tag with you yesterday, Paula, thought I'd go this route...didn't want to wake you in case you're sleeping off last nights' meeting with the Captain! I will try again later!! Leslie and I talked last night and want to visit on Tuesday...I know your parents leave that

day, Mark, so let us know if that is an accept-
able day for the Cheer-Wagon to visit! Anyone
out there who'd like to join us, we'd love for you
to come along! "God is great, beer is good and
people are crazy"!! Love and strength to you both!
Judie-Boodie

Mark and Paula,

There are two sayings that help me when
I feel discouraged with life that might bring a
moment of comfort for both of you, it is "Two
steps forward and one step backward" and the
other is "It is darkest before the dawn." I hope
you get some good news today. I am praying and
hoping for a more encouraging day for all. Mark,
this is bigger than you are. I commend your effort
and courage so far. It is amazing. I hope that you
can let go and let God care for you during this
challenging time. Sheri

Paula and Mark,

You are in our thoughts every day. Keep up
the faith. Thank you so much for your updates.
We pray that Mark will be home with the family
soon. We love you! Love, Lisa and James

Paula & Mark,

Thinking about both of you this evening
as I wind down from a busy week and catch up
on your journal. God is truly amazing and I can
see Him in all the miracles, both big and small,
that you share with Mark's progress. I may not
post often, but please know you are in my prayers
frequently throughout each and every day. Even
though it will be a rollercoaster ride to full recovery, it is obvious God is right there every step of

this journey. And we know He will be faithful to see you through, one day at a time.

Paula, especially now, be careful driving; stay focused when you're behind the wheel. It's easy to get distracted with everything you have going on.

Getting through the tough times makes us appreciate that much more what God has done and continues to do for us. May He raise you both up today—physically, mentally, emotionally, and spiritually. God bless, Terry

Hey Mark and Paula,

Sorry it's taken a few days for us to get on this site, but we thought there was a "secret" password that no one gave us (LOL!!) We want you both to know that you have been in our daily prayers for courage, strength, and healing through this ordeal. We know it's hard to do because life doesn't seem to stop when something like this happens, but just take it in baby steps and you'll get through. We got lots of positive reports on Mark's progress from Vince and friends after their visits. Even Mitchell seemed to be doing great at the Middle school field trip Wednesday. I know Paula will get a kick out of the fact that the day they go to the park for a water fight it rains in Ridgecrest! Coleen dedicated her adoration hour Wednesday night to Mark's recovery and for your entire family. We will continue to keep you all in our prayers (especially for no more W family accidents). If there is anything we can do for your family in any way just let us know, we are available.

Also, here is another Spanish lesson for you. Tell Mark that "El Nino" is Spanish for "the Nino". (that's our daughter Megan's favorite Chris Farley quote—I'm not sure why but it makes us laugh!) How come no one's drinking Margaritas?????

Love, Ed and Coleen

*Reflection*

*It was difficult to update friends and family when Mark's progress was very minimal or when there was none at all. The response was always more prayers and encouragement. I never felt defeated for long because I had an army of loved ones supporting me. As I look back on this day, I can sense sadness while reading between the lines. But then, when I read about Msgr. Cleary visiting us and lightening the mood, I am reminded of my faith as a child, a young adult, and now a wife and mother and how my relationship with my parish priest was one of friendship. I had known him since the fifth grade. Msgr. Cleary (Irish, of course) was our priest at St. Ann's for many years and was one of a kind. He unfortunately passed away in November in 2011. The support I felt during my stay in Fresno was very spiritual.*

# Being Uplifted by Others

**June 6, 2009**

Good Morning. Thank you all for your uplifting notes! I woke this morning wanting to go back to bed and have someone wake me when it is over but then I started getting ready like a big girl. When I got on the freeway my "Poker Face" song came on and I perked up! I don't know if I told you that my sister Ruth left yesterday and my brothers David and Vince came. They are here for the weekend and I am so grateful. Dave and Delores (Mark's folks) have been by my side since Tuesday. Can you believe it has been a week already? People have been traveling so far to see us. It warms my heart to know we are loved. Mark is getting his dressings changed this morning; not a big appetite yet, but he is choking down the Ensures. So we pray for an appetite and strength. Love to all, Paula

Hey Mark,

The other Mark here. I check in here a couple times a day to see how you're doing…tell Paula I appreciate the updates. I look forward to the day she posts the news that you have gone home. Take care and we think of you often. The K. Family

Mark and Paula,

Our thoughts and prayers are with you. We think of you often and hope things are ok. I know this road will be long and hard and full of twists and turns, but you will get through it. May God bring peace and love to your hearts. Please let us know if there is anything we can do to help you. You are the best boss a man could ask for. Thank you for pushing me when I needed it the most. I appreciate everything you have done for me. We love you and pray for your speedy recovery. God bless. Tad and Tara

Here's to healing up ASAP! God bless you all and we're praying for you. John

Hey there Mark & Paula,

Just wanted you guys to know that you are in our thoughts and prayers. It's really great to be able to log onto this website and get a daily update when you have been wondering throughout the day, "Hmm, I wonder how Mark's day is going?"

So, thanks for the updates. They mean a lot to all of us out here in cyberland, who would like to be there to give a smile, a few words of encouragement, and good slap on the back, er, uh, well maybe no slapping (yet)! I look forward the day when I can slap your back again, my friend.

Hey, hurry up and get well. We just bought a house and I need you to build me (another) back patio and patio cover. Is next week good for you? I'll have plenty of Ensures and I'll hold the umbrella to keep the sun off...

Just kidding. I got smart and bought a house that already had a patio and a patio cover. Lucky for YOU! Take care! Bruce

Dear Mark and Paula: I continue my pledge for Mark. I see the prayers continue to pour in. You deserve it. Keep up the great journaling. YOU GO MARK. I am going to call pat and see how she is doing. (My pledge can only go for 75 days :) Claire B

Hi Paula & Mark,

Hope things are improving today—we are praying hard for extra strength for you both— hope the hiccups are gone—that is not fun!! You have both been so amazing—such an inspiration to all!! I have all kinds of people at school praying for you—told a few of the seniors that had come back to serve their detentions about Mark—they all said they would say prayers for you. Glad David & Vince are there with you—know that many, many people are praying—take good care & God Bless you both. Love & hugs—Dorothy & Tom

Hi Paula and Mark,

We really appreciate the daily updates. I notified our daughter, Christina in Washington state, and she has added your family to her prayer list. I gave her the website as well.

We pray for strength on the not so good days and rejoice on the good days. Keep up the good work, Mark. Paula, hang in there and if there is anything we can do please let us know. We love you and you are in our prayers and thoughts. Linda & Hank

Uncle Mark,

I found this great quote. I think it pertains to you and Aunt Paula during this trying time. I love you guys. "You never know how strong you are until being strong is the only choice that you have!" Love you, Erin

Hi Paula and Mark—

You are in my thoughts and prayers daily. I promise to get to St. Ann's and arrange a mass for your intentions this coming week. Keep up the good work, Mark. We're rooting for you.

Keep your chin up, Paula. This too shall pass!
Love, Your fellow soprano who
can't sing right now—Dianne

Well, after a few problems with my inability to deal with computers…here I am. Whoever thought this website up was (and/or) is quite the genius. I hope this Saturday morning finds big Mark feeling better than yesterday. I've no funny stories to tell coming from a small family, but we are all praying for you and your families (all the driving…hoping everyone has a safe trip)! I know my Mom wishes you all well and a speedy recovery for Mark. I do love your family and friends and reading their funny little stories. How very fortunate you are (and I am) for knowing all of you. Take care and stay strong! Love you, Tami

Hello,

There isn't a minute that goes by that you two and your family aren't on our minds. We love reading your daily postings and keeping up with the good (and unfortunately) the bad days.

I am not sure where I read this (maybe a prior blog), "Hope sees the invisble—Feels the intangible and Achieves the impossible." Our faith, hope and prayers are with you all!

Grad was a little chilly. However a little hot chocolate and Peppermint Schnapps kept our little group going. (Yes we are the smart ones)

Saw Judie and she said that her and Leslie (and whoever else) will be heading up possibly Tuesday. So I am going to jump on the cheer wagon and be there! Looking so forward to seeing you and giving you a big hug. Stay strong— laugh, and keep taking the "Two Steps Forward" they have to get you somewhere! Chin up baby! Love to you all! Teresa, Rodger and Family

Mark & Paula

We are leaving for a few days and will be unable to access a computer to check in on Mark's healing. However we ALWAYS have access to GOD. Rest assured you will continue to be in our thoughts and prayers. I think you said on a previous post that the kids are coming on Sunday. Let's all pray that Mark will have a good day on Sunday. I'm sure you both are missing them as they are you. Our caring thoughts and prayers remain with you. Patti

Hi Paula, I visited with Katie N. yesterday and she gave me this website. Sounds like Mark is making progress and has a lot of determination. I am concerned about you and how you are managing to "adjust" to this whole experience. Sometimes when the nurses etc. say to you "do you have any questions?", you don't even know what questions to ask since this is such a new experience. If you want, please call and we can chat about what is happening. Like everyone else we are praying for you and all the family and thinking of you, I look forward to visiting with you. Love, Katy M.

> So this is what I'm thinking...
> IT has been a week!
> It HAS been a week!
> It has BEEN a week!
> It has been A week!
> It has been a WEEK!
> ...and all that goes with that...
> I miss you and love you
> Your friend, Hope

Paula and Mark,

I hope today is the day for things to look up. Hard to believe it has been a week. Keep the faith and you will get through this. Maybe once Mark sees the kids his spirits will lift!!! It sounds like you'll have a busy weekend with family there. We love you and miss you. If all goes well Judie and I will see you Tuesday. Love, Leslie

Uncle Mark,

I hope today brings you a mighty appetite and some strength. Keep your head up, you are already so far ahead of the game in terms of your progress. We are so proud of you. I love you, lots of prayers headed your way! Auntie, Hang in there! YOU CAN DO THIS! You are one tough cookie. Just like Uncle Mark you too are allowed to have rough days. I'm so glad you have such a great support system. I love you. Erin

Hey Mark & Paula,

Sad to hear you got a couple of rough days, Keep your head screwed on right. Everyone is here for you and the nurses will help get you through. Love ya, big guy. Lynn

Hi Paula,

I got the update from Katie at work a few days ago, and then Mitchell was pretty happy talking about his dad and his progress the other night at the Luau lockdown (lockin?…middle school…it's probably all the same). Just a note to let you know that we're thinking about all of you and keeping you all in our daily prayers. I make the kids pray an "Our Father" and a "Hail Mary" everyday in the car on the way to school. Of course Jenn says it's because of my driving, which is partly true, but we do it as a way to start out the day and to include intentions. Now Mark is part of our daily prayer intentions. Mark is very lucky to have you by his side. You're strong and you're funny and you're definitely not a Debbie Downer! I didn't know you were friends with Elaine. We had some laughs about some of your antics the other day! Also, when you all are back home, we would like to do meals for you. It's something that military wives do for each other whenever someone has a baby, or gets sick, etc. etc. So, we want to extend this great thing on to you and your family. I don't know if anyone is planning this for you, and if they are we want to be added to the list. If not, then we'll start a list! I have a bottle of wine with your name on it waiting for you when you get home. Take care and just know that you and your family are in our daily prayers. XOXO Gina and Family

Paula,

You probably don't remember us but... Erik and Dena here. We went camping at some crappy campground outside of LA with other families and us (and Grace/Kate) and had a blast. I believe you and Mark picked Grace up on Sunday and you were pregnant at the time...I am the NCIS Agent on the base in China Lake if that rings a bell. We think the world of Kate, and of course her twin, Grace, and will always think of y'all as "extended family". I have lots of friends that work at Coso (Will G, Don B, Dick A) and we are all praying for you at the Inyokern Church of Christ where we attend. Get that big boy of yours better and come visit us at our next duty station, Naples, Italy!!! Kirsten and Marcel would love travel companions and we would love to see you!! Sorry to ramble, but we love Y'all!!! Erik, Dena, Braden, and Jake

Good Morning,

I'm so sorry to hear it has been a rough(er) couple of days. But you know the staff is right, with all of Mark's amazing recovery days, there will be some downer days. And lo, on that you get Monsignor:) He can bring a smile to anyone, huh? He always gives Brian a slap across the back of the head to say hello to him. He also married Brian and I, 14 years ago. Our kids go to Immanuel, so I have passed the prayer requests on that way too:)

Know we are all continuing to pray for you all. I can only imagine how bad all of your buddies at work want you back...to poke more fun at you:) Some of these entries are cracking me up...it sounds like you guys are REALLY in good company, know how to enjoy life and each other. Blessings, Toby

Well, I just don't understand why everyone was saying they were so "cold" during the graduation? The cutest toddler in the world was just as toasty as could be dancing with her backyardbuddy friends on Nick TV. Just cuz those "grown-up" people were silly enough to go out in the weather and watch a bunch of hooligans toss flat hats around!

The future dance major practiced her moves to "Samari-Pie" while taste testing Starbucks oatmeal. Kinda skeery when a toddler consumes more calories than her Dad! Better get cracking on that Dad! Genevieve wanted to read "Ten Things I Wish I'd Known Before I Left Home" (or something like that) but we decided the fuzzy barnyard animal book would be better...it had color pictures with fluffy fuzzy fur stuff!

Everyone's entitled to a bad day or two now and again...nausea and hiccups...but now it's time to get back to the recovery! I'm sure family visiting is a huge encouragement so get to it Dude! Praying for you both—strength and Godspeed (success of the journey!).

Tammy

**Good Evening! It ended up being a pretty good day for Mark! First, my friend Sara P and husband Frank showed for a visit, it was so good to see them. Frank brought Sara all that way so she could hug and see me! They stayed for about an hour so my brother David called her husband a saint. Clara arrived just in time for lunch at the cafeteria! After lunch, Clara**

and I headed to the room to find out Mark had just finished five laps! He looked so much better. We started to visit and I decided to shave him again. Using his electric shaver on him is awkward so I ask him how to do it as I am shaving him. I decided to ask him when he thought he could do it himself and he grabbed the shaver and said "right now!" and started shaving himself. He was being feisty :)

The doctor came by a little later to say his white blood count was high and they were starting an antibiotic. It did not mean he had an infection but they would take that precaution. They will test his blood and urine and if they were clear they would stop the antibiotic. He also said Mark would most likely have surgery on Tuesday to clean up the wounds and add allograft back to places that needed it.

Then the speech therapist came in to look into the hiccup/gagging problem. She had him eat soft foods and then some solids and asked him lots of questions. She determined it was not a wind pipe problem. He did experience all the symptoms in front of her and said he knew now he was not crazy. They will hopefully get to the bottom of this problem soon but they are a little perplexed. He promised he would drink the 5–6 Ensures a day. My brothers visited him after Clara and me and got to talking to him about his work. They decided to go and print off maps of his work and will talk shop in the morning. I am loving all the entries, they are my drug of choice. KKLL (Kiss Kiss Love Love), Paula

Sista, I am really surprised. Personally, I feel you are quite handy with a razor. Especially in those hard to reach places. You were very careful about the twists and turns. I was often reminded of your skills walking around Europe. It pretty much made the whole trip for me. Mark should feel very lucky he has such a skilled craftsman as yourself to do his shaving for him. I know I appreciated your special techniques. I love ya! Sista Sue

*Reflection*

*I can remember early on in my childhood that I always looked at prayer as a conversation, sometimes heated and trying to get my point across and then sometimes light and airy and casual, so I have always found it easy to talk to God. I am a firm believer in also saying what you mean and mean what you are saying. This also can get me into trouble, ha ha. But I like facts and specificity so people closest to me know that I shoot from the hip and call a spade a spade. As you have noticed that is how I tackled requesting prayers for Mark.*

Prayer is not optional, it is essential. Without it the spiritual life languishes, suffers, dies and though life may remain in the body, lost is the central purpose for living at all: communion with God.
—Johnette Benkovic, *Experience Grace in Abundance*

# God's Timeline

**June 7, 2009**

Good afternoon, Mark is having a pretty good morning. He ate all his breakfast but still has the hiccups. Doctor increased Thorazine (anti-psychotic drug that is also prescribed for chronic hiccups). I yelled "BOO!" Nurse Tim laughed and Mark said "What?" about 20 seconds later. It was comical! But the hiccups are still there. I got to see him walk 2 laps and then head back to bed. He will try to pace himself today and do that 2 more times. David and Vince are with him now looking at the map of Coso. My children will arrive around 2:00 p.m.. Thanks Auntie Amy and Ann. The nurse already said all but Genevieve can see him and we all can go together. I am blessed to have Tim who will bend the rules for us. Chandler really is not old enough but he is allowing him to see his dad. David and Vince will leave today and my sisters will stay on with my children through Tuesday. Visitors are the best, the days are long! May God bless all the travelers! Keep the prayers up and love you all, Paula

Mark

I can't believe I really typed this. I've been thinking about what happened to you, it could happen to anyone out there. I believe you are without a doubt the one person that will overcome this and grow from it. Hope to see you home soon. Tony C

P.S. It took me 20 min. just to type this that is why you & Bruce got to do the computer work.

Hi Mark and Paula, Just to let you know I will be reading your updates each day. Love reading what others wrote even though I don't know them. What fabulous people you guys have in your life. I'm glad today was a good day. I still pray for you and the family. Hope the kids visit was a good one. Love to you all. Edie

Paula,

We are winding down here after graduation weekend (and Molly's 18th birthday was yesterday, too). I am really tired but I keep thinking how tired you must be, Mark must be, your Mom & Dad, his Mom & Dad, your kids & all your family. I'm praying that God gives everyone all the strength & energy that they need to get through each day—and that each day you move a little closer to the goal of Mark returned to good health & fighting form. So glad that you've had so many visitors & that your kids are there now.

Hang in there. Love, Katie N

Hi Mark & Paula:

I was just checking in and wanted to let you know that our family continues their prayers for you daily. Thank you for the updates. Colleen

Hola! Amigos, Welsh,

It was so good to see Mi Amiga Paula, and meet her good looking brothers. Mark I will see you next time, I just didn't want you to feel uncomfortable. Paula keep up the good work, you truly inspire me with your faith and strength. Remember we have a date. Spanish word of the day "Enriquecer" means to enrich, and I do feel enriched by our friendship. amor y besos, Sara

I finally figured out how to read your jounal entries...Yes I'm a goof...Now I know what all happened to Mark on that cruddy/miraculous day. I'm a bit slow on the computer stuff but getting better. I hope today finds everybody doing ok. Just got home from work so I thought I'd give you guys a shout out that I'm thinking of you. Glad to hear that the kids arrived safely with their Aunties. Tell Mark I said Hi and I hope he gets to go home soon. He's going to need some sort of cage to keep Genevieve from throwing herself and all her love at him...extra baby gates or a big kennel maybe??? Take care and I will write again soon. I will have big glass of vino for you...that's a promise!! Love to all of you, TAMI

Mike arrived safely in Japan—said he cannot log on from his iphone to the website so wanted me to tell you and Mark that prayers and thoughts from all the H family (Japan to Illinois!) are coming at you. I am having psychosomatic symptoms just like I did when Karen had Adam and I had to go into labor, too—will let you know if my skin starts peeling—we love you all so much—enjoy your family today! Love, Ruth

Mark and Paula,

School is out but I had to let you know that the first graders went to the Grotto every day on our last week of school to pray a decade of the rosary for you, Mark. On Sports Day, as I was reaching for the bag of rosaries to pass out, I said, "We will be going out for Sports Day" meaning after we prayed at the Grotto for you, but they cut me off and about half the class said, "But we have to pray for Mr. Welsh first!" I almost lost it, but, assuring them that is what I had planned to do, passed out the rosaries with teary eyes. I had a great visit on Saturday with your mom and dad, Paula. What role models they are—ALL of you are. God bless. Chris

Paula,

It is so wonderful to hear that Mark is doing so much better. You sound much better also. Everything will be just swell. I hope that the visit with your crumb crunchers goes swimingly as well. I'm sure it will. We are all missing Mark at work, me the most, there is a very large presence missing from this place. But, we will see him here soon. Well, you take care. Best wishes to you and yours. And hey, don't worry, I have a whole network of Catholic old ladies praying for you all from Buena Park to Bishop. Dave

Hey Mark,

Glad to hear that you are doing better. Keep up the good work. You have been in our prayers everyday. Yes, even while I was at a Yankees game, I was thinking of you. God was looking out for the Yankees, they came from behind to win and then there was the Lakers. They beat the pants off the Magic. So I know He is there for you. If there is anything I can do, let me know. Alan and I wish you the best. Hang in there. Alan and Kirk-o.

Good Morning—what a difference a day makes!! So glad to read your good news this morning—We are planning to come up & see you next Saturday ( if you are still there—you may be back in Ridgecrest—who knows??) I'm sure you are enjoying the kids about now—Hope Mark had a good night & continues to be "feisty"— good for you, Mark!! You are in our prayers every day—I talked to Tom's sister yesterday so prayers are being sent from Winnipeg too! Know that we love you lots—Take care of yourself Paula—Love & Hugs to you both & to the kids too. May God Bless you all—Dorothy & Tom

Paula,

I have no idea how that note was dated June 11!!! That was written on the 6th. I guess my age is showing, but I can drive!!! Paula said soooooo. So happy to hear yesterday was better. There could be 4 or 5 of us coming on Tuesday. We would love to see Mark but it looks like he'll be a little busy. Can't wait to see you Paula. We had a great party for the Seniors. We missed you both alot. You are in my thoughts and prayers daily. See you soon. Love. Leslie

Mark,

We've been thinking of you often, and keeping you in prayer. As I was sitting in Mass this morning behind your family, I was wondering how you were doing, feeling, and what was going through your mind. I'm sure your children are at the top of your thoughts. You are very blessed to have such nice kids and a great extended family to take such good care of them. Your kids all looked happy, healthy, and full of the Holy Spirit. Work hard and heal fast. Take Care. Shawn

Hey Paula,

Just got home from church and Nancy came for the first time in months. She had Adam with her as he stayed the night and slept on poppy's side of the bed. It is good for her to have him visit. She does not do email, so I told her I would send the message that she is home and praying. We sang acapella—at least there was quite a group of us—not sure what else to say. (Walt did not say we sounded bad, so that is good!)

Hugs and kisses. Margie and Walt

Mark and Paula,

We don't have the pleasure of knowing you, but as members of the St. Ann's Parish family, and good friends of the O family, we have been receiving your updates, and of course now I consider myself a "virtual" friend! You can't have too many friends who are praying for you, thinking about you and sending love your way! Many arms are reaching out to you both from Ridgecrest, and ours are among them. Keeping you close to our hearts. Love, Ruth and Larry

Hey Mark & Paula—

The whole St. Ann Parish is praying night and day for your speedy recovery. Michelle, Robert, and I think of you often. Hang in there.

Bet you'll never want to see another can of Ensure after this. Take Care…Tom

I'm with Sue…what the heck, Leslie? I'm having a hard enough time keeping up with everything witout you jumping ahead! Slow down, girl!! You'll miss your visit at the rate you're going!!! :) Hopie

So glad to hear you are had a good day yesterday! Hope today brings you the same strength and determination. Love you, Erin

Paula,
    I am glad it was a better day for you and Mark, yesterday. I pray each day for continued progress for you and Mark. I hope that you get to enjoy your children today. I am keeping an ongoing gratitude/miracle list for Mark and his recovery and at this point I have 33 entries. After this, I will add more. Sheri

Mark & Paula,
    Just doing my normal check in to see how things are going up there. Paula we really do appreciate the postings and updates back here in the Ridge! Sorry to hear about the small setback, but I am sure small setbacks will be easily overcome by you, Mark. It sounds like you have some quality caregivers there. When we make it up to visit, I will hopefully get to thank them in person. I can bring up the "Week in Review" sheets if you like. That way you can keep your finger on the Coso pulse. LOL…On second thought, you focus on getting back to yourself, and we will deal with Coso. Keep doing what you can, but

don't overdo it. We will be thinking and praying for you and yours. Take care my friends.

Snowy & Dawn

Mark and Paula,

So glad to get your message this morning and hear that Saturday was a "better day." Also glad to hear you are getting "feisty", Mark. Tell David "Hello" for us. Love, Joe and Pat

**Good Evening!**

**My children arrived safely around 2 p.m. I took them to the room and Mark was kinda groggy. They were very brave and strong as they have to pass other patients to get to their bandaged dad. Nurse Tim was so good with them and took their picture for Mark. Mark ended up only walking the two laps which was kind of discouraging until I spoke with the night nurse Mike. He explained that Mark's body is reacting to the trauma with sleeping, hiccups and energy some days and not so much other days. He also said how hard it must be for a pretty independent guy to be so dependent. We pray for the hiccups to subside and strength to appear. Genevieve was so happy to see me and so jolly the whole time in the waiting room; I wonder what tomorrow will be like? Thanks for the care package everyone, I was out of vino and it magically appeared in my car. God has blessed me with such a prayerful team! Paula**

**P.S. Dave and Delores, Genevieve and I attempted to go to 5:15 Mass at St John's Cathedral but it was standing room only due to 1st Communion. We gave it a good girl**

scout try but Genevieve wanted to run wild during the homily. I know God understands

*Reflection*

 *There's an old Yiddish proverb that says "We plan, God laughs." I think most logical Christians would agree that God is in charge. God tested my faith a lot during Mark's hospital stay and it was difficult at times to be patient and be grateful for the small steps forward.*

 *I have a few vivid memories of certain days in the hospital, one being Mark's on-going hiccups. Mark was so frustrated, his appetite was not good, the hiccups were not ceasing.*

 *Come to find out, hiccups are common when someone has had something tragic happen to them, or an illness. They are a stress response.*

Suffering is the fire that refines the
gold that is your character.
—Matthew Kelly, *Perfectly Yourself*

# Renewed Comfort and Family

June 8, 2009

Hello, it was a busy day for Mark. He started off the morning with three of his four children saying good morning. Then three co-workers stopping by for a visit-Andy, Justin and Tad. I know it lifted Mark's spirits. Israel, wife Isabel and their three children arrived around noon. Next, Jim, Susan and Sam stopped by for an overnighter. Mark was able to see them all before a bandage change at 3pm. Last but not least April, a co-worker, arrived around 3:00 p.m. and was able to see him around 5:30 p.m.. We all trekked to dinner at Hero's, it was delicious. Now about Mark, he is still having the hiccups and did not get out of bed today. I would say he is a little feisty, just ask April she got to witness it. He will go to surgery around noon tomorrow to replace any allografts that have come off and wash all the wounds. He has been so groggy due to all the drugs he is on so I do not even know if he knows he is having surgery. My prayers are that he comes through surgery with flying colors (literally) and the hiccups disappear and his appetite reappears.

Our children will head home around noon tomorrow. I have loved having them here

**even though it is very boring for them except maybe when they went to Jim and Susan's hotel to swim. Good night! Thanks for all the thoughts and prayers. KKLL, Paula**

Dear Mark and Paula: Maria just showed me how to get to your web site. I think of you both at least every hour—sometimes that's all I think about, and each time I pray for you both. I am so sorry about the accident.

I just finished reading all your journals, Paula. I am so proud of you. You have great strength so you can help Mark and everyone else who is hurting for you both. You know you both are loved by so many and we all hurt so much for you and Mark.

Thank goodness you have such a close, loving family. I have always admired the strength of your family bond.

Melanie says to tell you she knows a sure-fire cure for hic-cups. If it is still a problem, give her a call. I think she is having computer problems.

Love and hugs and kisses, Ron and Nancy and family

I have done everything I know how to change my time zone from when I was in St. Louis—UGH!!!

Just a quick note to say that we are all praying for a successful surgery tomorrow and that our Gentle Giant (Mike's name for Mark) comes out of it peacefully.

Know that if you need anything, I am just a telephone call away. Love, Ruth

It is with much love and prayers that you are gaining the strength to continue on to another blessed day ~ God gives us only what we can handle ~ Life is a cycle of true ups and downs and it's moments like these that we are reminded of how precious the ones we love so dearly are so vulnerable to what could happen in a split second ~ You are all in our thoughts and prayers ~ With Love The R Family

"WHEN THINGS SEEM to be going all wrong, stop and affirm your trust in Me. Calmly bring these matters to Me, and leave them in My capable hands. Then, simply do the next thing. Stay in touch with Me through thankful, trusting prayers, resting in My sovereign control. Rejoice in Me—exult in the God of your salvation! As you trust in me, I make your feet like the feet of a deer. I enable you to walk and make progress upon the high places." JOB 13:15; Psalm 18:33 Colleen

Dear Mark and Paula.

Just a quick note from me and your second favorite Mark. I am here helping him with Sophea and Jackson. Casey has the boys. Mark says stay out of the vino and baby your husband. I have been reading him all the entries and trying to add the voice to go with it. Like Tommys and Tami, I can do Tommy pretty good. Tell Mark the first chance I get I will come visit and read to him. Last week of school. Again my prayers were heavy for you Sunday night. (I walked by my case of Coronas.) Keep up your faith and will write more soon. Your buddy Claire B...0 proof in my glass

Hey Paula and Mark,

Hope you are doing good today and hope for Mark's sake the hiccups have subsided!! I'm done with work for the day and put some food in the oven, since the weather is a tad gloomy here in Corona. I bought cookies for the crackerjacks so I could have some peace for two minutes… trust me two minutes is all I'll get before some crying ensues. Hope the kids are doing fine after seeing Mark. I'm sure that took alot of courage!! Thanks for the everyday updates and we'll give the good Samaritan an extra special blessing for filling the car with wine, my kind of friend!! You guy's all take care, get some sleep and we'll keep praying! Love you, Tami (the zoo keeper) ha ha

Well the big road trip is tomorrow. Looking forward to seeing you. Looks like we'll have a van full. Judie, Ann, Donna, Theresa, and me. Donna and maybe Ann will ride up with Karen. I know we all really wish we could see Mark. Karen said he'll be back in surgery. Has to be done but we will miss getting to see him. Let's pray it's a good day and hopefully the kids are providing that. See you tomorrow. Love Leslie

Greetings from Lake Elsinore (I prefer "smells some more")!

We are sorry to hear of your situation-all of us are in your corner cheering for you!

There is a tremendous amount of people sending you positive thoughts—Aedan and I included! Tom and lil' Aedan…

Mark and Paula we are praying for you and your family daily. We are all pulling for you to come back soon. Please let us know if you need anything we have a pretty big family to rely on. Perry.

Hi Mark and Dad

Gendhgdssnieve is trying to help write a get well message sdff gjehell

Love to you dad and I really want the other little girl's bottle in the waiting room. grandpa and grandma are taking me for a walk outside for distraction. She's back and running! Love and prayers. Ann

Hi Paula…

Glad to hear the kids arrived. How long will they stay? Last week of school for our gang… yeah! Mom said she talked to your Mom after church yesterday. Your Mom said she has "taken to the bottle", then pulled Genevieve's bottle out of her purse.

I hope you guys have a good day, full of encouragement and strength.

Miss you & will talk to you soon! Give those cute kids a hug for me. Connie

Hi, Welsh family—

Tracy and I just got back in to an internet zone since Thursday—just finished catching up on the updates—thank you—it's great to get the haps with a few keystrokes. We are both sorry to hear about the rough days. Hoping and praying they are behind you as we write.

Mark—when Dave and I came to visit last week, I had prepared myself for the bug eyed monster michelin man! But laying there talking was the good old Mark we all love—just wrapped in 50 lbs of gauze in your new multicultural state. It was so good to see you—and better to hear your will power was up to it's usual. Yeah—we all expect you to be stubborn and push on as you always do, just wish you were not being tested to this extent. Happy to see you pushing so hard—even if it pushes you over the edge once in a while. No one knows their limits until they experience them. Keep both hands on the wheel through this rough ride, you'll end up on top at the end of it.

I'm looking forward to the turnovers to come where we have both been too busy to remember much and the office is a pile of ongoing business—both promising to clean it up someday…uh huh! Keep fighting the good fight brother—Mike and Tracy

Dear Mark & Paula~

Up & down & Up…so glad to hear that the nursing staff says that is to be expected.

A week down though!!! You are getting that much closer to the end of your hospital time, as you work out all the pesky kinks, along this healing journey.

My prayers for you on this day: that the hiccups subside, the white count goes down, taking in real food feels more comfortable, & your laps are easier.

Sending love to you both, Tracy

Hi Paula,

Well, it is Monday morning. I wonder how Mark is doing and how those hiccups are? I bet your children were so very happy to see you and Mark. So you are a vino girl now. I goofed on

Fat Captains. What kind of wine do you prefer? Friday nights graduation was typical for Burroughs. windy. I heard Safe Grad was on the cold side. What kind of song is "Poker Face"? Country? Here is the big question: Do you have a feeling when you and Mark might come home? I love that the Monsignor came to see you. Well girl, be strong. Stay positive. You and Mark have another day ahead of you. Love, Elaine & Gene

Hi Guys…

I just caught up on your journal from the weekend. Hiccups…what the heck??!! I loved the "boo" story. I can totally see the look on your face as you did it!!! Glad to hear you are getting lots of love and support! I am soooo proud of you and appreciate you keeping us all posted! Big hugs, lots of love, and best wishes!! Sandy L.

*Reflection*

*It was difficult at times for me to comprehend all the medical lingo and I felt anxious at times with all the unknowns. Hospital noises and smells along with the other burn patients were overwhelming at times. I look back at my children's young faces and am amazed to see how happy and calm they look. They were just eager to see their dad. I believe their guardian angels were working overtime.*

*I felt at peace for most of my stay in Fresno. The only explanation has to be prayer and miracles. It was a tragedy but not an awful experience.*

Our response to suffering may give God
greater glory and get Satan to shut up.
—Dave Earley, *21 Reasons Bad
Things Happen to Good People*

# Gratitude for Community

June 9, 2009

Good Morning, I should have brought the vino with me today! Mark was so groggy this morning talking in his sleep. Chandler, Mitchell and Grace got to see him and kiss him before he left for surgery. They will not see him until he comes home. The physical therapist was working with Mark right before the surgery nurse came. He was going to get Mark up to walk because he might be laid up for a day after surgery so they all decided to have him walk to surgery. Mark kept saying, "let's get this over with!" Mark may have setbacks after surgery it's anyone guess. I have been told that his surgery will not be as long as his first one, but they did not even give me an estimate. It is hard for me to digest because I like to know EVERYTHING. Pray, Pray and Pray. It is going to be long day and my stomach is feeling like the first day. Love to all, Paula (my sissies will take the kids home around noon so Genevieve will take a nice nap, she has been cranky.) Karen just called and my girlfriends have arrived.

Well, (that's a deep subject) Did everyone get that? I am in a fog right now. Mark's surgery took longer than expected but I am so glad I had the distraction of my girlfriends. We cried, we laughed. I gave them an educational tour of the hospital, had some Margaritas and beer and some more laughs. I finally got called at around 4:30 pm that he was in recovery and I could go talk to the doctor. He told Karen and I that it went pretty well. The good news is that Mark's upper extremities are healing well especially the hands, they are not bandaged anymore. They are little crusty but they are healing on their own. His arms, chest and back and thighs are also healing as expected but are still covered with some synthetic skin and some allograft. The bad news is that below his knee to his ankles are very deep 2nd degree burns and will most likely need skin grafts. That means a longer time in the hospital. The doctor said his elevated white blood count might be from his lower legs being infected so he cleaned them real good. In 7–10 days Mark will endure this surgery again. They have taken him off the Thorazine and will put him on a strong antacid to help heal the hiccups. He has the feeding tube back in until he gets an appetite back. When I saw him at 7:00 p.m., he had a pretty pink inflatable blanket to keep him warm after being in surgery all day. He looked better than I thought he would. I am grateful for all the generosity that people have shown me. I know I cannot do this alone. Mark's folks have to leave in the morning and are very apprehensive about going. They have helped me tremendously with relieving me of some of the daily burden at the hospital. I will miss them. The prayers are working and we move on to tomorrow. I know tomorrow will be a better day because I bought perfume on

**my way home tonight so if the odors at the hospital start to get to me I can sniff myself. Good night, Paula**
**P.S. Karen is here until Saturday!**

Hi Mark & Paula,

For fun I googled—hiccup cures—the link below takes you to a site where this person has collected 250 cures for hiccups and is trying to test what works and what doesn't. Maybe one will work for you…if not it is pretty interesting what people have tried.

http://www.musanim.com/mam/hiccup.htm

Glad to hear your crew came to see you probably a good healing step for all of you. I like many find myself thinking of you often then choke down the lump in my throat and say a little prayer. I'm sure God is hearing.

As you might know I went through a unexpected life changing trauma many years ago. People still ask how did you get through it— my answer is always—not alone, someone more powerful than this weak soul gave me strength, led the way and kept me on the right path. You will too. Take care. Diana

Dear Paula and Mark,

Angels all around you both!!!! You have been in our constant thoughts and prayers!!! I am so glad you have such a wonderful support team around you, of both family and friends. I have some water from Lourdes, France that is believed to be healing water. Would love to send it to you, but need your address. My parents brought it back last year when they visited. You can drink it and put a little on Mark's burn areas—even over the bandages. Love to read about the miracles that have taken place so far. Thanks for letting us know you needed prayers. God Bless!!! Katie, Dave, Holly and Paige

Good evening Paula/Mark.

Love and prayers to you. May the day's surgery bring relief and another step forward. You guys are always on our mind.

Current info for you—Sam graduated from Redlands and Casey will graduate from UCR Saturday. Sam is going to grad school in Boston

Sophea and Jackson (who live with us now) are joys to us (though it is very tiring so I understand Pat's scotch at nights). So glad your family is able and willing to be there for you. Claire and I will work out a time to come and visit you and or the kids. Thanks for keeping up with this site, Paula. It is good to know what is going on without having to bug you. Your friends are so delightful. Peace, love and Bobby Sherman. Rose and gang

Mark and Paula and kids,

Just wanted to say hi and hope Mark's surgery went well. I hope he is not in any pain either. (keep the drugs a com'n)

Glad to see you all had soooo many visitors to help pass the time…that's so awesome!! Got nothing going on today just best wishes and prayers for all of you!!

Take care and hope to see you all when Mark gets home and situated. My Mom sends her love to all and I know you know she's praying hard. Love you guys, Tami

Paula and Mark—

You are in our thoughts and prayers daily. Stay strong and keep the faith…God's grace will get you through each day. Mark is a fighter and we know he will come through with flying colors. All our Love, Uncle Wayne and Aunt Rose

Dear Paula & Mark—got your updates today, Paula—hope the surgery is going well—I am praying hard especially today—I'm sure you were glad to see your kids—it will be hard to say good-bye to them—Hang in there—there will be good days & bad but in the end it will all pay off—You are so loved—take care & God Bless— Love, Dorothy & Tom

I heard about Mark from Leslie over the weekend and wanted to take a few minutes to send our thoughts and prayers your way. I will keep checking back on your journal, Paula, what a wonderful way to keep us all informed on what's going on. I know I wouldn't call for fear of bugging you or interrupting. I think once Mark's on the mend we need to start planning another cruise. Love to you all. Lorin and Shelly

Paula,

You must be wearing out. I will hope that Mark's surgery goes well and that the skin under the allografts is rebuilding. Courage, girl. If you are having problems sleeping, the doctors caring for you can help you out. Just ask one of the nurses—they sound like they are a terrific group of people. I'm really enjoying reading the guestbook—took me a long time yesterday to catch up. What a wonderful group of friends coworkers, everybody that writes! Teresa K

Hey Guys—just thinking about you. Hope your procedure goes great today Mark, and hope you can get something down tonight besides Ensure…Ugh!—Mike

Paula and Mark…I'll offer my hour of adoration up just for you two and your family. We pray all went well with the surgery. So do you now have a new driver in the family?!! Take care. Sally

Hey, Paula!
I hope and pray Mark's surgery went well today and that you're feeling better now (as better as you can). Here's a joke to share with Mark when he's recovered from the anesthesia. (Cath. Dig., 8/06, p. 21):
Posted outside a monastery: "Next Sunday afternoon there will be a procession in the monastery grounds. If it rains in the afternoon, the procession will take place in the morning."
:) Mary G

Praying, praying, praying…as requested, dear Paula.
…For it to 'go quickly today' (for Paula), and 'smoothly today' (for Mark).
Actually, I guess you'd both like quick & smooth & the BEST most POSITIVE outcome possible!!! Prayers for that, OK??? Tracy

Paula, Here is my prayer for you and Mark.

Lord Jesus Christ, in your ministry you healed many with frail and diseased bodies. Be present with Mark, your servant, as he undergoes surgery. Bless him and Paula with faith in your loving-kindness and protection. Endow the surgeon and the medical team with alertness and skill so that, if it be your will, this surgery may help Mark to a speedy restoration of health and strength. I pray this in your name as you live and reign with the Father and the Holy Spirit, one God, now and forever. Amen

Remember, we are all with you today and throughout the remainder of this trial...I am so happy to hear that Mark is still his feisty ol' self, we wouldn't have him any other way. I am also glad to hear that you have many close friends around you lifting your spirits, and helping you drink them...LOL. It was great that the nurse allowed all of your children in, I am sure it lifted everyone up. Big Hugs!!!!! Lisa H

Hi there, Paula and Mark,

Still continuing to pray you through this tough time. Keep the faith sissy...it is all gonna be better. Hang in there, Mark, God is with you through it all. Hugs and Kisses, Jill

Hey Paula,

We know today is a hard one. We just wanted to let you know that we are praying for you and Mark through his surgery today. We are also keeping everyone who is traveling in our prayers for a safe journey. Hope this short poem helps you through the day:

Be still, my soul! the Lord is on thy side;
Bear patiently the cross of grief or pain;

Leave to thy God to order and provide;
In every change He faithful will remain.
Be still my soul: thy best, thy heavenly Friend
Thro' thorny ways leads to a joyful end.
—Katharina A. Von Schlegel
God Bless, Ed and Coleen

Mark and Paula,

You are still in our thoughts and prayers. Alan and I will try to make it out next week. I'm glad Mark is doing better. I know it is hard for him to depend on others for everything. He can be so stubborn. That is one reason we love him so much. I hope the surgery goes well today. Please tell the kids that they are in our prayers also.

Alan and Kirk-o

Glad to hear things are steady and Mark's doing ok. We definitely want to come see you guys, but we will wait when he is doing a bit better and not so prone to getting infections. If you need anything at all, please hollar. And you know our home is open if anyone needs a place to stay. I'm glad you're doing good Paula! You being so strong is what's gonna help make him have hope and strength. Prayers, thoughts and love are with you! Justin, LaRay, Matt & Luke :)

Uncle Mark,

Lots of thoughts and prayers coming your way today. I hope surgery goes well for you. We will continue to pray no infection! Love you. Keep up the great progress. We love you. Ben, Erin, Charles and Ella

Hi Paula,

I am a little mopey that I'm not in the van to go up to see you. BUT, I'm glad you're getting so many visitors!!Our Pastor told the congregation Sunday about Mark and he is still on our church wide prayer chain. I took Katy to her orthopedist yesterday and thankfully, no major issues. That was until we went shopping. YUCK!!! You can take her next time, okay? KKLL!!! Your friend, Hope

Thinking of you both often, but especially today. Praying the latest surgery goes well. Keep up your strength and sense of humor. That, with friends and family will get you through this. (S.A.S.S.)

Thanks for the updates. Every morning the guys here at Beowawe want an update. We are all behind you and pulling for you. I wish there was a way we can help. If you can think of anything let us know. You are in our thoughts and prayers. Andrew

Paula,

I came into work this morning wondering how Mark was doing. I looked at the clock and it was too early to call Karen and I remembered she told me about this website. I have found myself engrossed in reading your daily entries (instead of working!). If you don't feel like you are a strong person, go back and read what you have written. I don't know that I could have even managed that. You, Mark, your children and all the family are in my prayers. Keep being a big girl even though there are times when you don't want to be. God will help you and everyone get through this. With Love, Darlene

Paula and Mark,

God bless you both today. I so hope the news is encouraging for you after his surgery. I heard a good analogy about God's love at church on Sunday that I found encouraging. Here it goes.

An eagle takes her babies up to the mountain when they are ready to fly. She lets them go and watches to see if they are okay. If any of her babies struggle she swoops down beneath them and catches the struggling one(s) on her back. And stays with them until they are able to fly safely on their own.

I pray that you may feel the support of God's wings in your lives today and each day as you forge the road of Mark's recovery. Sheri

Hi Paula,

We're saying extra prayers this morning that Mark's surgery will go great! It's a good thing Mark is feisty...how else can he keep up with his feisty lil' wife? I think you have been amazing through this entire process and we keep you and your kids in our prayers too. Thank you for taking the time to update all of us with this journal. I know it can't be easy for you to go through the day, and then relive it again at the end of the day by putting it all into words for all of us to read. Like I said...you're amazing, and so strong. I think I better have 2 bottles of wine waiting for you when you get home! Take care, and keep going strong Mark! Gina

*Reflection*

*I am experiencing raw emotion re-reading my entry. I remember that day, the surgery took*

*6-7 hours. You wait patiently to hear how it went and how much of his burns had healed. I also see the Holy Spirit's work through the love and prayers offered from our community. Their continued support gave me strength to journal on difficult days.*

# Keeping Frustration at Bay

June 10, 2009

Hello, Mark is still groggy and not making any sense, kind of like before the burn but worse! Karen and I were with him this morning for an hour and then took a break. When I went back up, the nurse was getting ready to give him 2 units of blood because his level was 7.1 whatever that means. I am feeling a little frustrated today. I will go back up for a visit in a few minutes. Mark's folks flew out this morning. Mark's sister, Sheri and husband will arrive on Thursday and his brother on Sunday or Monday. I am hoping that he will grow stronger and stronger daily. KKLL, Paula

Good Evening! Mark is doing better this evening than in the morning. His right leg was bleeding and they did not know it. They knew his hemoglobin was down(a normal range for Mark was 13.5-17) so they gave him two units of blood and eventually found the bleed. He got a few stitches and a rewrapping of his right leg. The nurses act so calm which makes me not worry when I guess I should have been a little worried, see how well the prayers work? The nurses keep telling me he is doing well for such a big burn. The nurse gave me cream

**that I can now put on his hands and feet, it makes me feel useful. He is, however, acting a little goofy, drunk out of it. I do not know how to describe it but it does make me have to look out the window and laugh. Karen and I do a lot of conversing with our eyes! He is not trying to be funny but he just is. I think he is waking up and gonna have a fighting day tomorrow and I look forward to it. Hiccups are a little better and hopefully will be gone by morning. Love, Paula**

Sending some good smellin stuff your way! Hospital smells are BAD!!!! Blessings! Toby

Hello Paula and Mark—we heard what happened, and we are just in shock! Paula, I've been reading some of the journal entries, and it looks like you guys have soooo much love and support, and so many prayers, Mark will make a full recovery. You guys have such a wonderful support system, but if there is anything you need, please don't hesitate to ask, I can go to Fresno or Ridgecrest in a flash, I'm on summer vacation tomorrow!! (But there's this little boy and girl who keep following me everywhere asking me for food and clothes, don't know what that's all about!!) All kidding aside, we pray for a full recovery for Mark, and that all of his future procedures go very well!! We love you guys, please say hello to all your brothers and sisters and your mom and dad. Please Paula, if you need anything or just want to talk, just call me and I will make you laugh, that's medicine for the soul!!! With all our love and prayers, Tina and Greg

Paula,

I'm glad to know that you made it to the hospital okay this morning when the traffic was so bad! But, I wish that it wasn't such a frustrating day. We said another "rosary" for Mark & for your whole family that you will soon be through this dark time.

I found a few Scripture passages tonight that I used to have taped to the mirrors around our house when we went through a difficult time awhile back—though I am sorry to say that you have won the "prize" for difficult times with this situation—anyway, I hope they will be a comfort to you.

*If you feel overwhelmed by a situation, know that "all things work for good for those who love God, who are called according to his purpose." (Romans 8:28)*

*If you feel worried, know that you can "cast all your worries upon the Lord because He cares for you." (1 Peter 5:7)*

*If you feel you can't figure things out, know that you can "trust in the Lord with all your heart, on your own intelligence rely not; in all your ways be mindful of Him and He will make straight your paths." (Proverbs 3:5–6)*

*If you feel you can't go on, know that the Lord says, "All who call upon Me I will answer; I will be with them in distress; I will deliver them and give them honor." (Psalm 91:15)*

*If you think you can't handle a situation, know that "I can do all things in Christ who strengthens me." (Phil 4:13).*

Hang in there girl. Love, Katie N.

They say that "God only gives you as much as he thinks you can handle." Sometimes I wish he thought a little less of me! A prayerful chuckle from the east coast. Hoping each sunrise brings a brighter day. Love, Pete and Loren

Hi Paula and Mark,

We are still wondering about the wonderful weather we are having in good old Ridgie. Told Walt I ordered 3 mos of it. In the 80s and some cloud cover—whahoo. Then, being the realist, I think that maybe that means it will be 100 degrees for Halloween.

We are sorry your day was not so good--at least you smelled good with your new perfume:) We keep the prayers going and constantly think about you all.

No choir practice tomorrow—only doing that every other week for the summer.

Love and hugs, Margie and Walt

Mark,

We just wanted to let you know we are thinking of you and hope you're feeling better. There may be bumps in the road, but we know with the power of prayer, family and friends you can get through anything. We will see you soon. Love to all, Karen & Tony

Uncle Mark and Aunt Paula,

You would not believe the weather out here in Kansas. We have been under tornado warnings, hail, thunderstorms and lightning for the last few days. Ben has began flying out here and getting to know the new terrain. I'm holding down the fort as usual:-). There is not a day that goes by I don't think of the two of you and say a little prayer. Ok big prayers! LoL. I love you both and hope that this healing process continues to move forward. Much Love, Ben, Erin, Charles and Ella

Dear Mark & Paula,

Just a quick report from the Welsh compound! We (Chandler, Mitch, GiGi and I) took the recycling to the new place Mitch swore you take it to now! Can we all say "scary"? Holy Buckets…but the boys were troopers and even answered the guy who wanted to know if they both recently graduated from Burroughs…Oh Lord…hurry and get back in the car! Stranger danger for sure. LOL

Right now, Chandler is off riding his bike with a friend and Mitch and Sam are riding their bikes. GiGi is sleeping and Dad is napping too! I sent Mom off to Kristen T to get her hair cut :) Grace went on up to volleyball and I am manning the station! Wahoo!

Mary and Lew just picked up your cards to bring to you, so that will be nice! Aunt Sheri sent some very cool bears for the kids and they love them :) Thanks Sheri & Family!

We are all praying for strength and courage for you both…and always for peace of mind :) Lots of love, Dad, Mom, Amy, Grace, Mitchell, Chandler, Gigi and Ebony!

Dear Paula and courageous patient Mark,

Wow, I just got caught up! Sounds as though you are through the immediate pain and scariness, and I pray that you will make it through the "rollercoaster" ahead—though, of course, you will. Happy to hear that Grace, Mitch and Chandler got to see their daddy. :) I know, P, that you are surrounded with an amazing team of pals and Weidenkopfs, and a skinny pirate. Sending you much love and cheering you on from Big Bear. Take care, and God bless. xoxo, Cathee

Paula and Mark,

May today find things back on the right track. Although the news from yesterday feels like a setback, think of how far Mark has come. The community of support surrounding you reflects how beautiful the two of you are. It's quite a thing to witness, and we can 'see' it way out here in the Midwest. And your spirit throughout this, Paula, is just as awe-inspiring as Mark's progress. The two go hand in hand. I look forward to seeing the two of you soon, and the extra incentive is the sight of Mark in a pink blankie…precious.

I heard a report that Genevieve is quite feisty! I can't wait for Kaysa and Genevieve to meet. They must be cut from the same cloth. Kaysa is already "expressing" herself when her brother tries to take something from her. She holds her own ground. Things are getting interesting between the two of them if you know what I mean. Love, Craig and Wendy

Paula and Mark,

You are my heroes! The determined spirit that you both show is such an inspiration for so many of us. Mark's feistiness is a positive sign— He is willing to fight and work very hard to get back to his family as soon as possible. I'm sure that being able to see your children was a wonderful gift you needed right now and continues to give you the strength to keep climbing that hill. Blessings for you and your entire family. Marcia

Guten Tag Mark and Paula,

Sounds like you have been through some courageous days. God is with you both and holding you in his hands, Just remember to rest when you can and keep your strength up. I am sure that the Wine does that for you!! It won't be long before you are walking right out of that place to be an inspiration to someone else in the same shoes. Hugs and Prayers for you and the fam. Jill

Good Morning Mark & Paula:

We are praying for God to give you additional strength during this healing process and good wine always helps too. Hoping God brings you many blessings today. Colleen

Mark and Paula,

Glad things are going well. When Mark is ready, we can send some pink pj's to him to go with that pretty pink blanket of his. We can get the ones with the feetsie's and the butt flap in them, and maybe some nice yellow duckies too. Sounds like you're filling up that 'well' of yours with cocktails. Try not to overflow it, don't want to have to clean up that mess. Speaking of that other comment about not being able to handle things alone, for one I know you're stronger than that and you also know that you are never alone, even if you can't see them. You know what I mean. You and Mark keep up the spirits and faith, God and the rest of us are right there for you. Tell Mark that we love and miss him. See you soon. Alan and Kirk-o

Paula,

Even though your voice is upbeat in your post regarding Mark's surgery yesterday, and his healing in the upper extremities is going so well (AMEN to that!), I understand you are in need of prayers for a number of set backs you've encountered.

I'm certain Mark will be mad as a hornet today when he finds that feeding tube back in...and I'm sorry to hear that his lower legs are preventing him from getting the 'early release' you were so hoping for. Frustration! I know he was doing so well with the walking several day ago, and that has diminished too. He just may need more TIME (and that's a stickler) for all this trauma his body has experienced.

Please know that you don't have to be cheerful for me here...I'm checking in here to know WHAT to pray for you & Mark. So, you just save all your CHEER up for him! Love to you, Tracy

Paula & Mark,

Good Morning! We're back from our mini reunion and as promised, our first toast was to you & your family, for strength and blessings to help you through this. Many prayers were offered. Lots of vino was consumed. Glad to hear Mark's surgery went well.

Blessings to you and your family. Love, Susie & Vic

Paula,

Hang in there. I am so glad so many people are writing and visiting. It's a testament to how much you care about others. We are praying that Mark will get through this very soon. He is so lucky to have such a strong support system. I know we've thanked you for keeping up this site, but again…thank you so much! I check it at least twice a day and I'm always happy to get an update. Say 'hi" to Karen for us! Here's hoping that tomorrow's a better day! Love, Lisa and James

*Reflection*

*I probably scared some of my friends and family in the medical field when I said his blood count was 7.1. I would get information from the nurses that wasn't always explained to me. He was losing blood. Those reading my journal felt my frustration and prayed harder, and sent more inspirational words our way. They lifted my spirits more than they will ever know…*

# Distractions

June 11, 2009

Good morning, I wanted to let you all know a couple of cards have made it to Mark's room and they will let me hang them up so I wanted to pass on the address:

Fresno Community Regional Med. Ctr
2823 Fresno St.
Fresno, CA 93721
Attn: Critical Care/Burn Center
Mark Welsh Rm 528
KKLL, Paula

Hello, Karen and I arrived just in time this morning to see Mark get out of bed and take two laps. He was even walking flat-footed and putting his heels down. He has his catheter out too. His hands are looking so good! They have completely (look out for this big word) epithelialized! Which means his skin has new growth. He has been tired all afternoon but the nurses keep telling me this is normal. Karen and I headed back to Kingsburg @7pm. We had some interesting people in the waiting room today. A family was wailing all day in their chairs. Moaning and what not. Some family members were snoring on the ground.

**Also, we had some visitors. Mary, Sharon, and friends brought wine, bills (ugh) and some good smelling lotions (thanks, Toby).**

**We need to pray Mark gets his appetite back and his hemoglobin rises. Love to all, Paula**

Hi Paula and Mark,

I think about you two everyday and your children. I pray for you all and hope the recovery period is a quick one! You both are very strong people and I know that you will get through this difficult time. In all your journals Paula, you sound like the same ol' Paula from high school…comical as ever. Keep it going… it will get you through the difficult times. From reading some of the journals, there are a lot of people praying for you both and your family. Everything will be just fine with God on your side and all of those prayers coming your way! Hope you have a good day tomorrow!!! With Lots of Love! Love, Tonia, Robert, Rashel, Andrew, Emily, and Anthony

Hi Paula & Mark—hope your day went well—have been thinking about you—hope Mark is feeling better—I am sure it will take a day or so to re-cuperate after the surgery—sounds like the nurses are on the ball and I know God is looking down & sending you both strength to get through this—you are both an inspiration to all of us—we appreciate your daily updates so much & I am sure you don't feel up to it some days—May God Bless you & keep you—Stay strong—We love you lots—Dorothy & Tom

Paula and Mark,

Judie told me what is going on with Mark. One word that sizes it up is "Un-believable". I thank God that Mark is doing so well. I'll pray for you both. It sounds like your families have stepped—up' and have made a huge impact on a bad situation. I love families—and you guys have great ones. Kudos to all of them!

Paula, I'm glad you are getting some R&R away from the hospital even if it just a few hours. Have a skinny capt. for me...and I'll have one and send you the love.

Mark drink the Ensure, take your happy juice (medications) the pain killers will allow you to move more so you will have less complications later. And...this is not the right way to get some time off.

My thoughts and prayers will be with you both as you continue this journey. May God bless and keep you both close during this time of need. Love and kisses to you all!!!

Leah

Mark and Paula,

You both are in our prayers! I am glad to hear Mark is doing better. Call if you need anything. Love, Selisia, Michael and Emily

Dear Mark and Paula,

Glad to hear Mark is making progress physically if not mentally (haha). I'm happy to hear that Karen is back there with you helping out. I'm sure the room is filled with you two giggling at Mark's expense (haha). Going to San Diego with my Mom and Auntie and Uncle Jon for Pam's son Nathaniel's graduation at Point

Loma Univ. Friday morning before dawn cracks. Leaving the Corona area at 7:30am to be in S.D. before 10 am. Weather will be nice and cool. Good to see your sense of humor has stayed with you throughout this ordeal!! You all take care and I'll be doing my part with the praying!! Love you guys, Tami

Well hello from the Welsh Compound! Again, GiGi is napping :) I have to tell you, I turned on her music first before I got her situated and she hauled a** out of the bedroom and into the kitchen...and had she not stopped to check out something on the kitchen floor, she would have been on one side of the table before I got in there!!! She is too much!! LOL!

Dad is napping, Mom is at the store, Mitch is in his room...Chandler is at a party and Grace is at practice...it's all quiet! Wahooo! MaryKay called to find out if we wanted raisins in our cinnamon rolls she was bringing us...and I am sure you know what your kids answer to that was!! I was with the kids on that one! No cooked fruit LOL

Ann will join us for dinner tonight...dinner time is great fun here LOL

We are all praying for you and Mom and Dad can't wait to come see you both!!

Much Love, Dad, Mom, Amy, Grace, Mitch, Chan, GiGi and Ebony...ruff. LOL!

Glad to hear Mark is making progress. Especially with the hiccups. ONE LESS THING TO WORRY ABOUT. We really missed you and Karen last night. I do agree with Katie. Pretty funny the table is turned...I'm so glad you haven't lost your sense of humor. Let's hope and pray that all starts to fall into place for Mark. We could all use good news. Love, Leslie

Mark,

I had a serious talk with our special angel, Chris, told him he needs to "lift" you up and help with the healing. Then I slept soundly knowing that when I do pray to him especially somehow they are always answered! So know today Chris will be your guardian angel, helping with the walking, pain, hiccups, and keeping all infections away! Love, Ruth

Dear Paula,

Our thoughts and prayers are with you and Mark and family. Lots of prayers are being sent your way. Love, Pat and Buck

Paula,

My how the tables have turned when it is Mark "acting a little goofy" & you're the quiet one! Hope today is a good day. Love, Katie N.

Paula and Mark,

Glad to hear that the hiccups are residing and how positive your attitude is. It helps me to feel encouraged and your situation continues to increase my faith. Also, love to hear the nurses say that he is doing well. I pray for Mark and you today. I hope it is a fighting day.

Also, we are flying in Vegas around 7 p.m. We thought we would spend the night in Barstow. Then maybe meet someone at 4 corners in the morning and then get to Fresno later Thursday morning. We are flexible, though. I will call you tomorrow with all our travel information. Sheri

*Reflection*

*One thing for sure was that I felt the need to be myself and that my sense of humor stayed intact. A good friend of mine told me I was the same person I was before Mark was burned. I am not going to lie, at the beginning I didn't know how to act and react. I was feeling lost...but she reminded me Mark and I were still the same two people.*

# Thankful for the "Good Day"

June 12, 2009

Today was a long but good day! Karen and I saw him first thing this morning and he did one lap! He is still recovering with his blood loss but his hemoglobin is on the rise! His hiccups still come and go but I think they are slowly disappearing. He had a few bites for breakfast which is more than yesterday. We had some surprise visitors today. Bruce and Chris came up and brought Monsignor Cleary over. I took Monsignor up to see Mark and I think Mark was showing off and ate half of his lunch. The nurses started the dressing change @ 2:30 p.m. and it took until 5:30 p.m.. I was expecting a groggy Mark when Karen and I came and saw him because they drug him good because of the pain involved, but he was chatty and his left arm, stomach and back were not covered! He is healing so well they left those uncovered. I hold on to such good news because you are never sure what tomorrow brings. The night ended with a good dinner at Joe's Steakhouse with Bruce, Chris and Monsignor. We had some laughs, drinks and good food! The visitors help us kill time! Karen leaves in the morning and Susan and Katie come for a slumber party for 2 nights!

**God bless you all for the prayers, support and good thoughts! KKLL, Paula**

Prayers towards the appetite & hemoglobins~CHECK!!!

How about the hiccups…are they gone or only subsided slightly?

Prayers too, for you who are sitting all day around the hospital…that your neighbors behave a little bit better in sharing this community space!

Sending love to Paula & well wishes to Mark! (and Cheers to all the Weidenkopf clan who are supporting you in so many ways) Tracy

Good Morning Mark and Paula,

Glad to hear his hands are healing and Wow what a huge accomplishment of walking flat-footed. Enjoying your children every evening! I think we are going to have a movie night tonight. as long as Genevieve has my purse we are good to go. She was sharing it with Grandpa last night!

You are all in my thoughts and prayers. I still pray for strength and patience for both of you. Love and miss you! Ann and Jerry(Doug)

T.G.I.F.!

Hi; hope you're in good spirits today. Sounds as tho' yesterday was a good day.

Here's a joke for today (CD, 06/01, p. 87):

My 3-year-old daughter, Zoe, struggled to adjust to life away from Mommy at St. Bernard Catholic Preschool. By the end of the 3rd week, though, she seemed to be having a wonderful time. She came home every day bubbling with stories about her new adventures—especially about the trip to the fire station.

One day, Grandma asked her what she had learned so far.

Zoe bowed her head, made a perfect Sign of the Cross, and said, "Father, Son, and Holy Spirit...stop, drop, and roll."

Hang in there: healing takes some time, even for young, healthy guys! Hugs & prayers, Mary G.

Hey Paula:

I'm finally catching up on things, including your updates on Mark.

What a long week you've both had. So happy to hear the visits with the kids went well, and that you continue to be surrounded by family and friends. Although we can't get there to visit, you continue to be in our thoughts daily. All our prayers are being sent your way. Being the patient is difficult, but being the caregiver is a huge thing. Don't forget to take care of yourself :) Hope the coming week brings more healing and positive news. Love, Julie and Dave

Hey Mark, just dropping by to let you know your still on our minds and in our hearts here on 'C' crew. We miss you boss! Oh, and don't worry, Mother is keeping us in line while you're away...LOL.

Glad to hear you're progressing well, and I hope you continue to, I know you will. Miss you man. Elvis

Paula and Mark,

So glad to hear your hands are healing, Mark. I can hear your body say "I'm working on this part so just be patient about the rest!" We're still praying about the hiccups—is that getting any better? Paula, thank you again for taking the time to communicate with all of us. It means so much to us. I know it can't be easy to write at the end of an exhausting day. Love, Pat and Joe

Mark and Paula,

There is not a day that goes by we don't think and pray for you both and your family. I am so happy to hear that Mark is eating a little. Paula you are so strong and it must be hard but I know it helps both of you get through the days. If there is anything you guys need please let us know. I am not sure what your children will be doing during the day now that school is out, but if your family needs any help with your kids please don't hesitate to ask. I am home and would love to have them anytime or drive them here and there. Love you both, Brittany, Will and Sawyer

Hi, Mark and Paula!

Like Brittany, I think of you two every day and continue to remember you in my prayers. So glad to hear Mark has some of his bandages removed! You, Paula, are such a great cheerleader and I know it's helping Mark cope through all this.

Many, many years ago while pouring boiling water into a glass pitcher I saw a hair line crack in the pitcher and in that instant the pitcher shattered and the boiling water burned me from the tops of my legs to my knees. I had 2nd degree (NOTHING as severe as Mark's) and "sunburn". I had to have my dressings changed every other day, and it was so painful. No wonder you are sedated, Mark! And, Mark, I can hardly wait to show you my "no scars"! Any lines or crinkling skin you may see is from old age and lack of exercise!

Thanks, Paula, for always taking time to keep us updated on Mark's progress! Love, (Auntie) Claire G

Paula just to let you and your stong man know that we are praying for you. The we is Kristi, Lynn and Neil, his church friends and myself. Carl went throught a period of 3 weeks of the hiccups a couple years ago. They make the person tired. I will pray that they leave the building. As you know God is always there and so we need to pay attention to this small voice. Love you both. Willie

Good afternoon from the Welsh compound. GiGi just pooped her pants and no one wants to change her LOL. Mom won the short straw!

Mitch and Chandler are fishing in Lone Pine with my new bff Mark N! Go Mark go! We pray no one ends up in the creek! We also pray not too many lines get wrapped up in branches… as some children tend to cast away like they are at a lake versus the small creek HA!

Gordy has been busy here this morning and just finished the blind in the babys' room :) I just fixed lunch for Adam and him and Mom and Dad…

Miss W offered me adult beverages last night and I should have taken them LOL Instead, I went with Ann and had a beer at Chris's pad!

We have had some good laughs here… entertainment 24/7!

Please know we all pray a Hail Mary every night at dinner, right after we say grace for you both! Ann holds GiGi's hands while we pray and she tries to bite Anns' hands...which in turn starts some laughing but I think God understands.

Much love and prayers! Dad, Mom, Amy, Gord, Adam, GiGi, and Grace :)

Hi Paula and Mark...I'm back!!! Had a several day "pity Party" for myself and "the elbow"...don't laugh...I actually offered up the pain for Mark...it helped give my elbow a "reality" check...anyway IT STILL HURTS...saw Dr. S last week, it was too swollen etc. for a cortisone shot, went to therapy and begged pain meds from Dr. Bill (Theresa is a witness to my story!!) pain meds, therapy is helping, see Dr. S on Tues...I did not put myself on the prayer chain!!!!!! So, just wanted to momentarily take your mind off of your problems so you; can focus on my elbow!!! Now...all the "visitors" know about my elbow...I'll be expecting sympathy calls! Seriously...I think of you a lot and always in my prayers...I keep updated from various people, those who have made the pilgrimage to Fresno (sounds like I am missing out!!!!). Mitchell and Pat had a swimming event at Leahs' (actually invited boys!!!!...) will get a Leah update today!!! Take care...I am thinking I should become one of the pilgrims and come see you...Mr. Nobody of course would come along...hang in...we love you..." too embarrassed to "sign my name" due to elbow complaining!!! Charlotte

Hello my loving couple!!!!! Wow, good job Mark. I'm glad all these prayers are working.

(I won't take credit for how many times I said a prayer for you or stopped and thought about you; I had a long week.) But in the end you deserve them all. I hope to see you soon. Please order Paula around today. John sends his prayers too. We will be at Korrie's Graduation today. YOU GO MARK! Claire B

Paula and Mark,

What great news about his healing. I am so glad that some good news is coming your way. I continue to keep you and Mark in my prayers and I will continue to hope for more good news to come your way. Sheri

Hey Mark & Paula,

Regarding hiccups: I just remembered something that you might try. A couple years ago I had the hiccups for about 3 days. A temporary solution, the ONLY thing that finally worked, was to drink something (preferably carbonated)—enough to make you want to burp—but to NOT burp—keep it in. As long as I had that pressure in my stomach, I did not hiccup. It was like an OFF switch for the hiccups, seriously, as long as there was enough pressure in my stomach. The second I let out a burp, even a small one, the hiccups came back, so I'd have to do it again. It was uncomfortable to keep the pressure in, but it was better than hiccuping constantly. It's a normal reaction to burp after a big swig of beer/soda, so you might have to concentrate on keeping it in (I had to, or I'd let it out without thinking). But keeping that pressure inside really did the trick. I tried it with water too, but to make it work I had to try to swallow as much air as I could with the water, which was harder than just using beer. I suppose you could just swallow air, if you know how, and that should do the same thing. But it wouldn't be near as much fun as beer...(OK, soda, Mark) Good luck, hope it helps, and glad to hear about some good healing going on there!

P.S. If Mark pukes all over himself trying this, it's not my fault...OK, maybe it is. ;>) Bruce

Hi Paula,

Mark and you and your family are in always in my prayers. I really think you need to change Mark's initials from MW to WM (walking miracle).

You are both such strong and faithful servants of the Lord!!! Kelly and family

*Reflection*
*Prayers were being answered on a daily basis. So many Christians witnessing them right along with us.*

# Blessed with Support

June 14, 2009

Hello. Saturday was an okay day! Mark is looking better each day and all the nurses and his physical therapist remind us he is doing remarkably well for a guy with a 73% burn. He ate a little bit more today but still needs to increase his appetite to be able to get off the feeding tube. He was having hiccups again today so we need more prayers that those GO AWAY! He did however get in a lap this afternoon. I had to say goodbye to Karen this morning but Katie and Susan will be with me for two nights. Our good friends, Tom, Dorothy and Lisa made it in time for dinner at El Torito and will see Mark in the morning. Marks' brother Craig, will be here late tomorrow. I found out from the nurses that Mark will have his surgery on Tuesday. I feel blessed to be surrounded with love and support! Paula

Greetings!

Our visit with you and Karen was like being on a faith-filled, day long retreat. Bruce, Monsignor and I can only admire the strength of Mark, Paula and all of the family members. You are all definitely using every bit of the graces God is pouring upon you daily. Even though we can-

153

not be there daily, our prayers are with you daily. I know Monsignor will surprise you again with a visit. I will do some research on the patron saint of getting rid of hiccups. God Bless! Chris

Hi Mark and Paula,

Hank and I would like to come to see you both on Friday. We probably won't get out of RC until about noon which means we should arrive in Fresno about 4 pm with traffic, getting gas in Bakersfield, etc. Paula do you have a cell phone number where we can reach you? Thanks and see you soon. Linda and Hank

Mark and Paula,

Thought you might appreciate a little humor...

Superman, Sleeping Beauty and Pinnochio are walking down a sidewalk one afternoon in Los Angeles. After a bit, they walk by a sign that says "World's Most Beautiful Woman Contest." Sleeping Beauty drops her mirror and runs in. After 20 minutes or so she emerges from the building and says "It's true, I am the most beautiful woman in the world!" A bit later, they walk by a sign that says "World's Strongest Man Contest." Superman busts down the door as he enters. He emerges 30 minutes later exclaiming "no contest" as he flexed his bulging steel biceps. Right next door there was a sign that said "World's Biggest Liar Contest." With his nose already growing, Pinnochio enters the building. Forty minutes later he comes out with a snubby little nose bawling his little wooden eyes out. Superman and Sleeping beauty asked him what happened and he whimpered with great perplexion "Who the hell is Nancy Pelosi?" My mom, the biggest liberal in the Ridgecrest, told me this joke and laughed her butt off!

Hope this finds Mark in improving health and Paula in strong spirits. Know that the East Coast continues to pray for strength and healing for all of you, especially Mark. Pete

Greetings!

I said I would look up the patron saint to cure hiccups. I found on one site that Saint Jude is often implored to help rid a person of the hiccups…so as I go to bed tonight, I will have a conversation with St. Jude, mentioning that he needs to take care of Mark fast. Good night and God bless. Chris

Hello from the Taylor Compound! Grace, Mitch and Chandler and I are raiding Aunt Ann's stash of scrapbook stuff! The kids are making cards! Aunt Ann said they could use WHATEVER they wanted, so it is a free for all on the kitchen table! LOL Aunt Ann has 50,000 kinds of paper so choosing was a little psycho for some :) The creative juices are flowing…

Mitch and Chandler washed Grandma and Grandpa's car for some cash…and Princess GiGi has been a little freakshow today. Aunt Erfie came over and took her for a walk around the neighborhood so she was the favorite…until she made the walk down the hall to the bedroom…then she didn't want her anymore! Whoever is new in the house that she hasn't seen for two weeks (like anyone but Mom, Dad or I) she immediately goes to and tells on all of us! Little heathen ankle biter. LOL!

Mom cooked the fish from last night… fresh fried trout…it was FABULOUS!! Thanks, Mark N…you rock for taking them! Only it was too short…my mom and I were hoping you were going to keep them for a week…or maybe just around the alcohol hour which seems to be getting earlier every day!! LOL! Just teasin' ya!

Dad, the boys and I will leave in the morning for Big Bear :) Mom, Grace and GiGi are going to have slumber party…do each other's hair and nails and discuss boys and relationships! HA HA HA!

Mitch just said Aunt Ann was "centuries old"…that is hilarious!!

If he had said that about me, I would have had to sock him up, but since it was about his OLDER Aunt, it's all good :).

Okay I am signing off…please know we are all praying for you and the cards will be in the mail soon! We love you muchos…even Ebony sends a lick or two. LOL! Amy, Grace, Mitch and Chandler

Paula and Mark,

Glad to hear that Mark is doing so well. That's so awesome that the bandages have been removed! That is really great news. Thanks, Paula for all the updates on Mark. I'm able to keep my Mom in the loop also if she has not spoken to your Mom for the day. Gotta get her a computer that works soon. All went well at my little cousin's graduation…it was very nice!! My Mom said I got all my praying in for the next few years{it's a Christian high school}. It was a very nice ceremony and the principal was funny also. We were on our way home and my Uncle Jon had a genius idea that we should stop and do some wine tasting!! So we did!!! We had fun and Mom bought some wine and gave me some. I scored!! Please take care and love ya. Tami

Paula and Mark,

The boys and I had a good day fishing in Lone Pine yesterday, they are such a hoot to talk with! As for Mitchell falling in the stream, it wasn't very deep, and I was near by, o.k., not very near by, but I was downstream so I would have grabbed him as he came by!

I am glad to hear that some of the bandages are coming off, and that Mark is doing his laps again. We have a daily rosary going for his speedy and complete recovery, and for your peace of mind, Paula.

Since Katie is up there visiting with you I decided to try the guys suggestion that wrote in earlier about beer and hiccups, I didn't actually have the hiccups when I started the test, but the beer still helped!! O.K., that was my sad attempt at humor for the day. You and Mark are in my thoughts and prayers. Mark N

Hey Mark,

I have read through the journal entries, and it seems you have improved greatly after last weeks' surgery. I hope you continue to get better each day. You need to eat! I have seen you eat and know you can put it down :). I'm glad to hear you are still getting at least a lap in each day too. As I have said before, you can never sit still, so I know not being physically able to bounce off the walls is driving you nuts. Hang in there, and only take on as much as you can handle. You're doing great. Thinking of you often, April

Paula and Mark,

Glad he is having more good days. I sent the Lourdes water Friday. I pray it makes it to you in one piece. So glad more friends and family keep coming to keep you company.

XOXO Katie H

Hello Paula,

You don't know me but I am Hope's sister, Margaret Ann. I live in Fresno. I am going to be telling my small-group about your husband today and we will start to pray for you! I will also be coming to the hospital with Hope on Wednesday and will give you my phone number. If there is ANYTHING we can do to help you, please call! Margaret

Hey Paula,

Just a quick 'hi' to all of you. So happy to hear you had some girl time. You of all people really need the companionship. You and Mark are in my thoughts and prayers daily and I can't wait to go back up!! I look forward to the progress reports every morning. Mark is doing very well. Remember each day brings new hope and maybe a few rough patches.

Rachel and I are off to Lancaster for a little shopping. She needs a few things for her summer job. She starts on Tuesday and it's about time!!!!! Love to you both. Hope to be back up there soon. Love, Leslie

Hey, Dad it's Chandler. I went fishing yesterday. I went with Pat, Mitch and Mr. N. I caught two fish. Mitch caught one. Pat caught two and Mr. N caught three. It was a lot of fun. We had lunch at the Pizza Factory. I had cheese. We cooked the fish for dinner, of course Grace did not eat any :) Genevieve is crazy as usual like a wild Indian. Hope you get well soon. Chandler

Dear Dad.

It's Mitch. me, Chan, Pat and Mr. N went fishing on saturday and it was fun. I fell in the freezing cold water it was invigirating. Then this one fish kept on eating my bait then eventually he broke my line so i said i'm done with that fish then we left and had lunch at the Pizza Factory and it was deliciousthen we went home. Love Yuor son

Mitchell

Hello, Paula and Mark,

Well, Mr Home Depot, Walt was frequenting his favorite place (I told him the store should employ him as he is more help to other customers than the employees) and low and behold your Dad is there searching for washers (I think). soooo Walt assisted him and Dad was appreciative and told me so after Mass on Saturday. That is Walt's contribution to assisting those in need:)

I told Amy, I love reading her guestbook entries. Scott returned from the busniss trip in Vegas and says that is a "young persons'" town and not for him. (See what happens when you turn 40—and you will be there soon.) Beyond that, he sends his love and prayers to you both. He is reading the journals as I am forwarding them to him and quizing him to make sure is really reading. Once a Mom, always a Mom. Today, I am supposed to make cookies for Walt but we slept in and now I am behind so we will see. Prayers and good thoughts. Margie and Walt

Good Morning, Paula

I woke up early thinking about you, Mark and the kids. "Praying without ceasing"…comes to mind. I'm looking forward to seeing you on Weds. and have been asked to carry care packages already!! I hope it makes it okay!! I will stay with my sister unless of course, you need some company! My sister has a friend at the hospital so she is anxious to find out if you have met her. I'll get more details when I get up there. Can't reiterate enough how much we, and everyone else, are praying for all of you, in all kinds of specific ways. Love you lots and will be with you soon. Love, Hope

p.s. My sister's friend is a nurse, not a patient!!!

Paula and Mark,

You are continually on our minds and in our prayers. Last night after Mass, I went into the choir loft and gave Karen a big hug, so I hope you felt it being transferred to you through God's blessings. It was good to see Karen but we sure miss you. We saw your Dad after Mass as well. Hank was talking with your Dad when I came down from the choir loft.

We leave Friday to drive to WA to see our other grandkids but you will still be in our prayers and thoughts and we will have the laptop to stay abreast of all that is happening. It will be tough to leave Megan (granddaughter) here in Ridgecrest for three and half weeks as we will miss her dearly but we will have fun with Alex and Abby in WA.

Have a blessed Sunday. Love, Linda and Hank

Mark and Paula,

I looked it up and we need to pray to St. Jude. Apparently, he is in charge of hiccups (patron saint of lost causes). So that is what we will do. Glad to hear that he is slowly improving and that prayers are being answered. I have a feeling that the more Mark improves the appetite will return, so we will be grateful for things such as feeding tubes until his body takes over by itself. Take care, sleep well. Mike and I would like to come up when he gets back so I'll be checking in with you later this week. We continue to pray, pray, pray—all our love, Ruth

*Reflection*

*The hiccups would not go away and I think it's funny and interesting that that is what I was focusing on, not the 2nd and 3rd degree burns. God has a funny way of giving us distractions to help us cope and it definitely took my mind off the surgeries and burns.*

*This website was a powerful means of communication. I was able to reach so many and spread the good news about answered prayers. It also revealed that miracles come in all shapes and sizes.*

# Grateful for Others' Help

June 15, 2009

Good morning, I was too tired last night to journal so let me catch you all up! Yesterday morning Katie, Susan and I started the day with Mass. I was able to talk to the priest and he will be praying for Mark. When I go into Mark's room in the morning I always kiss him and Sunday morning he put his left arm around me and gave me a hug! It meant so much, I think the fog is lifting! He ate better yesterday too! But I was feeding him and then later got scolded by the nurse, he is to do everything on his own. His nurse, Toni, and I have a love/hate relationship. He did two laps yesterday, so that helps all his muscles. Tom, Dorothy and Lisa stayed for the day and got in a visit with Mark. I am so grateful for the company! Mark's brother got in @ 6:00 p.m. and saw him before the nurse changeover. Katie and Susan have to leave today but have made my last few days full of laughs and comfort. I am grateful they put up with me! Craig will be here through Thursday and then their sister and husband will be here Thursday afternoon. Mark will have a dressing change this afternoon so his new doctor/surgeon can survey his wounds for tomorrow's surgery. Dr. Dominic is on vacation but I am told Dr. Kaups is also one of the best! This morning when I walked into Mark's room he was in the chair and had eaten most of his breakfast and was hiccup free! I hope they continue to subside. We actually had a conversation about maybe getting him an Ipod and he also wants a new cell phone when he gets out. I will hold onto these moments because he could be down a few days after surgery. Craig was able to assist Mark on his laps this morning. Mark is pooped out now and will rest up for his dressing change. God bless all the people praying for us and for all the travelers. Paula

P.S. Everyone that knows me knows I like to know everything and people might consider me nosey but yesterday when I went to visit Mark he was concerned about his neighbor because he had seen a lot of the nurses run to a room. So, later when a nurse peeked in to check on Mark, he asked if he could be "nosey". It was the cutest thing and, come to find out, a visitor had fainted. It was not the patient. Mark was relieved.

Hi Paula and Mark…I know you are dying for an update on my elbow!!!! Actually…there is someone who cares out there…Mary G. called and left a message and has an ointment that may help…thank you Mary…I'll be calling…things have been hectic!!! and of course you want to know how I hurt it…I am blaming pulling 50 lbs. of suitcase through LAX and SeaTac filled with items of "total necessary" needs for the Alaska cruise…including 10 bottles of "2Buck Chuck" for emergency needs aboard ship!!!! Thanks for the journal updates…I am with you many times during the day in thoughts and prayers…Mr. Nobody is seriously considering visiting…he has his white Dr.s Lab coat complete with name on the front "Dr. Nobody"…take care…Go Mark!!! (and Paula too!!!)…Love…Mrs. O>

Dear Paula & Mark—it was so good to see you both—Mark—you really are amazing & we were so glad to be able to see you—I hope & pray that the surgery goes well tomorrow—I pray for strength for you too Paula—you are one special lady—we love you both lots & lots—call anytime & know that we are praying hard that all continues to go well (& that the hic-cups stay away) Take care & God Bless—Love and Prayers, Dorothy & Tom

YOU GO MARK!!!! Glad to see you are hiccup free. I won't say which visitor scared you so bad, but I bet it was the man with great stories. My family wants to send more prayers. You get a special one from brother Tom. He just flew in to see family. He hasn't changed. He said he will take Mark surfing when he is ready. I have been praying hard this week and really hard. Then Tommy and Aedan stopped by to add more fun to our full house. YOU both are always on my mind. LOVE and Prayers, Claire B.

P.S. I want to hear more about how you are taking care of Mark. How is the shaving coming along?

Mark and Paula,

Wow what a wonderful web site!!! Sounds like you are doing good. Thank God! In all my nursing experience I think burns are one of the most painful injuries there are. You must be one tough cookie. We are thinking of you many times daily and praying also.

We thought of you quite a lot this weekend as we were camping up at Glacier Lodge out of Big Pine. Remember Mark's birthday that we celebrated up there? Anyway it was a fun weekend! This weekend wasn't as celebratory but was nice. Caught lots of 14 in. fish, nice weather, with family and did S'mores. What else can ya ask for? Well, besides a speedy recovery for Mr. Mark. Funny story about fishing this weekend…Shawn, Bryson and a friend were crossing the creek on a log. I was following them by quite a ways. I walked by this fisher dude with dark glasses, total fishing clothes, funky floppy hat and he was yelling at Shawn and the boys! I thought to myself what a jerk! They weren't going to fish in "his" hole, just crossing the creek to get a football they had thrown across the stream. So I said to him we weren't going to fish "near" him just crossing the stream to retrieve a toy!:( I continued on thinking to myself, "man that dude takes fishing way too serious". Then I turned around and the rude dude was still looking at me and I thought "WHATEVER". When I got across the log, Shawn said that guy yelling at us kind of looked like Jim L. I walked back over to take a look and low and behold…It was. That rude fishing dude with the weird clothes on WAS Jim who, by the way was yelling nice things at us. Moral of the story… hard to hear with loud roaring water in creeks!!!! So we had a nice rest of the weekend visiting with him and his friend. Take Care, best wishes, lots of prayers your way. Shawn and Sondra

Hi Mark & Paula,

Just a short note to say—even if we don't write every day—you and your family are still in our hearts and prayers. Mark, sounds like you are doing really good—keep it up—and hug your wife more!! God bless. Diana

Uncle Mark and Aunt Paula,

We made it to Montana! After two days of driving with the kiddos we were pooped! The kids did great! Ben fished the Big Horn River today and caught 5 fish! He is loving it. It is so beautiful here!

I am so glad you are doing well Uncle Mark. Paula I'm sure that hug felt like a million bucks. Uncle Mark you will continue to be in my thoughts and prayers. I love you both. I will be thinking of you tomorrow during your surgery. I'm sure you will get through it with flying colors. I love you. Ben, Erin Charles and Ella

Paula and Mark,

It was so great to see you both this weekend. You are both so strong and I know this will make you even stronger! We will be praying especially hard tomorrow for the surgery to go well. Paula, remember to take good care of yourself! I can't wait to read how the surgery went. It was also fun meeting Susan and Katie! Thanks for all the laughs!

Love, Lisa E

Hi Mark and Paula,

Just wanted you to know that Alex had "sympathy hiccups" all through mass yesterday and on and off through the day. He said the way to get rid of them is to bend over then drink some water upside down. Since Mark probably can't bend over, we thought maybe he could watch Paula try this trick!! Paula, let us know how this works out. Love, Coleen

Sounds like the Lord is at work in your hospital room. Sounds like Mark is turning a corner, that is good in medical speak. God bless you guys. We continue to hold you in our prayers. Dawn

Hello Mark 'n Paula,
Glad to hear things are going well. I still plan on coming up for a visit next week, that is if Mark is still there. (Kinda hope not) Anyway, Alan and I are praying and thinking of you guys and the family every day.

Kirk and Alan

Hi guys. I am soo happy to read such good news! Awe. He wants an ipod and a new phone, huh? He reminds me of a little boy when I read that! Too funny! Amy and Ann are cracking me up with what they write about your kiddos!! Life is never dull for you guys!! It's constant entertainment at the Welsh house!! LOL! You guys are such great people and you have wonderful kids!

We are doing good here in Bako. Enjoying this beachy weather we've had for the past few weeks. Justin lives at work at the moment. I'm ready for a change of pace in life, feeling like a single parent! Me no likey. LOL! Matt & Luke are ornery boys...they take after Justin so much it's not even funny!! I feel for Cindi! Justin drags out his BBgun we just got him (early Fathers' day present) and he has been teaching the boys how to shoot. They euthanize the annoying little birdies that poop all over our patio!! LOL!! As for me, I decided to try out wakeboarding…Naive me…I didn't know what was coming. I feel like a truck hit me! I went last week on Wednesday and I'm still so sore. I think I might have strained my hamstring, so I'm slowly recouping from that. I also took up running with a friend. Hoping to do a marathon with her and other deputies' wives. Should be a good time :) Well, Aunty Paula and Uncle Mark. I love you so much. We think about you always and looove reading the updates! We hope to be one of your fun guests soon!!! Our prayers are with you, Mark and your surgery tomorrow!! God is awesome and He's going to take good care of you!! After all, our lives are in His hands!! Hugs and loves…Justin, LaRay, Matt & Luke

Hi Paula!

We are so thankful to hear that the last few days have gone pretty well! Mark and your whole family have been in our prayers since the day we heard about the accident. We'll start praying that those hiccups subside as well! With so many family and friends in Ridgecrest, I know you have a lot of help and support, but please let us know if you need anything at all! Our hearts are with you. Stay strong! Love, Josh and Abby

Paula,

I'm so glad that Mark is healing. I'll be sure to keep both of you in my prayers tomorrow for his next surgery. Wish that I was with you along with Katie & Susan (hello!) instead of here at work. It was nice to have Chandler at Chris' b'day party Friday. They all had a good time. I didn't get a chance to go over to your house last night to do Scrip, but I'll get there today. People are going to be SO glad when you come back. Anyway, every morning here several of us get together for a quick morning prayer and you all are always remembered. Take care, Missy

Hi all,

Greetings from Tallahassee, FL! Wow, what a shock to finally get on email and find out about Mark's accident! We have checked out all your journal entries and you have been through quite an ordeal. You're right, those prayers and support from family and friends are what help you make it through each day. I can see why your parents need a Scotch at the end of the day, the children are very active and "quick" and us "older ones" are slowing down!! Being with Redd, a very active 22-month old, and Addison, a 2 ½-month old and Taryn, a very, very active 2-yr. old, has let us know we need a couple of beers @ night! Must go—the swing battery just went south! God bless you all! Paul & Sherry:)

Good Morning Paula and Mark!

Hope that this day brings you both new strength for this new week! Last night I was able to visit at the Welsh House! Popcorn and Milkshakes and Movie night too! It was great! Fun was had by all.

The boys and Grace had a good time making cards yesterday. Sorry I had to miss all the creativity. I was with Ridgecrest Cares painting 3 mobile homes! UGH! I would have much rather been making fun cards!

Genevieve went to bed like an angel! I wanted to get in her crib with her! The boys are excited about going to Big Bear. I am sure it will be an adventure for all!

My thoughts and prayers are always with you. Miss you both. Love Ann and Jerry (Doug)

Hi Paula, Mark, and Family!!

I had to catch up from the weekend and went through a bunch of emotions, as I am sure you do regularly. Your updates are amazing. It is likely therapeutic for you, Paula…it is comforting for those of us who can't be there to be with you to be so thoroughly informed of the recovery process and how you are handling it.

Those damn hiccups…I can't believe they are still an issue. You need to make more "BOO" attempts…unless, of course, you are so scary that his body is uncomfortable from the leap.

I am so happy to hear that some of his bandaging is off and that his body is recovering in some areas. What a road you are traveling! I will continue to pray for you and send loving thoughts your way! You are a strong woman and I admire you so much!!

Keep the faith and good humor…I can see your eye conversations…you were always good at those!!! Big hugs to you and yours! Sorry if this was too lengthy folks!! Sandy L.

Thoughts & Prayers to you both, Paula & Mark, as you start off a new week on the road to recovery.

Extra prayers for Mark to build up the needed strength today in preparation for tomorrow's surgery. I sure hope that they find your lower legs have made some significant progress in healing. Tracy

Good Morning! I am gathering my things before I head over to your house to pick up Dad and the boys :). We should be heading out around 9 a.m....although that could be delayed. As you know, we will need to make at least 4 more trips in and out of your house for things forgotten... LOL! Actually, I am going to think positive... and go for no trips...just pack and head out. If I plan it right, I can arrive and Mom and Dad's car will be packed and I just need to throw my own trash in. LOL!

We have been trying to sit outside a bit at night with Gigi in the front yard. However, every night she wanders a little farther, but she looks back at us, wondering who is going to come get her. Last night she ran in the garage and got around the car as I got in there. That little twerp knew which way I was going too...but as luck would have it, she always finds something on the ground to stop and pick up so I can get to her!! She is too much and getting more independent every day! We need a gated community in the front yard...she is totally Nancy the Nosy Neighbor...if anyone is out in their yard...she wants to know what is going on. LOL! I wonder who she gets that from??

All right, have a great day! We are sending the cards up. I think you both will love them. They are a hoot! They all did great!

We watched "Ferris Bueller's Day Off"...
and I think Mitch was taking notes the whole
time. LOL! I had forgotten how funny that
movie was!

Much love and encouragement to you
today! Amy

Hidy Ho from the mountains in Big Bear
where Dad, myself and your two hilarious boys
are freezing our asses off! LOL! Mitchell, of
course, forgot his sweatshirt, so he is hanging in
Dad's flannel shirts... which is actually kind of
sweet! We got up here and it clouded over and we
couldn't even hardly sit out while Dad BBQ'd...
it's like what the hell?? So Dad found the wine,
and after I found my sweats and socks and a
sweatshirt, I found some beer. LOL! Wahoooo!

Okay, the trip here went by very fast as we
played games in the car...we made Dad play too
so that was entertaining! The best line up here
was by Mitch... My mom's maiden name begins
with a "W" and my Dad's maiden name begins
with a "W"...Where is Charlotte with the supposed hurt elbow...I think you should get your
money back from Kindergarten...Mitch got
juiced on some basic information. LOL!

Then Dad took a rest after watching
"Finding Nemo" with us and we played "Phase
10". Now I have to tell you...I am laughing as
I type this. The cards were dealt for the round
and Chandler was first. He literally picked up a
card and went out before Mitch and I even had
a turn. What made it so funny was he kind of
jumped a little in his chair out of excitement and
farted...well, hell...that was all she wrote...my
maturity level matched theirs for about 20 min-

utes…It was hysterical…Mitchell was holding his stomach and tears were just streaming down his face…we just busted a gut. LOL! It was just the best :)

Everyone is now in bed and I am headed there myself…tomorrow is another day. I am making pancakes in the morning…they waited until after I had a beer to ask…and I couldn't say no…I think Dad was pretty excited too. Dammit. LOL!

Glad the McCarthy's and Susan and Katie got to come…did Dorothy cry? *smile* Mom is excited to be going up there tomorrow…and we will be on the extra prayers for surgery and more safe travels. Much Love, Dad, Amy, Mitch and Gas-X

P.S. And speaking of the hug you got…I have been giving Grace crap about her hugs…this little pitty pat on the back crap is just wrong. LOL! I told her from now on I wanted a real hug…and she laughs and tries to tell me this is just how she hugs…it was hilarious!

**Mark's dressing change started at noon and went until 3:00 p.m.. Craig and I came for a visit right afterward. Mark was pretty groggy but hiccup free. Dr. Bhakta came and talked to us about the surgery for tomorrow. Mark is scheduled for surgery between 12–1 p.m. It will be a long one—probably 6–7 hours. The surgeon and doctors will debride (clean) his burns, excise (cut away) the wounds and put allograft where burns are not yet healed. Any burns that are clean and ready they will start to autograft which means they will take healthy skin from his upper shoulders/back and cover**

his wounds. His lower legs, knees to feet, all need to be skin grafted. The graft site will need to be protected from external trauma so he will be casted and immobilized, (restricted from bending) to protect the graft. The cast will be on for three days. The doctor said where they take his healthy skin will be very painful for 2–3 days because it will feel like a burn also. We pray the autograft takes, the hiccups stay away, and surgery is successful. Mark will have more autograft surgeries. Hard to tell how many, but the good news is it can be an outpatient surgery so he won't necessarily be in the hospital. I am so grateful for all the gifts, love, prayer, support and visitors. I cannot begin to think what it would be like without all of them. KKLL, Paula

*Reflection*

*Those of you who have had to be away from your children for any short period of time (that was not planned) know how hard it is. My siblings and parents jumped right in and it was peace of mind for Mark and me. I was able to focus on Marks' healing and knew the kids were being loved and well taken care of.*

Sometimes houses and health seem to be important but suffering has a way of adjusting our perspective—especially our view of God.
—Dave Earley, *21 Reasons Bad Things Happen to Good People*

# One Day at a Time

June16, 2009

Hi! This morning was so different than last week's surgery. He was sitting up at 9 a.m. when we came in. Ace had him walk three laps. He shaved himself and brushed his own teeth and I washed him up! Then he got out of his chair by himself and got into bed! Ace keeps telling him he has to be independent and then he won't have to go to rehab from ICU—he can go straight home. The staff is so proud of Mark and knows how hard he works at the littlest task. He will be able to go outside soon and get some fresh air.

Mark is in recovery now! Everything went as well as expected. Lower right leg anterior was autografted. They autografted 9in × 12in area from his back and they thought it would go further than it did. Dr. said he is a big guy! We can expect this type of surgery every Tuesday until both lower legs and tops of feet are done and then we can go home! That was hard to swallow. I will journal more later. God bless these doctors and nurses. He is so well taken care of. Bye for now!

Good evening. So, most of you know he went to surgery at 12:15 p.m. and went to recovery around 5:45 p.m.. Craig and I were

able to meet with Dr. Bhakta post-surgery. Parts of Mark's right arm were re-allografted (a word I made up) and some smaller wounds were left to heal on their own. They had enough allograft to do his stomach and, hopefully, it will not need autografting. His thighs were also re-allografted. Like I said in the previous post, his lower legs to the tops of his feet need the most work. But I know prayer is powerful and maybe God will heal some of the deepest burns and he will not need as much autografting. His back is doing well and the autograft sight is covered with a type of foam. He will feel pain in a few days, but I know God will be with him every step of the way. I received the Lourdes water from Katie H today and will take it to Mark's room in the morning. Thank you, Katie, from the bottom of our hearts! Tomorrow is another day and I will not think about Tuesdays now until Tuesdays arrive.
Love to all, Paula

P.S. Craig and I were able to see Mark a little before 8 p.m. He was shivering and very groggy but within an hour he was resting peacefully and I felt we could leave him in peace.

Most of you do not know, but I had received a couple bottles of Lourdes water. Every night before I would leave, I would put drops of it on all of Mark's remaining wounds, mark a cross on each one and then we would hold hands and say the Hail Mary. We did this every night until he was able to go home. We believed it would heal him, and it did.

*Lourdes water* is water which flows from a spring in the Grotto of Massabielle in the Sanctuary of Our Lady of Lourdes, France. The location of the spring was described to Bernadette Soubirous by an apparition of Our Lady of Lourdes on February 25, 1858. Since that time, many thousands of pilgrims to Lourdes have followed the instruction of Our Lady of Lourdes to "drink at the spring and bathe in it." Lourdes water is considered nonliturgical holy water.

Good Evening from freezing Big Bear! What a day! After Mitch had his two cups of coffee, he and the Chan Man were ready to rock! They went to town on some chores and did a fabulous job! The decks and railings never looked better :)

We didn't have pancakes this morning as Mom swiped all the eggs...BUT Dad went and got some for the boys so we could have pancakes in the morning :). I am telling you, I think he is equally as excited for them! LOL!

Tonight as we were watching TV, one of those new commercials about bullying came on. This girl was giving a serious talk about stomping out bullying. I was watching both of the boys to see what their reaction would be to it or if they would comment. At the end, Mitch's comment was "Boy, she sure has weird legs" LMAO!! We all busted up...aye that boy!!

We played "Phase 10" tonight with Dad (after some wine) and now I have a headache from laughing...you know how Dad likes to talk alot when its his turn...he is talking to himself about what he is going to do or what card he might play and Mitch said "All of that talking isn't going to change the outcome"...we all just roared. LOL! About 3/4 of the way into the game, Chandler notices about 5 cards under his chair from 2 hands prior to that. LOL! They are just too much!

We said our prayers all day today for you and Mark and all the travelers...and they will start again tomorrow! Be safe and get some much needed rest...we head home tomorrow after lunch and the boys said tonight, they don't want to go...I think they are liking the alone time without their Sistas. LOL!

Much Love, Prayers and Blessings...and wine and beer :)

Amy, Dad, Mitch, Chan, the bunny out front, and the scrappy looking coyote that keeps hanging around

Hi Paula,

We want you to know that you are all in our thoughts and prayers. My husband works in a scary industry also and I am praying so hard for you and for what you are going through. Please know that this whole town is praying for Mark. I hear conversations about him all the time. God Bless! Stacey, Carlos, Elijah, & Alexia

Paula,

I'm so glad that the surgery went well, you've been on my mind all day. It stinks about surgery every Tuesday, but it sounds like they know what they are doing. I'll be remembering you in prayer tonight and tomorrow also. I'm just about to join Katie in spirit with a glass of wine, wish you could join me. Love ya, Missy. It's fun to play with color!

Paula and Mark

When your hut is on fire...

The only survivor of a shipwreck was washed up on a small, uninhabited island. He prayed feverishly for God to rescue him. Every day he scanned the horizon for help, but none seemed forthcoming. Exhausted, he eventually managed to build a little hut out of driftwood to protect him from the elements, and to store his few possessions. One day, after scavenging for food, he arrived home to find his little hut in flames, with smoke rolling up to the sky. He felt the worst had happened, and everything was lost. He was stunned with disbelief, grief, and anger. He cried out, 'God! How could you do this to me?' Early the next day, he was awakened by the sound of a ship approaching the island! It had come to rescue him! 'How did you know I was here?' asked the weary man of his rescuers. 'We saw your smoke signal,' they replied.

The Moral of This Story:

It's easy to get discouraged when things are going bad, but we shouldn't lose heart, because God is at work in our lives, even in the midst of our pain and suffering. Remember that the next time your little hut seems to be burning to the ground. It just may be a smoke signal that summons the Grace Of God.

P.S. You may want to consider passing this on, because you never know who feels as if their hut is on fire today.

THERE ARE MANY THINGS IN LIFE THAT WILL CATCH YOUR EYE, BUT ONLY A FEW WILL CATCH YOUR HEART... PURSUE THESE.

In God we have faith. Just had to share with you. Margie

Dear Paula and Mark,

Glad to hear Mark's surgery went well. I am sure the idea of this every week is a lot to take in, but baby steps, and one day at a time. He is doing so well. We will continue to pray he continues to heal and that you are well supported. Your family and friends are amazing!!! Love ya tons, Katie H.

Well, I'm afraid I've had 2 glasses of wine already…rather large ones, I must say…and I just want to say, "oh sh#$" about the surgeries every Tuesday. I've been praying for a miracle since my hour last night (this morning) at 2 a.m.. I guess the miracle is that you & Mark are staying strong & that the good Lord is meeting your needs each day ("give us this day our daily bread"), just not giving Mark the grand, overwhelming instant cure that we all are hoping for.

Know that you have been lifted up in prayers & thoughts by so many people today.

Hang in there……(that's an expression) Love, Katie N.

Hi Paula—

Checking on Mark's progress daily. Good to see that he's progressing well. All of you are in our prayers daily. I know you have lots of family and friends helping out, but if you need anything, we would be glad to help! God bless! Debbie, Dennis and Family

Paula & Mark,

It's wonderful to read your journal. What a gift you have for writing! The church office is as busy as ever. Most people that come in, ask about Mark & you. I get to direct them to the website and those that don't have a computer, I get to relate your stories.

Keep up your strength. Say 'hi' to Mark. from the Jensen and Lara families. We celebrate Victor 8th birthday on Thursday, as well as our wedding anniversary. What an Anniversary present Victor was! Prayers constantly from us. Love, Susie & Vic

Mark. & Paula,

You continue to be in our thoughts and prayers. I read your journal daily to see where the prayers are needed the most. So very thankful that the hiccups have left, hopefully leaving the body for good. We just can not imagine what all Mark. is going through. Paula, you now know more about burns than you ever thought you would and I am sure you will continue to educate yourself once Mark. comes home and his healing continues. We pray they give Mark the good drugs after surgery and while he is casted so he can sleep through the pain. If he can't do his laps and he still has the feeding tube in, I say leave him be. But I know how the doctors and nurses like to poke and prod. I pray it won't be as bad as it sounds and that God continues to give you both the strength you need to get you through this. Our prayers are with you both. Bill & Patti

Paula,

It's a cloudy day in the desert, but I'm sure there are some rays of light from heaven blessing Mark. during his operation today. He has been in my prayers all day. Tell the big guy I said hello when he wakes up! God Bless, Mark N.

Mark and Paula,

As I write this, Mark would be in surgery and people all over this country are using "God's Internet"—prayer—to petition for Mark to have a successful surgery and that he heals quickly, and for you to keep your strong Catholic faith and your awesome sense of humor! God bless both of your families. Chris

Dear Mark and Paula,

I am back from visiting my son and grandson in Seattle. Have read that surgery is today. My prayers are with you and hope that all goes well and stays that way in the next few days. Much love! Edie

Dear Paula & Mark,

I am so so sorry to hear what happened... Aunt Claire just told me about it this mornin'. Can't believe my Little Verbal Diarrhea Sister Judie didn't tell me, and I saw her yesterday.

You both are in my prayers for a speedy recovery. Mark, I know you don't know me, but it sounds like you are a strong man, physically and spiritually. I'm sure that's why you are doing better than most...keep up the good work! Paula, I will be thinking of you tonight as I have my glass of wine! Hang in there baby!!! Terry

Dear Mark & Paula—Wow—I just read your journal—extra prayers are being sent your way—it will be a long day & you will need extra strength to get through it—I'm glad your Mom & Karen will be there along with Mark's brother—they will be good support for you. I just can't stop thinking about how strong you both are. Amy, I did have my moments, but I managed to hide it better than I sometimes do—I did not want to fall apart in front of Mark. I will check in with your Mom tomorrow & see how things are going—Lisa & I won't be near a computer for a couple of days so will have to catch up on Friday—take care of yourself, Paula—like I said you are amazing & such a good caregiver—extra hugs to Mark. Many prayers & God Bless you both & your kiddles too. Much love—Dorothy & Tom

Paula,

I thought last Tuesday was a long day!! Sounds like today will be especially long. At least they are able to start on the autograph. That must mean good progress. I am just amazed at what a process this has been. Not one any of us ever want to go through. My thoughts and prayer will be with you both all day. And for all the travelers too. Glad your Mom and Karen are there today. Love, Leslie

Paula,

OOPS spelled autograft wrong. My good thoughts were there at least...

Love ya, Leslie

Happy Monday! Mark, we're praying your surgery goes well and were elated to read how well you've been doing recently (of course, I haven't been reading in a timely fashion: I have to contend with 2 other computer users on the weekends!).

Paula, I'm glad you are being buoyed up by prayer (and vino, too); surgeries and hospitalizations of family members are traumatic for the whole family.

Here's some mind medicine! (C.D., 11/07, p.23): Lady to waiter: "I'm going to order a broiled, skinless chicken breast, but I want you to bring me lasagna and garlic bread by mistake."

(ibid., p. 28):

A Sunday school teacher asked her students as they entered the church, "And why is it necessary to be quiet during Mass?" One bright little girl replied, "Because people are sleeping."

We're all waiting hopefully for Mark to be released, so he can come home to Ridgecrest (I don't know how much he'll rest: a whole lot more of us will be able to visit then!).Hugs & prayers, Mary G.

OMG Paula, What a big day for Mark today. The skin graft surgery sounds intense. I can't believe he has had to endure so much. My thoughts & prayers. Love, Gene & Elaine

Hello Welshes,

The pre surgery praying has begun on this cloudy day in the desert. The Ladies from our singing group will be here tonight, and will wrap up with prayer for Mark, you and the family. I am leaving early bird time tomorrow for the trip to Fresno, so will call you when I'm in the neighborhood, probably around 10. In the meantime, sure am enjoying being nosy and reading all the entries! Continuing on the journey with you,

Your friends, Russ, Hope and Katy KKLL (Hope only)

Hi Paula & Mark,

We are continuing to pray for less pain, no hiccups, and better eating...wierd combination huh?? Well it doesn't matter as God knows what we are praying about!. I can't imagine what you are going through and even reading about it makes my stomach churn. Keeping up the prayer vigil for you all. Hugs, Jill

Mark and Paula,

Our prayers are still coming from Tennessee. I admire your strength and determination to move forward with healing, Mark. I know it has been a long, painful journey already, but you are a re"mark"able hero! Paula, I wish was there in body, but know that I am there in spirit everyday. Love, Emily

Paula and Mark,

I will continue to pray very hard for Mark and you during this part of his recovery. Both of you have done so well dealing with such a challenging situation. You both are such an inspiration to all. May you find that peace that passes all understanding today.

I look forward to seeing you both on Thursday. Sheri

Dear Mark,

God Bless you! You are such a good person & we are all keeping you in our prayers. God Bless & good rest during & after surgery.
Dear Paula,

Just want to let you know it is ok to stay in the fog for a while. That is why everyone is pray-

ing for you to help you during this time of need.
Love Always, Ann

*Reflection*

*I remember those surgeries and how long those days were. It was a little too much sometimes—wondering how much of the burn sites had healed. And if they would be able to shave that healed skin and use it on the deeper burns and now he would have a new kind of pain on the shaved sites.*

*But that day so many guests reached out to me which helped pass the time and gave me hope.*

*I remember another good friend telling me that Mark was an inspiration to others on those surgery days. He was feeling no pain under sedation not really knowing what was happening to him. But all those praying for him were focusing on God. What a gift prayer can be.*

The world is a heavy place and we can't
be all cross and no Resurrection.
—Carrie Gress, *Nudging Conversions*

# Prayers for Appetite Answered

June 17, 2009

Despite yesterday's worries, fret and help-lessness, today was a new day! Mark was alert this morning, eating almost all of his breakfast. His catheter came out in the afternoon and his port/cath in his shoulder area will come out tomorrow. Mark really had what I consider an alert day! [My friend] Hope arrived around 10 a.m. and we visited Mark for an hour. He talked and joined in conversation, now Hope thinks it is because of her. Craig took over "Mark duty" so I could go get a haircut with my new favorite guy, Josh. He washed my hair and then massaged my head and neck for 1/2 hour. It was HEAVENLY! He also told me about a website called YELP that gives reviews on restaurants. It came in handy because when I got back to the hospital he asked for Japanese food. I went to my office (3rd floor lobby) and looked it up on YELP. Hope and I took an adventure and found an authentic Japanese place called Tokyo Restaurant. Hope was scared driving the streets to get there but nothing really scares me anymore. I brought a Dragon Roll back to Mark and he scarfed it up! Hope now thinks that is because of her also. I was so proud of him. He even had one

**of Hope's sister's cookies! (thanks, Margaret). Craig left around 4 p.m. and I will miss his company and support. It was so nice having him here. Well onto to playing Beauty Parlor! Hope will help me color my hair, which Mark usually helps with (not willingly). I asked his brother to help the other night but he looked at me like I had 3 heads! Mark told Craig today it was a PITA (pain in the ass, that's an expression) I love you all and hope tomorrow brings more energy for Mark. KKLL, Paula.**

Mark,

Sounds like you are doing well. We are so proud of you. Keep up the hard work. Love you and you are in our thoughts and prayers! Love ya lots. Erin

Way to go, Welshes! Sounds as tho' today was a good day, in the long run; kudos to you both. Now that you've done it once, the subsequent surgeries will hopefully be less stressful (you know what to expect). Since these procedures seem to be painful, I guess that's the best you can expect and, of course, all of us who know what's going on will keep storming Heaven for you in our prayers. Mary G.

Hola! Mi amigos, Welsh,

Spanish word of the day. Vacaciones (vacation) that's where I have been. Didn't go anywhere. The computer decided it needed some time off. Anyway, I see that Our Lord continues to bless Senor Mark. Senora Paula you have a huge medical terminology vocabulary. You should become an Enfermera (nurse) when you grow up. Even though the uniforms are not as cute as they used to be. Did you ever play Dr's? Just curious. Mark you are a determined man, and I admire you, keep up the good work. Buenas Noches, Sara

Hello, Welsh Family,

We apologize for signing the guestbook so late, no excuses. Please know that from the first day when we heard the news you all have been in the Duhon prayers daily.

We visit the site often to get the updates on his surgeries and progress. It is so amazing to see all the well wishes and prayers everyone has sent. Paula thanks for the Journal updates daily, with as difficult as it is to deal with being at the hospital and then have to write an update I know how exhausting each day can be. Love your honesty and humor.

Wishing Mark a little more progress each day, and with you and your family by his side we know he has the best cheerleaders for recovery. Our love and prayers with you all, Mark, Theresa, Warren and Aunt Jane

Paula, Mark and family,

I am Katie N.'s sister Rene from Bellevue, NE. Just wanted you to know Katie has asked for (and we are responding with) lots of prayers for you. Your intentions are with the Perpetual Adorers at St. Marys in Bellevue and also with the Sisters of Mercy community (I am a Mercy teacher). Plus the whole Duffy family and all of our prayer links. As I know you know, prayer works miracles (as it has already for you). I'll let my sister and brother-in-law do the drinking for us (I know you will read this, Kate!), but do know that many, many people are praying for you. God Bless, Maureen

Paula and Mark,

Just a note to let you know that we're keeping you in our prayers today and everyday. We learned when we had children that God needs you to be specific with your prayers. (We only asked for healthy babies and He played all kinds of jokes on us with that one!!!) So we are specifically praying for your first Tuesday with no surgery to come quickly, then for your first Tuesday to be able to leave the Hospital to come soon after that, and finally for your first Tuesday when you can return home when your body has healed enough. We also pray for your daily courage and strength through this all. Lighting a candle at Church for you this evening. Love, Coleen

*Blessed be the Lord,*
*for he has heard the sound of my pleading;*
*the Lord is my strength and my shield.*
*In him my heart trusts, and I find help:*
*in my heart exults, and with my song I give*
*him thanks.*
*Psalm 28:6–7*

Good Morning Paula and Mark,

Hi, Craig! Hi, Hope! I am so glad that the prayers are working. We certainly will continue to pray for strength for the both of you on this long road to recovery.

Last night I had the pleasure to have dinner with Grace, Adam and Genevieve. We went to Kristy's after a lengthly decision making process by Grace! We enjoyed our dinner and our entertainment by Genevieve.

Grace has enjoyed her quiet time without the brothers! They return today. It will be back to a full house!

I enjoy the night time routine of giving Genevieve her bottle and putting her to bed. Sometimes she needs a bath before bed. She lays on her belly and kicks and splashes. I think she will be a strong swimmer. Just need to teach her to close her mouth as she puts her face in the water! She is an angel!

Mom thinks I drug Genevieve when I put her to bed because she has been sleeping in to 8 a.m. and this morning it was 8:30 a.m.! No drugs just a lotta loving!

I travel to Bishop today for work until Friday evening. I will miss my evening adventures with the kids. I even tried to get out of this travel.

I will keep you—all close to my heart as I travel. Miss you both!

Love to you both, Ann and Jerry (Doug)


Paula and Mark,

So glad the Lourdes water made it to you in one piece. I have been nervous since I sent it off. So glad to hear he is doing so much better than last surgery. Good for him for working so hard to get better. Angels all around you both. XOXO Katie H.


Hi Guys—

Happy to hear the procedure went well yesterday and that you're able to push to keep working toward independence. Paula said that in one of your groggy states you were worrying about making sure your crew was covered always thinking of others even now! Glantz is doing a good job heading the crew 'til you get well though I know your people miss you as do the rest of us. Just take care of you. We'll take care of the work stuff till you can come back.

I was just thinking about your legs after recovery. You in your shorts—looking like Sasquatch from the knees down (now having your hairy back skin covering them)! Hope they don't have to take any from your head or you're going to have the sexiest poke-a-dotted legs ever seen. You should start thinking about having Paula teach you to shave your legs.—Mike

Paula and Mark,

It just filled my heart today to hear he might get to go outside soon and all the little tasks he works at to get better. I heard a great sermon in church on Sunday that brought me encourage-ment and strength. The message was that little seeds of faith/christian acts are planted and some-times we think nothing is happening. But God works in these small seeds and creates a beautiful, awesome picture in the end. This made me think of Mark's recovery and how each little piece of healing in his body (and your acts of faith com-bined) are lifting Mark to a full recovery. See you on Thursday. Sheri

Mark and Paula,

We always say prayers for anyone who needs it at the end of our Knights of Columbus meet-ings, and have included you and your family since the accident. The meetings are on Tuesdays, and as rough as your Tuesdays look now, we'll keep doing it. So you'll have 15–20 grumpy old men (and myself, of course) pulling for you after every surgery. God bless, Jim

Good Morning, Mark and Paula,

The two of you have been on my mind a lot lately. Just wanted you to know I am continuing to keep you and your family in my prayers. You are both very strong people and with God's help I know you will win this battle. Hugs, Jo

Paula and Mark, just a small note to express to you how sorry we are to hear about this. Your family is in my prayers. It sounds like today was a good day and I pray for more. Remember that God deals out only what you can handle. You both seem to have a very close bond to each other and God. That is your strength for each other. To be home is the goal as you will heal faster, so keep up the good work, Mark and eat lots of protein. Listen to your wife. She will be your best cheerleader, and you will be home soon to recuperate with all your kiddos. Leave the prayers up to us. Sounds like so far He's been listening, so take care and God bless you all...love, Debbie B.

So many prayers—it just makes me happy knowing the power!!! Mike returns tomorrow and then we will make plans to come see Mark. I hope your hair turned out better then when I did it—I think we had to call Clairol 911—last time Paula asked for my help! Mark I could tell you how to mess it up—did you know I have your hair? Mark, know that we all love you and appreciate your strength—many men would have not been able to come back to their families. Eat, drink (okay Ensure) and be merry!!! Hope to see you very soon. Love, Ruth, Mike and family

Paula and Mark,

I can't believe it. I didn't know Mark colored your hair!! I thought we girls KNEW ALL...Looks like things are on a roll...Speaking of rolls. You may have started something, Paula. I hope that restaurant isn't too far. You might be dealing with much deserved craving!!! You go, Mark. We continue to pray for a quick release. Yesterday Rachel was just telling someone about how silly we all were for your 40th birthday. Parading around in diapers...Here's to more silly-ness in the future!!!! With Love, Leslie

WOW! You are really a true HERO! I am glad you are inspired to work so hard (ok, so I want you to come home soon so you and I can share a moment (Coors Light moment). Now really, it takes a strong man to have accomplished so much and endured so much too (and tolerate your wife lovingly). YOU GO MARK! Claire B

Hello, Paula and Mark,

Glad to know that Paula is taking care of her hair—all I can remember about self help hair color is that one night after church I came home to the teenage daughter with a towel around her head. It stayed there until bedtime. In the middle of the night I awoke and went into her room and low and behold, Stacey had carrot orange hair. We had to go to the salon immediately the next day to get that rectified. The joke at our house is if you feel the need to color some part of your body, paint your toes! We are so greatful for the journals and the progress that Mr Mark is making. Hang in there you two.

Love, Margie and Walt

P.S. I would not ever let Walt near my hair, he can put color on cars but not hair, so see how blessed you are?

Hidy Ho from the Welsh compound! GiGi is napping so Mom and I are enjoying some quiet time...sort of...as we watch Miss Jessica, Mitch and Chandler take a swim. Jessica is a doll :) She had a snack and then a hotdog for lunch...and didn't wrinkle her nose at the apples like her boy cousins did...she ate those right up. LOL! GiGi is loving her and leading her everywhere by the finger and also lifting Jessica's shirt up...doing the complete check and Jessica is a good sport for all of her cousin's craziness.

Grace went on to volleyball this afternoon. Yesterday I took her and showed her how to pump gas and fill her truck up :) So now she is completely independent...but she did tell Grandma today she would run to the store BEFORE she left for practice. I believe her comment was "I am NOT going into the store in spandex!" Isn't that hilarious!

Tomorrow we go to Vince's in the afternoon for some swimming out there...I look forward to it. LOL! Wonder if Vince has any Scotch at his house?? Lots of Love and Prayers, Dad, Mom, Amy, Grace, Mitch, Jessica, Chandler, Gigi and Ebony :).

Mark and Paula,

It brought tears to my eyes when I read that Mark helps you color your hair. What a wonderful partnership you share! I am so glad you are able to sneak away and take a little time away to renew your strength so you are able to continue to provide Mark with the support he needs at this time. You are truly an amazing woman. There is nothing like getting a shampoo with a head massage to boot! Awesome!! We continue to pray for you and your family daily. We are posting your blogs on the refrigerator in the Coso Junction office. Everyone enjoys the updates. Thank you for taking the time to include us in Marks' recovery. We had our SafeStart training seminar yesterday. Mark, you were in the room with us all day. We all miss you very much and are thanking God for your miraculous progress. With much love, Lisa H

YEAH!!! So glad to hear Mark's appetite is kicking in!!! He seems to have really taken a nice turn since this week's surgery…maybe the up & down cycle is over…Sending my prayers that the 'set backs' are now behind you and only the 'good days' lay ahead…and, of course, for your continued strength on this road to recovery, dear Mark & Paula. Please know that you are being thought of constantly…Tracy

What great news today! Hooray!!!! I know there will be ups and downs but while things are up Hooray!!! Hooray!!! Hooray!!! Thank God for the small steps as well as the big ones. Much love, Edie

Dear Paula and Mark,

I'm happy to hear that Mark is doing so well…keep up the good work Mark!! Paula, way to stay PRETTY for your man!! Just a little shout out this morning to let you know I'm thinking of you guys and praying away. Please take care, love ya, Tami

Dearest Paula & Mark:

I heard the news from my sister-in-law Gloria Avalos. She called to give me the news and make sure that I prayed! I am so sorry to hear about the accident. It has been a while since I have seen you ( missed you this year at Congress, but I went and visited your MOM!!) I am keeping you and your family in our prayers, also have some awesome Norbatine Sisters praying for Mark. My son, Justin, was burned 2 years ago. He spent 2 weeks at the Sherman Oaks Burn Center. He worked with a contractor at Cal Portland Cement Co here in Mojave. It was a long hard road 2 weeks, 3 surgeries later. God is good. Justin was burnt on his arms, back side, and ear. The Burn Center did a beautiful job. Be assured that the Lord will guide you all the way! Is there an address that we can send things to you? Kids getting out of hand? I will check in later, keep up all the good work! Love, Denise

*Reflection*

*We take our appetites for granted. It was diffi-cult to see a feeding tube in my husband. His appe-tite was so weak in the beginning and hindered his recovery. The hiccups didn't help either. The removal of the feeding tube was another miracle.*

*I also didn't know talking about how Mark helped me color my hair would be a topic of conver-sation, he had been doing it for years so unwillingly. I am glad I was able to post random things because I believe it changed the subject and gave people some-thing to talk and laugh about.*

# Continual Improvements or Miracles?

June 19, 2009

Boy, the time got away from us! John, Sheri and I have been visiting and catching up. It is so nice to have them here. They arrived at noon safely.

This morning Mark was sleepy but his hemoglobin was down so he did receive 2 units of blood and by the afternoon he walked 150 feet. Sheri and John visited with him while I ran some errands with the crazy Sizemore sisters! When I got back to the room in the afternoon I brought the water from Lourdes and I sprinkled it on all of Mark's bandages and we both took a sip. We said a Hail Mary and had a moment. I believe God is bigger than all of us and (although we are here for a couple more surgeries) the doctor informed us tonight that parts of Mark's upper legs where he thought skin grafting was needed was healed by the allograft. Time is on our side because the longer the allograft is on, the more healing can take place and we will come home with less wound care. I hope everyone seriously thinks about donating their tissue after they die. It has saved my husband from a lot of debriding and scrubbing of his burns—basically saved him from excruciating PAIN. God bless Dr. Dominic for working at this Burn Center. It was opened just 2 yrs ago!

Mark asked for chicken nuggets and fries for dinner and when I brought it back he ate it all gone. He then had a cookie for dessert!

David arrives on the 10 a.m. flight and will be here for the weekend! Hope and her sister have offered to pick him up. Then Hope will head home sometime tomorrow. I am grateful for all who have come to watch over me. Love ya, Paula.

Good evening! Mark started the morning with a visit from Ace, his physical therapist. He was able to take two laps in front of his sister and bro-in-law. They will leave in the morning so I was so happy that they were able to see his progress. Dick A from Coso, surprised Mark with a visit. My brother arrived safely from Seattle too. Mark had a dressing change after lunch and faired through it pretty well. Then the big news of the day is that his doctor approved him to go outside! We took him out for 45 min. The Eberharts showed for a visit and also got to see Mark outside. It was so nice to show Mark My patio, My office and all the surroundings. After a busy day, he managed to eat his Quiznos dinner too. My parents arrive tomorrow and John and Sheri head back to Oklahoma. Love you all and I can HONESTLY say I look forward to tomorrow. Paula

Mark's 1st trip outside was 45 minutes long??? wow! What a nice surprise. Glad to hear Paula got to show off her lunch venue… the change of scenery must have felt refreshing, even in the 1st day of our real summertime heat. Continued prayers for you both for a peaceful & healing weekend. Tracy

Dear Paula,

The delivery service made a stop to your house today. Mission accomplished. I have to confess I had a moment. I wished it wasn't me driving into the drive way, but you and Mark instead. I loved spending time with you…even though you risked my very life…and spending time with Mark was a real blessing. Glad that our family looked crazy compared to the Weidenkopf's…very comforting indeed…Love you lots, Hope

Dear Paula and Mark…thanks, Paula for your TERRIFIC updates…Mark (and you) were in my prayers on surgery day (extra prayers… as you are in them often during the day!). O.K, readers out there…I know you all want an elbow update!!!! Well…on Tuesday, I had "the magic shot"…hurt like H…but it all went straight to Mark!!!!

And then…wonders of wonders…the pain was gone and I could actually move my elbow!!! Now WHAT am I going to offer up for Mark. Just kidding, GOD…I don't want the elbow pain back…I'll find something else! Dr. Nobody was absolutely NO USE for my pain and suffering… but he is sure he could do wonders for Mark!… and by the way…I think George's skin has run out by now!!! Seriously…thank you Paula for sharing about skin etc. donors…so…Mr. N. is working on his summer schedule…DON'T be surprised…you know how he likes to fly under the radar…love for the HOT, HUMID desert…Char

Hi Paula & Mark,

Just wanted you guys to know that we've been keeping you in our thoughts and prayers! It's incredible how strong you've both been through this whole ordeal. May God continue to bless you and we pray for a speedy recovery! Love, Ben, Laura & Aiden

Paula,

I sold Scrip today & I don't think I screwed it up too badly…if I did, Missy will take care of it, I hope! A lady came in to buy Scrip and she asked about Mark. She had 4 little kids with her & she said that she did daycare for someone who works with Mark. I asked her who the co-worker was, and she said it was Kirk. I said, "Oh, you mean Kirk-o…then that cute little boy must be Alan!" (like I knew them!). It's nice to put a face—even a small one—with a name I see on this guestbook. Anyway, you're still the talk of the town although Mark's made most of the husbands look bad because they don't color their wives' hair. My husband colored <u>my</u> hair without any dye…just living with him turned it gray! (Just kidding, Mark…I mean, my Mark!). Hang in there…we're so glad that there's been some good days lately. Here's hoping & praying they continue to come more & more often. Love, Katie N

OMG—As much as Dave complains about how much I spend on my hair, he still would NEVER offer to color it. If Mark does hair color, he's definitely a keeper! LOL

Hope told me of the second surgery—I'm glad to hear how well Mark is doing—it sounds like his mobility and appetite are really coming along. We pray for his quick return home. Love, Dave and Julie

Good Morning Paula and Mark,

Sounds like things are moving along just fine, good news! Keep the faith, it will carry you a long way! FYI: I'm on the donor list for when I die, whatever is needed, organs, skin, hair…I would like to know if there is a place I can go locally (Chico) to donate blood in Mark's name. I have O-neg, everyone can use my blood… :-)

Well I'm heading off to Idaho today for a family reunion, going to meet relatives I've never met, that could be scary…Take care and big hugs to both of you, Jo Elaine

Hey Paula,

Just getting back from vacation and catching up at work this past week, so was finally able to spend some time this evening to catch up on Mark's progress. wow! How can anyone look at how far he has come and not believe that God is in control! Paula, thank you for taking the time to post. I can't even begin to imagine what you're going through. It's a blessing to have family and friends to help you through this. Loved your pictures too! It does help to put things in perspective when I think about Mark being able to finally spend 45 minutes outside. The things we take for granted...Both of you are, and continue to be, in my prayers. God Bless, Terry

Dear Paula and Mark,

My thoughts and prayers are with you during this very difficult time. I just heard about the accident and Leslie just gave me the website for CaringBridge. Your family has always been very special to me during my time growing up here in Ridgecrest. I know your family is there for you but please remember that you have an extended family that includes me. I will be praying for you all every day. I send big hugs to you and your husband and to all of your family. Love Always, Lisa M

Paula & Mark,

Love the pictures you added. Nice to see smiles, too.

Keeping you & your family in our prayers. Love, Vic & Susie

Thanks for sharing the great photos of you and Mark!—And, I see Linda E. got to give you a hug, Mark. NO ONE gives better hugs than Linda! Keep up the great progress. Love, Claire G

Mark and Paula,

Thank you for sharing time with us on Friday. It was so good to see Mark, and outside at that. What a blessing. Paula it was good to be able to hug you in person instead of just through emails. Keep up the good work (both of you). Love you, Linda and Hank

Good Morning from the Welsh compound! The transfer has been completed. I left the Taylor household and am now here to take care of your muffins! Mom and Dad are on the road and Chandler and I are watching cartoons. All the others are still in their dark caves fast asleep... must have been the busy day yesterday!

Mitch, Grace, Chan, Jessica and I went on up to Vince's to swim! Perfect timing as it was hot here. We first ran through Beansters to get a cold treat...3 chocolate milkshakes and 2 PB Mochas later we were on our way!

The swimming went on for 3 hours. With Vince's help, Grace figured out how to get the XM radio on so we would have music while we partied poolside :) Mitch showed me his "Big guns" (his muscular arms) while he wore his sister's purple sunglasses. Chandler asked me out of the blue if I knew if Romeo or Juliet died first... and I was pretty amazed that he knew that story and Shakespeare. So I told him "Well Romeo thought Juliet was dead, so he killed himself... but she wasn't really" and he gave me a very weird look. So I said "You are talking about the play aren't you?" and he said "No, I was talking about Uncle Vince and Aunt Cindi's cats" LOL! Nice.

The kids and I raced and played Marco Polo...but Grace lay out like a lizard sunning herself on the table in the pool! I will have to send that picture...it was pretty funny! Jessica swam like a fish and kind of took it all in. I would love to be a bug on the wall when she gets alone with her parents...I can just hear it now. "Man, why did you make me stay with those psycho freak shows!" LOL Welcome to family Miss Jessica!

The best part was (Claire hope you read this and it brings back a funny memory) driving in my car up to Vince's...with "Cecilia" (by Simon and Garfunkel) blaring and all of us singing at the top of our lungs...just like we did with the Canavans many years ago...it was hilarious... Jessica sung like a big dog!!

Well I am off to tend to my muffins and breakfast...missing you! We will miss Miss Jessica too...hope everyone has safe travels today!! Take care, Amy, Chan, Grace, Jess, Mitch and GiGi and Ebony too!

Dear Mark and Paula, Nice hair I hope that was after your salon visit haha. Well it has been 21 days for you Mark and I hope you are still staying strong (I am doing so so) I also want to know if Mark is thinking about his next remodeling job yet. Take care.

PS. Yes, Amy that was a trip I will never forget. Go Cecilia. **YOU GO MARK**_PSSS. Is David singing to Mark? Claire B

*Reflection*

    *I start to tear up as I begin to read my entry and all the guest posts because I am remembering that after a few good days that he takes a turn for the worse.*

    *It was a rollercoaster ride and it was difficult to take 1 day at a time. His progress was always changing. But I do remember that in the back of my mind I knew he would be leaving there someday in the future*

Your Pains are Spiritual Gold

—Anonymous

# Two Steps Forward, One Step Back

June 21, 2009

Happy Father's Day to all you daddies! Especially all of Genevieve's daddies :). The doctors told us there would be setbacks and Mark has had a setback. He has been bleeding internally since Saturday around noon and they are trying diligently to find the area. He has had 6 units of blood and is getting the 7th unit as I write this. He is coherent and understands what is going on. The doctors and nurses consider him stable. He had a bleeding scan at midnight but it did not show an active bleed. By this morning his hemoglobin was down again so around noon today they did an EGD, upper scope of the stomach with a camera and that did not show any bleeds in the stomach. So tonight he will get "Go Lightly" in his feeding tube and a colonoscopy Monday morning. They told me that this is not unusual for a burn patient to have this happen. There was a lot of trauma and stress to his body. He is being well taken care of. I guess our prayers now are for the doctors and nurses to care for him to the best of their ability, for the bleeding to stop, and for a diagnosis. Love, Paula

Hey Paula and Mark...HAPPY FATHER'S DAY...MARK...Chandler served mass with Leah at 10:30 and survived "dragon lady" Leah... who of course is ALPHA server!!! so happy to see your picture...hey, you look good...read about latest trauma so upped the prayers today...... next time I have to have a colonospy (or however you spell it!). I won't complain...waiting for good news on Monday...Laurie was lecturing Chris on how EXACTLY to fix the deep dish pizza they are taking over tomorrow so it won't be "soggy"...Chris almost listened!!! take care...love MORE>>>MORE>>>EXTRA PRAYERS>>>> Char

Hi Dad,

Wats up i heard you were really tired today so was sam and i. Me and sam did some yard work and wash a car and got 14$. So that means i have 242$ so thats good. Then tomorrow we are goin to wash some more cars and do Aunt Ann's and Aunt Amy's car so that will be fun. WELL i hope you had an Awesome Father's Day. Love, Your Son, Mitchell

Hey daddy its Grace. Happy Fathers Day!!!!!!!!!!!!!!!!!!!!

Genevieve says hi too. She was wearing my jacket and it is as big as her it is pretty funny. She is so styling with her sunglasses that her aunties got her. She can say please now so when she wants something we tell her that she has to say please...it's cute. Last night when i was going to put her to bed i accidently feel asleep in the chair with her for two hours so when i woke up my back was aching. Well i hope all is good up there, things are pretty quiet and everybody is waking up real late and staying in there pjs down here so everything is slow pace

hope to see you soon. Love, Grace

Happy father's day to all. Auntie Amy keep up the good job and posts.

Mark, you did a good job raising your children in spite of their mother (just kidding Paula). Paula your hair looks great and Mark you look yummy. (Yummy i got love in my tummy). Paula you actually let Claire use your email? Wow! Wonder what she added to your computer????? Thinking of you always with love and prayers.

See you soon. Rose and gang

P.S. GiGi's real dad says hi. Rose

Dear Mark & Paula.

**YOU GO MARK!** Today was a step back but you have been making big steps forward. Keep the faith. You are in my thoughts and my vision (ok I see you.) Enjoyed watching army movie with you. Stay strong kkkk no **horsing** around. Claire B

Hey Mark and Paula,

Wanted to say HAPPY FATHER'S DAY to Mark and to all the Dads out there. It's pretty clear how many great friends you all have and how well thought of Mark is at work!!! Sorry to hear about Mark's bleed but am hoping the great doctors there will have some good news soon. Good to hear from Amy how the kids are doing also. Everybody keep up the good work!!! You guys take care...Love ya...Tami

Hi Mark & Paula—Happy Father's Day, Mark!! You are doing so well—just checked out the pictures on the website—you look great— you too, Paula. I' m sure it was nice to get out of your room & be outside for a while—have been thinking of you all week—I talked to your Mom on Friday after our little trip—they will be there with you now so that is good. I'm glad your appetite has improved, Mark—it is just amazing to hear how well you are doing. God is all around you and our prayers are being answered—I hope that each day you are feeling stronger. Take care & know that God loves you & is taking care of you—lots of love & prayers—Dorothy & Tom P.S. Paula, Tom says you are not "Chopped Liver"!! Love you!!

As all of us are thinking today of our great dads, it's Mark who came to mind, too! Happy Father's Day, Mark!! Hope God has an extra special blessing for you today.

Russ, Hope and Katy

Paula,

We made it home without any problems. Thank you for hosting us while we were there. Jessica loved her visit. The photos are a meaningful touch to the website. We will continue to pray for Mark, you and your family as you continue to deal with Mark's recovery. John and I were both in awe of what you and Mark have accomplished so far in his recovery. It was like standing in the midst of an incredible miracle. I understand from you, Mark, and your family that his recovery will be long and very challenging and I am sorry for that. But something just kept nudging me about that—God does not give us so many blessings in a situation and then just pull the rug out from under us. He is there for the long haul. May you find more blessings along the way today. Sheri

Hi Mark & Paula,

Happy father's day wish it was at home for you. It's good to see you progressing forward, keep your spirits up. Hope to see you soon. Lynn

*Reflection*

*When Mark started bleeding internally I remember being mad at God. I was thinking if they could not find the source of bleeding, he could die and if he was going to die, why didn't God take him on the 30th. God was testing my faith.*

*And soon I realized it was not about me, it was about Mark working through the stress. He just told the nurse he had been there for 21 days and she told him, "yes and you could be there for 21 more". He didn't like that response. He had just gotten to go outside the day before for the first time. His worrying about it is probably what caused the ulcers to bleed. When you endure that kind of trauma and injury to the body, the body also internally stresses.*

*We were blessed that the bleeding stopped and never happened again.*

It is always difficult to be mindful of the fruit of suffering and to live with its hope, but that is where trust and faith grow and live.
—*Unknown*

# Being Loved

June 22, 2009

Hello, I know everyone is praying double time, triple time, and overtime! I appreciate it so much. Mark had such a long day today and also had to endure a dressing change @ 4:00 p.m., so when I went to see him @ 6:30 p.m., I did not expect to see him sitting up in bed and eating his dinner. He seemed to be in a good mood, too. The doctor said his burns are still looking good and surgery will probably be Wednesday or Thursday. Ace will have him walking tomorrow, with any luck. Claire slept over last night and headed home this morning. And then Clara came for the afternoon and stayed for dinner! My folks will leave in the morning and Rose G will come for a day and Karen will come for a few days. I could not have orchestrated the visitors better myself :). I will be able to get to bed early tonight. Love to all. Paula

Good afternoon,

Good news! Mark's colonoscopy was clear and Dr. Kundu found no active bleeding. The doctors will watch Mark closely and if any more bleeding occurs they will look into the small bowel area. Dr. thinks it might have

**been a blood vessel that bleeds and then stops on its own. We pray Mark's hemoglobin will rise, rise and rise, and his appetite resumes so the healing can resume. KKLL, Paula**

Dearest Paula & Mark:

First of all, thank you Paula for keeping us informed, all of us here in Tehachapi are praying for the both of you as well as the entire family. (I know they are the support staff!) Since Fresno is rather far for me and the clan (that is 6 little boys still at home, we have decided we will wait til you get home to see you!) My family loved the pictures; it makes it nicer for the children to actually see Mark and you in person. Those rosaries get kind of long for kids! Be assured that we will continue to keep you in our thoughts and prayers daily. I pray that Mark continues to get stronger; he is amazing as are you! Love, Denise

Hi Mark and Paula,

I sure enjoyed reading all the guestbook entries from your family! Decided it was time to add a word from Colorado.

We are glad that the Colonoscopy was clear—hope you don't have to do that again for a while. We'll keep our hopes up for the hemoglobin (sp?) levels to rise.

We just had dinner with Scott, Steph, Kenzer, Livi, Cady, Papa Joe, Grammy O (that's me) and Mike. Scott flew in from Oklahoma City and will be here until tomorrow afternoon. Steph brought the kids over and it was such a joy to watch them greet Scott in the front yard. We had a wonderful time—I'm so thankful for the opportunity to be together. Kim, Chuck and Kate arrive later this week. We'll all be thinking of you.

Love, Pat and Joe

We are so happy to hear about Mark's test. Hopefully his appetite is back...Dragon roll, anyone? We just finished cracking up over Amy's journal entry...Your kids are hilarious!

Thanks for the updates. We will keep our thoughts and prayers going...Love, Lisa and James

Okay Paula, I hear you! That's what we'll pray for... Rise, rise, rise! (...frustrating that it's still a big 'unknown' as to where the leak is/was coming from...maybe that's all over now?!) My prayers for that too. Tracy

Hi Mark and Paula,

Happy to see that Mark is all CLEAR or Clean? (haha) What a nightmare to have to go through on top of everything else. Hope that is all of the bleeding he will have to go through... keeping our fingers crossed!! I guess you're being entertained by Claire, so that's helpful!! Hope you all have a great day and Mark is able to eat a little something to keep up his strength. Take care and much love to ya, Tami

happy fathers day mr welsh! i am praying for you all!

pat n

Great News!!!! :)

I am home and thankful to visit with you. I understand that each day things change and will call to see when I can visit again. I understand how hard it is to know your plans each day. LOVE & PRAYERS kkkkkkk be the horse like my smile Nurse Claire B 2nd wife

Well helllllo from the Welsh compound! It is a good thing I type fast as it's all quiet right now. They are all still in bed, asleep! So I can do this in peace...and no, they don't all have bed sores from staying in bed so late...and Grace was including everyone in her late mornings. LOL!

We had a FABULOUS time at the McDonald's house! The Sliders and hotdogs and great salads were a hit! Katie, Mark (my new BFF), Molly for a bit and Pat joined us, along with Auntie Jo :). I have to say my favorite part was a glass of wine... thanks Katie!

GiGi was in her element...she led Mark and Jim around the yard by the fingers at the same time...it was like a newer version of "My Two Dads"...she needed some attention...you know she hardly gets any...please look the other way as I roll my eyes! She sat like an angel on the couch while SD (Surrogate Dad) Mark read to her from a travel magazine...talking to her about San Luis and Morro Bay...SD Jim held her and BBQ'd... she has sucked us all in. LOL!

The new bedding is on and looks great! Grace, Karen and I got the dust ruffle on without too much huffing and puffing...and the boys helped me make it up, with Mitchell arranging those new pillows just so. Then I slept in it...it was HEAVEN! I made sure I slept on both sides to wear it in evenly. LOL!

Yesterday we had a lazy day after church... Grace and I watched "America's Next Top

Model"…there was a marathon. When the boys got home, they watched some and I have to say, watching it with them was entertaining as hell. They had lots of comments about the one judge…Miss J (who is a man of African descent with ponytails). Mitch said they weren't ponytails…they were clumps…and Chandler added they were clumps of junk. LOL!

Then it was time for the boys to say goodnight. Chandler went to hug and kiss his big sister Grace…which she immediately had stinky face, then Mitch jumped in to hug her too…and she yelled out that this was like a horror show. LOL! You have to love family affection…then they began to wrestle all 3 of them on top of the couch…I needed a camera…the boys were trying to be snuggle bunnies with their big sista… and she had that same look on her face as she did at the hotel with one dude…STRANGER DANGER!! It was hilarious!

We loved the visit from Miss Hope…GiGi looked like an ewok in that black sweatshirt that went to the floor, with the hood on and her sunglasses…then Grace tied the sleeves to the back and she looked like she was in a straight jacket. LOL! She is our source of entertainment…no wonder she is exhausted at night! Hell, no wonder we are all exhausted at night! Ha Ha!

I should tell you I have stopped and started this 10 times now as Princess G is up and she is high maintenance…sheesh! Ann will come later and the boys will wash cars for more money…I had told them both earlier last week to save their money big time because I don't have any children and I will need them to take care of me…and they both answered that Grandma will take care of me...Mom about choked on her scotch. LOL!

Oh and driving home from Big Bear, Mitchell informed his Grandpa and myself that he wished he had a tail...one coming right out of his tailbone. I of course, did the honors and asked why he would want that...and he said, laughing "So I can smack people with it" which made us all laugh...then Dad said "Well you won't be smacking too many people because you'll be in the cage with all of the other monkeys". LOL! Now we know where we get some of that quick wit from!!

Okay off to have a great day with your muffins...lots of prayers being said all the time for better days and healing all the way around. We love you and we have you close in spirit always.

Much Love,

Amy, Ann, Grace, Mitch, Chan, GiGi, and Ebony (who put her head up to the living room window and looked in...as if to say "What the hell is going on in there...I don't recognize anyone".

Hi Mark and Paula,

Sorry that you had to spend your Father's day away from the kids. We are still praying that you keep fighting and keep getting better. You'll be home soon I am sure of it. Drank some Red Zinfandel for you both last night...it was good; I will have to bring you a bottle. Keep up the great work, and don't sweat the small stuff... We continue to pray for you all and for your strength to get better every day. Hugs to you and the fam, Jill

Happy Fathers day daddy!!!!!!!!!!!!!!!!!!!!

Yesterday I went with Aunt Karen and Uncle Gordy to 4 corners to drop off Jessica. We went to the McDonalds house to eat dinner. We had mini burgers and hot dogs. GiGi says please now. Today Mitchell and I made some money at the McDonalds house. Bye for now. Chandler Welsh

Happy Father's Day Mark! Hi Paula!

Sorry to hear about the rough adventure and hope the future brings new smooth adventures. I still pray for strength for your next adventures!

Enjoying being with your children all have a great sense of humor, even Genevieve with her new Please and getting right up to my face and batting her eyes with a whisper "please". The boys of course had a wonderful day with the McDonalds thanks Susan, Jim and Sam for sharing your Father's day with them. They truly enjoyed their time off with us girls!

Us girls hung around the house and watched a movie and Miss Hope came and visited. Three of the neighbors stopped by to see how Mark was doing. It was very sweet.

Tomorrow will bring us all new adventures to share with each other!

Hi Claire! Hi Mom and Happy Father's Day dad! Love, Ann

Paula,

I continue to pray for Mark and your family. Thank you for posting the pictures. You have an adorable family. I love having a face to go with my prayers. I hope everyday will bring Mark closer to a complete recovery and going home to those adorable children. I would be afraid to leave them with Amy too long; she may teach them how to sock someone up. LOL! Just kidding, I love her to pieces and can't think of anyone more fun to hang out with. She is the best. Take care and know that your postings are read aloud to my husband, Vernon, every day and if I don't read them to him he keeps asking how is Mark doing? Is he OK today? You would have to know him to know what a great but sappy guy he is. Carmel

Dearest Mark and Paula,

We are so hopeful and prayerful that this medical nightmare with the blood has miraculously righted itself! May this Tuesday be spent restfully and peacefully as healing continues! We love you, Mike and Ruth

P.S. Mike thinks he can speak Japanese now. Okay, and Chamarro (official language of Guam)! I'm sure he will entertain you both this weekend when we come to visit!

Mark and Paula,

What a feeling it must be to read the emails that shout of the power of prayer from the untold prayers being sent heavenward each day! I am so proud of you, Paula, for learning how to post pictures on the web. When Genevieve is in first grade and you are my room parent, you can have the job of posting first grade photos on the web! I loved the pictures of the two of you on the patio. As for the hair coloring, if I ever decide I don't want to keep my gray hair, I will call Mark for an appointment. God bless.

Chris

Hi Paula & Mark—I'm sure you are glad
that yesterday is over—talked to your Mom
in the afternoon so I was glad to hear that the
test was over—hope the blood levels stay good
now. It is so unbelievable that after such a trying day that you would be sitting up & eating
dinner, Mark—like I have said before—you are
such an inspiration!! You are both in our prayers
every day—just wish there was more we could
do. Good luck with the walking, Mark. Take of
yourselves—& know that God loves you. Love &
Hugs to you both—Dorothy & Tom

Hi, Mark and Paula,

I've kept up with what's happening through
everyone else, but now I'm getting together
enough to try this on my own. I want you to
know that I've been saying rosaries and many
prayers for your recovery and for strength during
this time. You are also on my Mom's prayer
chain in Idaho—and they've accomplished many
miracles!

I've seen Genevieve a couple of times with
Ann and gotten that lightening smile from her,
so I can report that she's doing well. You are so
blessed to have such a supportive family. I hope
that you can force yourself not to worry about the
kids because they seem to be doing fine. Please let
the family know that I would be happy to help
watch kids anytime. If they all want to come visit
you together, I could keep the kids with me easily. The boys would have Eric and Sam to play
with since they live nearby. (However, they might
have to do some bargaining to get that little girl
back when they return.)

220

Mark, I hope the latest procedures went okay. Do you feel like two steps forward, one step back? From what the family tells me you're not in horrendous pain, so maybe that's the first miracle. I will continue to keep you in my prayers, as will my whole family. Although that's the best thing we can do for you, I wish there was more I could do. Mary G.

We were out of town yesterday but were able to check the journal (just couldn't post anything or email). I'm glad that there wasn't any big problem found with the colonoscopy...but know that even though that's good news, it's kind of frustrating because it's nice to have a neat explanation for why something happens. My Dad always said that doctors don't always have answers because they are only *practicing* medicine...they haven't gotten it perfected yet! (Did they ever find where the bleeding was from? If so, maybe inject the answer here)

I'm glad to read in other posts that other people besides me (& Leslie, with her future time traveling) have had trouble with the date & time thing! It's always a surprise what time posts on the entry even if it shows the right time when I'm writing it.

The shield of prayers & thoughts from so many people are still covering you. Hang in there & keep on keeping on. May the ups continue higher & higher and the downs become smaller & smaller. Love, Katie N

*Reflection*

*Our friends and family responded like clockwork after I would journal what was going on at the hospital. I still can't believe as I re-read through all the guest book entries, how much I had forgotten about all the people who wrote to me and lifted my spirits.*

*God does heal your pain, emotional and physical, if you let Him.*

*My heart does feel all warm and fuzzy like it did when I read these entries for the first time. I may not remember all the tiny details but I always felt so loved during that time.*

Suffering is the classroom of pure love.
—Carrie Gress, *Nudging Conversions*

# The Calm after the Storm

June 23, 2009

Hello, everyone. Tuesdays are not that bad after all! No surgery today! Mark ate all his meals today like a big boy! I put on my big girl panties and ate lunch all by me self! I had a couple hours between visitors. After lunch, when I went up to Mark's room, a lady named Sue stopped by. She had Lucy, a therapy dog. She asked if Mark likes dogs and of course he said yes and I of course lied and said that I liked dogs too! Lucy is a West Highland white terrier who Sue rescued a few years ago. It was so great to see Mark perk up! Later he did two laps with Ace. We spoke with the doctor and surgery will be Thursday or Friday and not sure if there will be autografting. If the burns are healed enough on the left leg then doctor will autograft. They will definitely debride, excise the burns and re-allograft where they need to. Karen, Rose and Tracy spent the afternoon with me and then we went for beer and pizza at Hero's. My folks made it home safe. TODAY was a good day! KKLL, Paula

**June 24, 2009**

**Good evening all.**

**Wednesday was not a bad day either. Mark has kept up with his eating. Anyone who knows Mark knows he will do what he has to do. I always ask him, Did that taste good? Are you feeling ok? Are you in any pain? The answers are all the same, "Not bad." I want to hurt him but do not worry I won't. Honestly, the prayers keep me calm as a cucumber. He had a dressing change that went well and I believe there are wounds that will be able to be autografted tomorrow. YEAH! He was able to walk 2 laps today and also sit up in a chair and eat his lunch. I do not know when surgery will begin but I will get the word out. Good night to you all. KKLL, Paula**

Way to go Mark! I'm still praying for you. Love to you and your family. Edie

Hi Mark and Paula,

Think of you often throughout the day! I am so glad yesterday was a wonderful adventure! You are still are in our prayers and even little Genevieve lets me hold her hands for prayers every night and do the sign of the cross at dinner. It is one of her many angelic moments!

I will pray for good healing and strength for both you tomorrow during his surgery. Love to you all there Miss you. Love always, Ann and Jerry (Doug)

Hi Paula,

I liked the photos on the website. You looked really cute (Mark looked pretty cute too). I am happy that Father's Day went ok for Mark. I was worried about his spirits. It is good to hear that Mark's eating was better and that he got to make a trip out to your patio. I think about you and Mark throughout every day. Love, Elaine

Dear Mark and Paula,

I've been catching up with the journal. I know how you feel when you say you "feel so loved". It's a great feeling to have so many people praying for you and expressing all their love. Mark I'm glad that you are holding up so well {most of the time}. Stay strong. You look great in the pictures. Paula your journal is great, so informative. My love and prayers are with you both. Lorraine

Paula & Mark,

I'm glad to hear nothing serious came out of the bleeding. Just a big scare. But you my friend put it so well when you said "nothing scares me anymore" Sooo true.

I am getting a kick out of Amy's daily logs. I see a lot of the same humor you have…Your family is doing such a good job of keeping life normal as possible. And some good has come out of that. They might not have gotten to spend this much time all at once with your kids. Mark keep up the good work and keep eating. KKLL. Leslie

Mark & Paula,

Glad to hear yesterday was a great day. We continue to keep you and all the family in our prayers. Be assured that God is with you and the whole family every day. I know how touch and go it can be, it seems that Mark is really making a lot of progress. Mark you are a Hero!! Our children love the updates as does our friends and family. Our rosaries will continue to include both of you, the staff at the Burn Center, & your entire family, I always say, the Blessed Mother will look after all of us especially in our time of need! Stay strong. Lots of Hug-A-Bugs to Both of You! Denise

Good morning to you both!

Just checkin' on you, Mark and it sounds like you're doing good and moving right along. We are grateful to you Paula for doing a great job on keeping all of us up to date… All the guys on the department always ask about you and how your doing. Monty (O.C.F.D.)

Dear Mark and Paula,

Mark, I loved reading about your visit with the little white Westie dog and hope it did cheer you up. Paula, how can you not like those little critters? If Lucy returns for another visit, just fake it again for Mark's sake!

We have three little white dogs—only planned for two, but we inherited another from a daughter. I am thankful they are with us though because their antics are good for Bill as he recovers from his heart attack and open-heart surgery (6 bypasses!!!). It is literally a 3-dog circus around here! You should see me when I take them for their walks—people do think I'm crazy!

Our youngest daughter was married last Sat., and for the past few weeks, I have been sewing table runners for the reception tables. Making fourteen of these, at ten feet long each, gave me a wonderful opportunity for prayer for Mark as I sat and ran them under the sewing machine. The table runners actually became prayer cloths. I know you have so many others praying for both of you, but I believe each prayer is heard and is counted.

Take care of yourself, too, Paula. Get as much rest as you can to stay strong for Mark.

Marcia

Wow how wonderful it is to hear no surgery yesterday…does that mean that they will be getting fewer now that he is healing well?

Mark you look great and I bet it was a wonderful feeling to get outside for you!! Paula you look awesome too like always!

Great news and great updates, keep them coming! from working at the fire dept all those years I thought I knew so much more than I do about burn victims. Boy was that a wrong assumption. We are learning right along with you and if there is anything that you need to help you heal faster, please don't hesitate to call on us!!

You are all so brave and strong, and I pray every day that God shows you more strength and healing in your recovery! God bless you all, Hugs and Smooches, adopto sissy, Jill

Mark and Paula,

I am very grateful that you both had such a good day yesterday. I pray that you are blessed with many more. Sheri

Good morning! God is good! Isn't He:) You all are doing so amazing, I get goosebumps reading the updates! When I give my husband (Brian, Sharon & Tom H's son) updates, he shakes his head and just says, "And explain to me how people do not believe in God." Miracles happen. This is one! Keep up the great work! Toby

*Reflection*

*Mark had weathered a storm over the past weekend. Two good days in a row were exactly what we needed. God was starting to shine a beacon of hope. We felt the fog lifting and the sun was peeking through the clouds.*

# Learning to Trust

**June 25, 2009**

Good afternoon! Mark went to surgery around 1:30 p.m.. I have no idea how long it will take, but it will be at least 4 hrs. On another note, this morning Ace brought in a Physical Therapist in training to see Mark. Rueben was his name and he graduated from Burroughs in 1997! (He remembered you, Erin.) It was so nice to chat about our town. He is about 6–8 inches taller than Mark and Ace is 6–8 inches shorter, so it amused me watching Mark take his 5 Laps this morning with these guys on either side of him. Mark is able to do this now with NO help. He also can get from a laying position out of his bed and then stand up by himself. I will let you all know when Mark is out of surgery. KKLL, Paula

Dr. Dominic just called and Mark is in recovery. The 5 hour surgery went well. Doctors were able to autograft both legs so left leg is almost completely done and right leg is 3/4 of the way done. Knees and upper thighs are looking so good the doctors only re-allografted and think they may heal on their own. I know God knows what he is doing with this timeline. Love to all. Paula

Hi Paula...glad to hear that there was good news after the surgery today! I hope & pray that the next few days will be good as well. Love, Katie H

Hi Paula, :) Great news. Shout out to all my BFFS! David W.

Thanks for the Day today, Paula (& Karen)! I think you both helped me more than I helped you, though...I'm so happy Mark's surgery went well & I will pray that tomorrow is another good day. ☺.(Sorry, I just couldn't resist doing that!!!) Tracy

Dear Storybook writer. Great to hear Mark is getting to eat Sounds like prayers are being answered. Keep smiling and taking notes. <u>YOU GO MARK.</u> Love and kisses and kkkkkkk and sorry for horsing around. Claire B.

Good Morning to you both!! Glad to hear that Mark is doing well & extra prayers for him during the surgery today—it is good that he feels like eating again—& that he is able to do so much walking—way to go Mark!!! Good luck today—will be waiting for the update—Love & lots & lots of prayers, Dorothy & Tom. Take care of yourself, too, Paula.

Mark and Paula,
It is so great to hear that you are both doing so well. We are trying to hold it together here at work but without Mark, it is tough. Pretty big shoes to fill if you know what I'm saying. You guys take care and hurry home. David L.

Paula,

I will keep you and Mark in my prayers today. I am glad for the both of you that he has healed enough this week to have some autografting. That's great! Sheri

### June 26, 2009

Good evening. The day after surgery went very well! Mark ate all his meals today! The team of doctors okayed Mark to walk this afternoon too. Ace MADE me learn how to wrap Mark's legs. It was not easy. I may have had a fit and STEPPED in it! (That's an expression). Mark was able to get out of bed again with little help and did three laps. He sat in a chair for 1/2 hour when he was done with his laps and shaved himself. They have disposable clippers so I cleaned Mark up REAL NICE! Also, Karen burnt her leg on a clothes iron yesterday, it is .01 degree but Ace talked to Karen for 5 minutes about caring for it, now she thinks he is her PT, also. An occupational therapist came in and talked to him about what it will be like when he goes home. That sure boosted Mark's spirits! There is a light at the end of the tunnel!

Karen and I attract weirdoes around these hospital grounds, so there is never a dull moment. I know what you are all thinking, but we really do try to mind our own business. Donna arrives soon for a slumber party, YIPPEE! Thanks Margaret and Bernice Denice for the Snickerdoodles! All the nurses wanted them! KKLL, Paula

Hello Paula and Mark

Mark you are one tough guy and making great progress. (Probably have to so that Paula quells her desire to shave you, do your hair and lord knows what else.)

Paula, I miss you at choir—no one singing in my right ear. Nancy is back so I have someone to keep me on key. It is not as much fun without you there. Going to bed it is late and tomorrow is supposed to be a real sizzler here. Better rest up so I can get some dedicated pool time. Love you both. Margie and Walt

P.S. Amy is still my favorite blogger—go girl!

Hello Paula and Mark,

It is so good to hear that yesterday's surgery was successful. What a grand adventure. All of the prayers and extra good thoughts are awesome.

Enjoying the kids in the evenings. Genevieve is eating like a big girl with a spoon and manages to get most of it in her mouth. Mitchell was so proud that he had changed most of Genevieve's diapers yesterday, even the very smelly ones! He asked about the A & D ointment and I replied well is she red? He said Red where? and Chandler yelled from the kitchen on her booty! Mitchell gave me a look that was beyond his comfort level so I helped him out. He was very proud of taking care of his little sister as I was him for his help!

Mom is convinced I am slipping Genevieve something when I put her to bed, because she is sleeping till 9 a.m.! I just give her extra lovin!

Tomorrow I will be traveling to South Dakota to meet up with Doug. He assures me I will have cell coverage to check the site for the updates. I am looking forward to the trip but sure will miss my evenings with the children, Grandpa and Grandma and Amy.

I will still think of you both often and pray for continued strength and terrific adventures!

Love you both. Miss you. Ann and Jerry (Doug)

Hey Paula and Mark,

We are glad to keep hearing of all the improvements and milestones Mark is making. You both have been working so hard towards recovery and its working!!! We will keep the prayers going as usual. We are thinking of you and all your family continually.

Yesterday Alex and I had lunch at John's Pizza with Mitch and Chandler, and then they came over to the house for swimming and video games. Chandler was the jackpot ticket winner for the day but the prizes are less than stellar now. They both opted for whoopi cushions so to all the others at the Welsh compound we say "beware the whoopi cushion!!!" It was nice and hot for swimming @ 107 degrees so it looks like our mild June is over. Baby G was adorable as ever and Grace was working hard to download the music for Dad's new iPod. You can be proud of your kids and the grown-ups caring for them, they're all amazing! We had a good afternoon and we look forward to another visit soon.

Oh I also had lunch the other day with my visiting sister-in-law Dana and she invited none other than her good friend Hope "the Dragonroll lady". We had a nice time catching up and she talked a lot about her visit with you last week. Just goes to show it's a small world after all!!

Special prayers go out for a safe journey for Miss Donna who is traveling today for a visit. God bless you and keep you all. Love, Coleen

P.S. Loved the picture update, nice to see some smiles on your faces. Mark looks great!! Paula your hair looks smokin' hot!! When you get a chance, more, more, more pics! Love Coleen

Hello Mark and Paula from the Welsh Compound!! It has been a few days since I have had a chance to update you on the comings and goings of all of us!

I have some peaceful moments right now. Chandler is with Miss Jenny and Brendon on a road trip, Mitch is in his room on the computer, Grace is at Volleyball, GiGi and Grandpa are taking a nap and Mom is at the store :)

I have been waking up in the middle of the night wondering where the hell I am...I think it's the back and forth between two houses...I find myself listening for GiGi when I am at Ann's house...Coo Coo I tell you. LOL!

Despite the heat, we still have been able to go outside at night in your front yard with the Queen. She is still Nancy the Nosy Neighbor... any kind of action going on down the street and she sits right at the edge of the sidewalk, crouches down and checks it out. She comes back and tells us everything...in her own language of course... Oh, if someone could just interpret what she says...I am sure we would get the secret squirrel scoop. There is a lot of facial expression and eye fluttering when she tells it…it's hilarious.

Now, I have to tell you, that all of us in lawn chairs on the front lawn is rather trailer trash like…the only thing that keeps us one step above that is we actually drink wine out of wine glasses and not paper cups or straight out of the bottle. LOL!

Grace will go over to Katy's house tonight for some chick time. I would love to be a fly on the wall there. LOL! She and I have been chick flicking it up at night after all the peeps are in their beds. Last night was *Sweet Home Alabama*…a definite good one. She is getting better about her hugs. I actually got a one arm around me hug. Now granted the other arm was a dead arm, but she is getting better and Ann and congratulated her on the improvement :) Ha Ha!

Mitch and Chandler went to the N's the other day. They swam and then went "air-softing"(?) and Mitch spent the night as well…I believe a good time was had by all. I mean, how could it not be a good night at my BFF's crib?? LOL!

Chandler also served at a funeral this week…and all of the people there who knew you and Mark…were so impressed with that :) Saw Nancy R out front as I picked him up, so I had to jump out of the car and give her a hug! She sends her love up to you both and says she prays for you all day long :)

We are so grateful for everyone's help for us here…dinners from Michelle D, Susan, a fabulous afternoon with Colleen, and Chris S. is headed over here Monday…wahoooo! Sometimes by 5 pm we don't know what the hell to do…so this has made it easy for us...thank you, thank you, thank you!

We pray every night at your dinner table, including GiGi for both of you and all of the travellers and helpers. We all get encouraged by the little bits of good news we read...and they loved talking to their dad these past couple of days...smiles all the way around!

Much Love and Prayers Always,

Dad, Mom, Amy, Ann, Grace, Mitch, Chan, GiGi and Ebony (who is so happy that she has a poop-free environment thanks to her big sister Grace LOL)

P.S. GiGi doesn't like anything on her fingers these day...so if there happens to be a crumb of toast or a bit of turkey or a piece of lint...she squawks and holds her hand out to be wiped...she is getting to be more and more high maintenance every day...

Hey Dad

I went over Aunt Ruth's today and Earned 20$ so i have about 300$. Then she gave me and Naval weapon's book witch is cool.

So i heard you only have a little bit more for surgery then you come home. Love Yah

Love, Mitchell


Wonderful news! We continue to keep you all in our prayers. Mark, continue the amazing recovery! I love reading about what the Welsh children are up to! We miss them all! Love, Emily


Hi Mark & Paula—what Great news—I was so happy that the surgery went so well—Mark you are doing so well—5 laps—wow!!! We

are so proud of you—keep up the good work—
God is answering all our prayers. Today is our
anniversary so the good news makes it extra special—know that we are praying every day for
you—take care & God Bless—Love & Hugs,
Dorothy & Tom

Paula and Mark,

Awesome news. I am so happy for you and
Mark about the news from surgery of his recovery.
I hope the good news just keeps flowing. You both
have worked so hard and have been so faithful. I
admire and love you both. I'll keep praying. Sheri

Hey Mark and Paula,

Glad to hear things are going well. We will
try to make it up next week and see you both.
Give your kids our best and God bless you all.
Kirk and Alan

*Reflection*

*Another surgery day and I can tell my spirits
are much better than the first one. I had begun to let
go and let God. I had no control over Mark's healing
schedule and was resisting that in the very early days
of his arrival at the hospital. God does only give you
what you can handle, but it took a bit of time for
me to adjust to the load.*

*The days are long at a hospital and you have
a lot of idle time. Mark had so many medical issues
for God to fix and I guess I wanted Him to be more
efficient. I have learned trusting God is most difficult when someone you love is suffering.*

# More Encouragement

June 27, 2009

When Donna and I walked in this morning, Mark was already in his chair and waiting for his breakfast. He is waking up so much more energized. He took 2 laps after breakfast, too. He is awake for most of the day now and the nurses are looking into not bothering him after 10 p.m. until 6 a.m., they have to get that approved by the doctors. Tracy came and hung out with Karen and me in my office; we may have laughed a bit about what is going on in the news. We like to gurgle (google for the lay person) things and pass the time. Tracy and I then went up for a visit with Mark. I just know he is starting to like chit chat! Mark got out of bed and sat in his chair for dinner, too. Tomorrow 3 of our 4 children will come for a visit, a belated Father's Day. We hope to eat lunch together out on the patio. God Bless you all! It has been 4 weeks today and all the support keeps coming. Angels are among us! KKLL, Paula

P.S. Genevieve will stay back with family. Mark and I feel it would be too upsetting to her to peel her away from her dad. We will see her when we get home and we do not have to

**be separated again. Please pray our homecoming is SOON!**

Mark and Paula,

We just made it home from Montana. It was awesome! I have been getting updates but we have not had internet. Uncle Mark, I'm so glad you are getting such great care there. Rueben is awesome. I love the Wooley family! Hope you are having a great day and continue to have a good appetite. Love you and miss you. Erin

Hi Mark and Paula—

Well—this Saturday daylights is going a lot better than my last Sat daylights (knock on wood—that would be my head). And I'm sure it's much, much better for both of you too! Just wanted to say hi—we miss you around here. You two keep taking care of each other—Mike

Go, Team Welsh!! Sounds as tho' yesterday was a great day. You all keep up the progress and we'll keep up the prayers. Mary G.

Just a quick note from the Taylor compound…Ann is out running errands for last minute things before I take her to the airport :) I have to say, I am not at ALL surprised about the weirdo thing…well for you anyways…but I am surprised Karen has attracted that…she usually has a "weirdo" radar and heads south at the speed of light if someone might be approaching her…I think I know where Grace gets the Stranger Danger approach from. LOL!

This will make you laugh…Grace called from Katy's last night and Ann answered the phone…Grace said "Hi Grandma…" LOL! I LOVED that!!!! HAHAHAHAH! I hate when I sound like Grandma HAHAHAH!

Your neighbor Ken came over last night to get an update on you two! He sat out front with Dad for awhile and they talked about mutual people they knew on the base…I think Dad was ready for some dude talk…too many chicks in the house :) Miss and Love you both! Amy

P.S. Hope Don-nah made it there safe and sound!

Hi Paula,

It's so exciting to read about Mark's amazing progress! Thanks for all of the updates. We continue to keep all of you in our daily prayers. I had a friend who attracted weirdos just like you, and so we dubbed her the "weirdo magnet." Sounds like that's a suitable name for you too! You probably attract the weirdos because you have that nice Ridgecrest hometown attitude about you! That's not a bad thing, and I bet you probably make someone's day when you meet them. I think you're amazing in that you have kept your sense of humor through this whole thing. By the way, it's HOT here…we're starting to see (feel) a true Ridgecrest summer. Stay cool and stay strong! XOXO—Gina

*Reflection*
*You will be happy to know four years later, I still attract weirdos. I can sense by my journaling I was able to see the light. Mark was improving daily; we would eventually be heading home.*

*We couldn't help but notice that the young 18-year old, two rooms down would be there six*

*more months and he had already been there for four months. He had been badly burned in a car wreck; his 2 friends did not survive. He was lucky to be alive but his arm and leg had been amputated and his head suffered 3rd degree burns. Mark was going home soon and would be making a full recovery.*

If you don't have faith, you don't live it
If you don't pray, your efforts will fall short
Joy is the fruit of appreciation.

—Anonymous

# Recovery Continues

June 28, 2009

Dear All,

This morning I helped Mark get all spiffed up for our kiddos. He shaved himself again. He's getting really good at it because his hands are getting less shaky as the days go by.

The gang arrived around noon—Susan, Gordy, Grace, Mitchell, and Chandler. We brought Mark to the patio and enjoyed a nice lunch. The kiddos were able to visit with their dad individually. Mark was alert and full of conversation, so different from the first time the children saw him. They noticed a huge improvement too. Mark could only handle a couple hours away from his bed, so by 2 p.m., we needed to take him back to bed for a nap. Grace, Mitch, and Chandler then went on a venture to the TNT fireworks warehouse with Tracy and son, Jared, (Tracy's husband, Louis, works for them). They were given a tour, which the boys loved. They also met Tracy's daughter, Audra, who was helping at the warehouse. They came back with some fun goodies! They even took a TNT hat up to their dad. What a great Sunday! Gordy and Karen headed back

**home with kiddos and Susan will stay for a couple days. KKLL, Paula**
**P.S. There are some new pictures!**

Mark & Paula,

Love the new pictures. Looks like it was a great visit with the kiddos. We are still in Washington enjoying our visit with the grand-kids here. Keep up the great progress Mark. We so love reading Paula's journals so we can keep track of the progress.

Love to you both. Linda & Hank

Love the pictures!! Mark, you are looking great! Praise, Honor, and Glory to God for his wonderful hands that are healing our Mark! Miss you guys and love you! Thoughts and prayers are still coming your way daily! Justin & LaRay

Hey guys! Still here and thinking and praying for Mark daily. Really appreciate the updates. With all of the feedback from friends in

Ridgecrest, it makes me realize how special a place it really is. We do miss it there. Why does it take being separated from a part of your life to make you realize how good you had things? Anyway, Mark, we are confident that you will continue to excel in your healing as it seems you do in most things in your life, especially with your beautiful family. God Bless. Pete and Loren and the boys

Dear Mark & Paula,

You two are real Heroes to Jon & I. soooo impressed with your strength, your love and your Faith. Mark, the hills you have climbed are unbeliveable!!! So glad to hear the talk of GOING HOME, remarkable!!

Paula, my eyes are full of tears. I didn' have to go to ARGENTINA!!!!!, about all the strength you have shown. It was hard, lots of tears in reading the journal. Now that the news is soooo good I thought I would read some of the emails from your friends and family. Big tears again, I don't cry easy!!! I know all this LOVE & PRAYERS Caused this huge MIRACLE. OUR PRAYERS are with all of you every day. Jon & Joann Grandpa & Grandma "L"

Hey ya'll,

Glad to hear Mark is doing better. He's a brave soul. I pray that you will all be together in your own home very soon. Mark came out to visit for 9 days. We took a 5 day fishing trip down to a place called Grand Isle. We had a great time but oh my gosh was it hot! Good thing I had plenty of icy cold beverages! Take care and God Bless you all. Love, Malana

244

Happy Sunday—Hope your kids are there with you today—thanks for the latest updates—you are both amazing as I have said before—yesterday at Mass the priest said have faith & you will be healed—I was thinking & praying for you & it sure is true—God is good!!! It will be awhile before I can send a note again as we leave tomorrow morning for Maui—will check in with Lisa & of course your Mom to see how things are going—You could be home or close to it before we get back—Yay!!!!Know that you will be in our thoughts & prayers every day—Keep up the good work, Mark—you are doing GREAT!! Take good care of yourselves—Lots of love & hugs—Dorothy & Tom

Uncle Mark and Aunt Paula,

I'm sure you are enjoying the kids being there today. I can't imagine how hard it is for the both of you to be away. You are in my thoughts and prayers. Love you both very much. Hope you all have a wonderful day. Lots of love from Kansas. Can I just say hot and humid:) Ughh I would take the dry heat any day. Much love, Erin

Good Morning

Well, it sounds like it should be a great day today. Rachel and I were going to take Grace out for lunch yesterday but I didn't want to snag her from all the fun she was having at Hope's. Hopefully one day this week.

Alan and Todd went fishing for the night and I had 2 extras boys over to hang with Dylan. How did that happen!!!! I was looking for a quiet evening after cleaning for a large part of my day. I thought of you when Rachel and I slipped out to Miso's for dinner though…I think of you and Mark all the time and pray for a release date very soon.

I'll call about coming up after I figure Alan's travel plans this week. Love, Leslie

Good Sunday morning to the Welsh Wonders.

May your visit as family be filled with good stories and lots of laughs.

I thank you for giving me time to visit Mark during his appreciation month(year). Enjoyed Mark's spunk(still is no match for Paula's), Karen was as lovely as ever and meeting beautiful Tracy was great. Paula your love and devotion for your husband is inspiring. May your homecoming be soon and a smooth transition. Lots of love and cheers. Rose

Hi, Mark and Paula—

I thought I'd share info on Kristin T's wedding yesterday. You were certainly on everyone's mind. I'm sure you would have been dancing 'til the end with the rest of us. It was such a nice service at the place on base. The tables were all set up and you came in and sat at the tables. Kristin and Chris stood on a stage for the vows. The preacher did a very nice job…it turns out that Jim works with him. After the ceremony the wedding party went out to the golf course to take pictures and everyone else visited, had snacks and could get drinks. When the wedding party came back, we had a very nice dinner. After and during dinner people mingled until the dancing started. (Of course there was the normal cutting of the cake and toasting. Ashley and Jacob really gave the best toasts I've ever heard.)

The setting was very conducive to visiting with people and the atmosphere was relaxed and comfortable. As a wedding planner you would have appreciated it, I think. Jim and I, usually party poopers actually outlasted a few of the more hardy types. To me it goes to show that you can have a very nice wedding without agonizing over it for a year and a half.

We're glad to hear that you might be coming home soon. Many of us were thinking of you—especially during the exchange of vows. You are living out the commitment that these words ask of a husband and wife—caring and loving each other for better, for worse, in sickness and in health. You're a great example of what marriage is supposed to be. Take care, Mary L.

Paula and Mark, we were sorry the visit didn't work out last week, but from the sound of it we may be able to visit with you at home before long. So many positive steps right now. We know you'll enjoy this special day with your wonderful family. We're off to church right now…there's much to be thankful for!!! Sally and Gary

Paula and Mark,

We are all excited about Mark's progress including Jessica. She likes to keep up with the news too. We will pray for a quick homecoming and we hope your family visit today is a special one today. Sheri

Paula & Mark:

Sounds as if Mark is really making progress. I can only imagine the sister's running free around the hospital grounds!! Enjoy the family visit today with the children, lunch outside sounds great. We have the whole Avalos Clan praying for your family and the recovery (That is a small crowd!!!) Like you said, God continues to watch over you. He is an awesome God!! Stay strong. Love, Denise (A.K.A. Amiga's Buddy)

Mark & Paula—The pictures are all inspiring—you both are inspiring. I wish I could write screen plays because you, your family, your friends and your story could be one of those stories that would play out as a heart grabbing inspirational wonder. Keep moving forward and wishing for a speedy return home for both of you!! Diana

*Reflection*
*What a difference a week can make. Mark's recovery was just what we were focused on. His wounds were healing on their own and some would not need skin grafts.*

Praise is the language of Heaven.
—*The Shack*

# The Strength and Courage to Fight

June 29, 2009

Good evening. Mark had another great day! Dr. Dominic spoke with us first thing this morning and said that Mark is doing great and there will probably be a little bit more autografting (skin grafting) but certain areas were healing on their own with the allograft. Only time will tell when Mark will be able to come home. No one gives us any dates. It is impossible to know right now. Sandy was his nurse today. LOVE HER! She unhooked Mark from everything. Feeding tube has been out for a day and they are not going to put it back in except maybe for surgery days. Mark's neighbor has been entertaining, likes to shout things! I will tell you all in person, it will be funnier if I act it out! She is not playing with a full deck! Funny you mentioned the screen play, Diana. My friends and family have been joking that this could be a Lifetime movie, just needs to get a little bit smuttier. I would like Matthew McConaughey to play Mark and after many hours of thinking of who could play my part, I came up with MYSELF, DUH! So everybody start thinking about who you

**would like to play your part. Back to Mark now, his dressing change went well and his back may not need skin grafting after all but, ankles will need skingrafting. No surgery date yet! Susan, Mark and I had a nice conversation with Mark's night nurse, Mike. He just wanted to tell us how amazing Mark is. He is not the typical 73% burn patient. He is doing so well and will go home sooner than most! I know everyone feels the same as I do, he has amazing strength and courage to fight each day! Love you all. Paula**

Mark and Paula,

What a great way to start my day...your Father's Day photo on this web site!!! Yes, I cried. By reading other emails, I'm not the only one with a few tears. I had a nice visit with your family, Paula, tonight. Mitchell was working hard at a very impressive jigsaw puzzle...a million pieces at least! Your dad and Chandler were offering some assistance too, as needed. Chandler was also a big help to me when I arrived. It is always fun to visit with your parents and with Amy. I did not see Grace, but she looked beautiful at Mass on Saturday and in your web photo. With such a great family, you can't help but move forward each day with hope, a smile and that great faith all of you have AND give to others. Thank you for all you do through this web site. It has become a ministry to others. God bless. Chris

Good Morning Mark and Paula,

Just a quick note from Rapid City, South Dakota. I am glad you had a great visit with the kids. I miss them all and it has only been a couple of days. The pictures are AWESOME. Enjoyed them! Our thoughts and prayers are with you-all. Off to some more caves and the Badlands!

Have a good visit with Susan. Sending hugs to you both and Mark.

Love always, Ann and Jerry (Doug)

Great Pictures. Who has the dark hair? (GRACE) Happy for you both. Keep up the hard work. I will be thinking of you double time for the next couple of days as I travel to Washington. YOU GO MARK. LOVE CLAIRE & John and Veroinca, Serena and 9 years today John and Steven wow time flies.

Paula and Mark

Just got home from vacation with my family. They all send their prayers. Love the pictures of the family. Mark looks amazing and you Paula look lovely!!!! So glad to read Mark is improving a little each day. What a blessing!!! Lots of love to you all and continued angels all around you all. Go Lourdes water. Katie H

**June 30, 2009**

**Hello. Mark sat in a chair and ate breakfast this morning! This is so great. He started out the day with energy. Next, Ace had him up walking a couple laps plus doing some balancing activities. He was walking frontwards and backwards in a straight line and doing really well. He was also lifting his knees up high and balancing. Ace was impressed! Then the occupational therapist, Nicola, came in to see what Mark is able to do and also still needs to learn. They are called Activities of Daily Living! She**

**is going to push Mark to the limits so he can skip rehab and come straight HOME! Mark had lunch outside with Susan and me. Mark can do this as often as he would like. Cindi, my sis-in-law and niece Andrea arrived around 2 p.m. and Susan headed home! They saw Mark for the first time and were impressed! Also, thanks Mary for the cookies! KKLL, Paula**

**P.S. Do not worry about the time warps, it gives the website character! I love it! Paula**

Hola mi amigos Welsh, All I want to say is I want Julia Roberts to be me and George Straight to be mi esposo,(Spanish word of the day Guapo...Handsome) That is George Straight middle name. And to Mr. Mark you are the man. Keep up the good work. And message to Paula Smutty is my middle name. Sara

Hi Mark and Paula!
Thinking about you today and always! Glad to hear Mark is doing so well. Just got back from Colorado to see Colby. Look forward to another lunch so we can de-brief again, my mother was there! ha ha ha!!!!! Take care of yourselves! Love Ya, Selisia & Family

Mark & Paula:
Okay, I think you for sure have the right idea on the Lifetime movie, Mark is amazing!! Of course Paula, you may not be allowed to play yourself as you have already proven to attract the paparazzi! Our family is so happy on the progress, it sounds as if everything is really moving along! Oh, I just have to add the local priest used to come over and ask to just come in the house to

have a seat in any little corner. We would try and visit, he would insist on just sitting and watching our reality show as life unfolded in our house. I must send him to yours soon, as life with the Welsh Family seems to be anything but boring. Stay strong and we are keeping the prayers coming!! Love You, Denise

Hi Paula, I spent time with Mike & Ruth watching basketball at UC Irvine. I am thrilled to hear that Mark is on a upswing and that he is recovering so well. I am so proud of your whole family. I like the screen play idea. I am sure you can smutty it up a bit. You haven't flashed any doctors yet? This adversity has sure proven how strong your faith and love is. God Bless you all. Love, Elaine

Mornin' to ya, Mark and Paula

Just doin' the daily check on Mark so I can report back to the guys at the Fire house. Sounds like you are doing great and you guys might be home sooner than expected. That's great news and as for the life time movie. I'm not sure about Matthew McConaughey, great actor but I don't know if he could pull off playing "The mighty Mark Welsh" but I do believe Larry the cable guy could…GET-R-DONE!!!!!!! Now that's funny right thar, I don't care who you are…;-)…I'd watch it. Monty (O.C.F.D.)

Wow you guys are amazing!!

Hi Mark Hi Paula,

You crack me up with your movie… HUM…I could totally get into this too…

I think Sandra Bullock should play Amy… or…

Anyways, glad things are going so well and that there will be less and less grafting going on. Continuing to pray for all of you and for strength to get through all of this. Mark you have a huge heart and the will to fight, and that is good. The burn center just opened in Bakersfield a few weeks ago, so maybe when you are an outpatient, you will not have to travel all the way to Fresno.

Not sure if you have to stay in one place after being seen there or not, but it is worth checking into for sure.

Keep up the great work and the posts, Paula. You are totally awesome for keeping us all informed about what is going on and this website is the best thing ever.

Gotta go to work now, but just wanted to say 'Hi' and that we all Love you in T Town!!... Hang in there! Jill

Keeping you all in my thoughts and prayers. I continue to be so encouraged by your story and will be so jealous when you act with Matthew... he's my honey...well, when he showers.

I am very proud of Mark, his progress, and his wife...yes, that's you lil missy! You are amazing!!! BIG HUGS!!! Love, Sandy L.

Paula and Mark,

I just love to read about the great news you and Mark are receiving. That's great about the feeding tube. Another milestone achieved—thank you, God. I also think that the Lifetime movie is a great idea. Somebody from the Welsh family needs to do something exciting or all of our tombstones might read—"Nice people, but lead really boring lives." Just kidding. The truth is that my brother has always been incredibly strong, especially physically. It is a gift. He was amazing to watch growing up, but this blows the top off the house. I also think that you, Paula, are pretty strong, too. I know that my faith has been incredibly strengthened watching and reading about your story. God Bless, Sheri

*Reflection*

*Mark had been getting stronger and stronger by the day. He was so courageous and had a fighting spirit. There is an Irish proverb that describes Mark the best: Courage does not always roar, sometimes it is the quiet voice at the end of the day saying "I will try again."*

*Little did I know we were right around the corner from leaving the hospital. 10 days to be exact.*

*I remember those last days when Mark's physical therapy was going so well, he would be able to skip rehab and go straight home from the hospital, another miracle.*

*Talking about the Lifetime movie and getting the staff and all my peeps across the globe involved really helped pass the time. There still is no Lifetime movie in the works, but never say never. The nurses would stick their heads in and tell us what actor/ actress they would like to play them. It was a fun time, in a weird way.*

The greatest things you can share with others is a sense of your own peace and healthy perspective, but you can't share what you don't have.
—Robert J. Wicks, *Streams of Contentment*

# Bravery and Stamina

July 1, 2009

When we arrived this morning the nurses were just getting ready for Mark's dressing change. My sis-in-law was allowed in the room because she is a nurse and Mark was OK with it too. She was able to see the burn areas that had healed miraculously and the burns that still need miracles. She said that Mark is so brave and unbelievably courageous while he endures those painful dressing changes. I think Cindi was also pretty brave to watch because I cannot do it yet. Karen arrived around 1 p.m. and Cindi and Andrea left at 2 p.m.. When Karen and I went up to his room around 2:30 p.m. he was walking pretty quickly with a PT assistant. She told Mark he was walking better than her. He never ceases to amaze me! So many times after bandage changes he is down for the rest of the day, but he was not today. He sat in a chair for a while too. He will rest up tonight for surgery tomorrow. The nurses have not been bothering him for the last three nights and he is sleeping uninterrupted which also helps heal him. I will post the surgery time as soon as I know. KKLL, Paula

Hi Mark and Paula,

I'm sorry I haven't checked in sooner but I have been thinking about you two and and praying for Mark's recovery. It sounds like you're doing great and will hopefully be home soon. I wish I had something exciting to share regarding work but it's been business as usual. You take care of yourself and know that we are all praying for you. Sincerely, Sandy S.

Paula, let Mark know that everyone up here in the I&E shop are pulling for him. You have great strength, I feel like I know you although we have never met. We do have mutual friends that I never knew about. Since you are people of faith I give you this passage: Romans 5:3–5 **3** *Not only so, but we[c] also glory in our sufferings, because we know that suffering produces perseverance; 4 perseverance, character; and character, hope. 5 And hope does not put us to shame, because God's love has been poured out into our hearts through the Holy Spirit, who has been given to us.* This is a very personally uplifting passage to me. It is good to hear about Mark's constant improvements. I've only been @ Coso for a little over a year but, Mark is definitely a man with moral apptitude, and his presence is missed up on the "Hill". We will continue to pray for his continued success in his recovery, and for your continued strength. Will

Hi Paula and Mark,

Well, if I read things right...plus a little "between the lines", looks like Mark is moon walking! You knew someone had to start that up again!!! Might as well be mighty Mark:). We went to Miso's last night in your honor, Mark. I know they miss you two, also. Sure am liking all the possibilities on the movie. Leave it to all your crazy friends to think of all the possibilities! Sending well wishes, hugs and smiles. Russ, Hope and Katy

So glad to see that Mark is getting so much attention from Ace & the new occupational therapist too! Seems like you're really picking up speed, on this recovery road. Nice that you have some fresh faces visiting, Paula! Continued prayers from our family to yours!

Tracy

Hey Mark n Paula,

We knew Mark would get ahead of schedule and be doing well. You're talking about a Lifetime movie? I think this can make it to the big screen, with an-all-star cast and director. The Rock could play Mark and I don't doubt your acting abilities but maybe they could get Charleze Theron or Ashley Judd to play you (they might be willing to show some skin to get that 'smuttier" stuff in there that you mentioned), and maybe get Ron Howard to direct. You should be the one to write the screenplay and be the Excecutive Producer. That way you can control what is being said and control the money. Anyway, everyone here is praying for you and for Mark's speedy recovery.

See you soon. Kirk and Alan and the rest of the bunch on C crew

July 2, 2009

Good Morning. Mark was the first patient of the day and went to surgery at 8:30! I will let you all know when he is out. Thanks for all the prayers. They are working! Love, Paula

Good News! Mark is out of surgery. Doctor was able to autograft (skin-graft) Mark's ankles, hips and re-allograft other burn areas. On Monday, when they do his dressing change, they will see how everything is healing and if skin grafts took! Also, Mark did not need a blood transfusion. God is Good. Also, Mark was not shivering as much as he has on past surgery days. I will write more later. Judie, Katie, Mike and Ruth arrived safely. KKLL, Paula

Good Evening! Mark's recovery went well today! He slept for a while but then woke up late in the afternoon and was able to visit with all his visitors. Ace stopped by and told me that Mark walked to surgery today! What a determined patient. I am so proud of him! He was able to eat his dinner, too. Susie and Vic showed this evening with cupcakes. I took them up to the nurses and Mark and they scarfed them up. Ruth and Mike left this evening and us girls are having a slumber party again, we will try to keep it down for the neighbors! God Bless You All! KKLL, Paula

Paula and Mark,

Glad to hear that the surgery went so well and that no blood transfusions were necessary today. Mark you are a wonder and God is so good. Keep up the progress. Linda & Hank

GOOD NEWS!! Yeah for Uncle Mark. I'm so happy that he is doing well after surgery today. I pray for continued strength! Love you guys. Erin

I was so happy to read the surgery went well. Just bummed I couldn't make it up with Judie. It really sounds like things might have turned around for Mark. Well, Rachel is finally legal!!!! The big 21…so far she has had a good day. Dinner and then back to the house with friends for dessert…Wish you were here to help her celebrate. Hope to be coming up in a few weeks. KKLL. Leslie

Hope all goes well with surgery and that you don't have to go through this part many more times. Keep up the strength and the updates. We all continue to pray that you all will be home soon!! Go Allografting…Hugs and kisses, Adopto Sissy, Jill

Hey Mark and Paula,
Good Luck to you Mark and your surgery!! Great to hear you are doing so amazing!! Had Inventory this week. Of course Stater Bros. would schedule an Inventory day right before a major holiday!!! I wonder if Mrs. Puff is complaining about the lines in the supermarket as they keep cutting our payroll. I'm sure I'll hear all about it soon!! It is really fun to read all of the letters from your friends and family. I'm sure this brings it all home how wonderful people really are. Looking forward to later today to see how Mark is feeling after surgery. Hope and pray all goes perfect!! Take care and Love ya. Tami

Prayers for Mark on this 'surgery day'!!!
Sending smiles to Paula & Karen too…:0)

Tracy and family

Paula,

As always everyday, and today especially for surgery, you and Mark will be close to my heart and my prayers. Sheri

*Reflection*

*We had been there over a month now. The dark clouds were lifting and Mark was pushing himself harder and harder each day. Ace his PT had already told him how well he was doing and he would most likely be able to skip rehab. This motivated Mark and gave him the extra strength and push he needed.*

*Surgery days were so hard on me. These last ones would determine how many more there would be.*

*We adored and admired Dr. Dominic and the entire staff we came to know. In due time, we knew we were in the right place all the time.*

# God Bless the Visitors

July 3, 2009

Hello. Mark ate all of his breakfast this morning, Belgian waffles, sausage and juice. He actually said, "It tasted good!" He thinks his taste buds are working again. He shaved himself then Judie assisted me and we gave him a sponge bath. Juuust kidding! We only washed his armpits! Judie headed home late morning. Vic and Susie brought Monsignor over and he couldn't get over how alert and full of life Mark looked. Mark has improved so much over the last few weeks. He gave Mark another blessing which means so much to us. Then Susie and I visited with Mark. She assisted me while I wrapped Mark's leg all by myself. Susie thought I did an excellent job. Mark and Katie N arrived and they visited with Mark for a while. MY Mark was telling stories and actually laughing. By 2p.m. Katie, Mark, Vic and Susie were headed back to Ridgecrest. Then by 3p.m. Tracy came for a visit, bearing Starbucks! We love Her! She and Karen and I went for a visit with Mark. He is a regular "Social-Lite" now. I think he really is getting the gift of gab! I stayed with Mark until 7p.m. and headed to Kingsburg early! A Happy Belated 21st Birthday to Rachel! I will help you really celebrate when I get home :). Also a Happy 17th Birthday to my niece, Megan, in Seattle. Tomorrow, my niece Erin, in Kansas is 28, our firecracker in the family! Every family should have one! We hope to get Mark outside tomorrow evening for a fireworks show! KKLL, Paula

Hi Paula and Mark,

We are so pleased to hear that Mark continues to make remarkable progress. Paula, your role in that progress has been inspirational to me and many others. On my drives back from Fresno I was consumed by thoughts of your and Mark's individual and combined strength. The tears we all have shed are simply testament to that strength, such clear indication of the grace of God in our shared lives. We returned from our vacation (can't wait to tell you some good stories) just a bit ago, and the kids are on the floor playing with Polly Pockets who "are seeing bison." Your "peace, love and understanding" comment became "PLU" (courtesy of Greg)—the acronym of our trip! We love you and will miss you tomorrow. Jannerans

Hi, Mark and Paula—

I'm very glad to hear the surgery went well. I heard that with luck this might be the last surgery. That would be great!

I wanted to share that I was talking to someone whose husband works at Coso. She said that you are very highly regarded there, Mark. Kind of like the Rock of Gibraltar for the other employees. It's probably hard to imagine getting back to work, but they sound like they can't wait to have you return.

Paula, I can just visualize the slumber party. I've spent many nights at Pat's place curled up on her couch with a glass of wine or a drink. It was so cozy and nice, and such a treat every time I went to Fresno. I don't know what she left there when she moved, but when I was there it was very nicely furnished.

It is hot, hot, hot here! We were spoiled for a long time with relatively cool weather, but now it's making up for it. Jim did some wiring in the office today and even with the cooler on we were toasty. I've been trying to get everything set up for a handful of new students and the new teachers, but working around everyone's summer schedules is tricky. Can't seem to get everyone in one place at the same time.

We will keep you in our prayers so that you can come back soon. What a relief it will be to be with the kids together in your own home! Mary L.

Well, hello from the Welsh Compound!

Let's see...what in the hell have we been up to?

Chandler had diving class this last week and totally enjoyed himself and his instructors! Learned some new dives :). Mitch will start soccer camp soon and that starts at 7:30 a.m. I hope they don't mind me taking him in my jamas with a mimosa in hand. LOL!

We are trying to encourage Mitch to take the summer drama course as he seems to have a flair for that...but he won't do it!! LOL! He did fix the table all just so this morning and then told Gram that it better look just like that when

264

he gets back…Ha! He has been entertaining us with his baby pics and how sweet he was back then! He had Ann get he and Chan some "Suave for Men" Shampoo…I told them both, the only man I saw in the house was Grandpa. LOL!

Gordy is our new BFF! He picked up the 3 oldest this morning for the weekend festivities out at Don-nah's house! The kids were pretty excited about that. Grace didn't care for the 9am pick up time…she was hoping for noon…she has become a lady of leisure this summer…and the "early" mornings just about kill her. LOL! Maybe she should take drama with Mitch?? HA HA! She knows I love her more than my luggage…especially since the hugs are an upswing. LOL!

I took the boys on Weds to go pick up Aunt Ann at the thriving metropolis Inyokern Airport. As we proceeded to drive down Inyokern Rd., one of our favorite games is to guess what time we will arrive. The boys picked one minute apart from each other and I guessed a little later. I proceeded to slow down the car to about 5 mph, so it would for sure be my time…and their eyes about popped out of their heads…it was hilarious! Please note, that any crazy driving things I do, I do them in Ann's car and not my own :).

Grace has been taking her highness GiGi for a swim…and she loves it :) I keep praying she doesn't let a brown bomb loose in her little swimmers…so far…we are good! She likes to dip her head in the water and kicks her legs alot in her floatie…the backyard is new scenery for her… so to her its like we took her somewhere, but we really didn't. LOL!

Today was the ultimate for GiGi. Miss Tammy was over for a visit and she let GiGi play with her little tape measure. Well then Ann just started measuring different parts of her body and telling her how long her arms were, and such... and she stood there like an angel. So Ann and Tammy measured her bust (19 inches) which is ironically the size of her head...then her waist was 20 and her hips were 22...she is 34 inches tall...the whole time she just smiled and stood still...I am really starting to believe she is going to be high maintenance as hell...she likes being measured...which means tailored clothing. LOL! And we are sorry to announce to you, that since her head was 19 inches around, that does indeed mean she is a "fathead" and not a "pinhead"... your boys are "pinheads" but not her LOL When you and Mark are back, we might have to measure us all again like we did that night at Karen's house. LOL!

Tomorrow morning we are going to breakfast...and then at 5, we have reservations at Chez Weidenkopf...up there on Summit St...we are only responsible for dessert and fireworks... Wahoo!! We are looking forward to that :)

We are so thrilled to hear about Mark's continued healing...I am sure it has to do with my hour of Adoration I took for Karen. I prayed triple hard...and it was so quiet and cool in the chapel, I thought I should bring a cot maybe next time for a little rest time...I know, I know, I am going to hell for that. LOL!

Well the trailer trash has already set up camp in the front yard and there is a chair with my name on it...we just need to lose a few teeth and add some tats...and for sure the neighbors will be filling you in when you get home LOL.

Lots of prayers and love always, Dad, Mom, Ann, Amy, GiGi, and Eb :)

P.S. Ann was walking GiGi down your street and someone asked her if she was the Grandma…HAHAHAAHAHAHAHAHAHAAHAHAHA-HAHAHAHAHA!!! I loved that!!! Is that hysterical or what?? Go Granny Annie Go!!

Paula:

It sounds like God continues to watch over Mark—especially through the difficult bandage changes and surgeries. Each week as I read your journal, you mention some part of Mark's recovery that is improving or becoming less difficult for him. How is his pain level through all that? I'm so impressed with all the walking he's doing—it can only be helpful to his recovery. Hope getting him home isn't too far off. Julie

Paula,

I'm glad to hear Mark is doing so well! I've been a visitor in hospitals in the past with family members, and I know it isn't easy or fun. Your strength continues to shine through the overcast skies. Your positive attitude and your joking and laughing are by far the best remedies. I know that Mark is definitely proud of the job that you're doing by keeping everyone informed, I know that all of us on the outside are glad to have this websites, it takes all rumors out of play. Give Mark our best, and to the both of you, we're praying for God's hand in a swift and full recovery. I know circumstances are not the greatest, but, I wish both of you and your children and happy 4th. Will

Wow! That is really something for Mark to walk so bravely to surgery. It's cool how you are being so nice to the nurses and staff. Working in the burn trauma unit has got to be a difficult job. Wild and crazy slumber party huh? These times and stories will not be forgotten. I'm going on a road trip to Lyle, Wash with my friend Nancy. I'm excited and nervous. Well, Paula, keep on with your positive attitude and keep the staff laughing and Mark too. Laughter is the best medicine. LOL! Elaine

*Reflection*

*To find out I was inspiring others and lifting spirits with my sense of humor and sarcastic nature just egged me on. I was serious when I needed to be. Believe me, there were several of those days. I loved reading all the entries, especially my sister Amy's depiction of what was going on at the Welsh compound. I am eternally grateful to her, my sister Ann and parents for taking care of my children, especially when I needed them most. I missed my kids but did not worry about them. What a relief that was being so far away from them. I couldn't do anything anyways. My children have those memories and my journaling as a part of their history.*

*God was working in mysterious ways, one day at a time. The Holy Spirit sent more visitors North to Fresno!*

God and Satan are locked in a cosmic battle for loyalty and allegiance and often we are the battleground.
　　　—Dave Earley, *21 Reasons Bad Things Happen to Good People*

# Celebrating the 4th of July

July 4, 2009

Hope you all had a Happy and Safe 4th of July. Karen and I took Mark to the patio for lunch. There was a nice breeze and no one was around! While we were eating, Tracy and Jared surprised Mark with balloons and 4th of July goodies. We took some more pictures and I will post them tomorrow. Mark went back to his room and took a nap after his outing. Karen and I took turns taking a nap on my couch in my office (3rd floor lobby). We are starting to blend in around here. We really need to get out of here! We visited Mark late in the afternoon and he had been doing laps all on his own, so he was pooped. He did, however, perk up when his dinner arrived. He remembered he had ordered Tri-tip. Karen and I went and had a lovely dinner at Cheesecake Factory, the Bellinis (sp?) were scrumptious! We got back in time to take Mark outside for the fireworks. It was hard to see them from outside so we went to the 4th floor. We will never forget our 4th of 2009! My sis Ann and bro-in-law Mike share a birthday tomorrow, so Happy Birthday from Fresno! KKLL, Paula

Wow…I just can't tell you happy I am to hear how good Mark is doing!! Yeah!! wow… Mark a gabber…i think i'm gonna have to test that out next time i see the man. lol! I hope you get to get him out to see a nice fireworks show. That would be very cool. I can't beleive how many July babies there are in the fam! I just read Amy's news and was dying laughing. Your kids are too much! They are soo funny!!

Well let's see here…plenty is going on around our house and life. Justin is leaving the GSU. Just found that out yesterday. Budget cuts. Pray he gets put somewhere close and has a good schedule with good days off. With the way things are going for California…we are just very grateful he still has a job. He got tonight off… thankfully…because they are not wanting to pay holiday pay. No complaints here!! LOL! We are having a fun block party tonight with all our wonderful neighbors! Mobile margarita machine Paula…swing on by!!! :) Life is just flying by! I love reading your updates and it just really brings me such joy everytime I hear how good Mark is doing. Miss you and love you so much! Have a wonderful 4th!! I'm praying for super fast healing so you can be in the comfort of your home and with your kiddos again! With much love~ Justin & LaRay

Paula and Mark,

Happy 4th of July! I'm sure this isn't the holiday you expected, but what great news that Mark is doing so well! I will be sure to spread the news to mom and dad…every time I hear from them I let them know the updates! Keep eating! You sound like you're doing fabulous. I have more friends praying for you, so maybe you'll get home very soon! Love, Lisa and James

Mark and family, Happy 4th! That is great news that your spirits are up and we hope you come home soon. From the Salmonds family.

Paula and Mark,

Happy 4th of July. I pray that all goes well for Mark and you today and you get to see the fireworks. That's awesome that you both are so blessed and have so many visitors to look forward to each day. Still thinking and praying for you and Mark's recovery in Lawton. Sheri

*Reflection*

*We did have a good 4th. Mark, Karen and I will never forget. He was able to be out of his room and enjoy the fireworks and again change the subject.*

*Mark was becoming more and more independent so Independence Day took on a whole new*

*meaning for us. He was taking control and accomplishing all the goals the doctors' and physical therapists had set for him.*

# Renewed Energy and Independence

July 5, 2009

Hello. Mark had already taken some laps this morning before Karen and I arrived. He seemed energetic, so he shaved himself. Then he got in a chair and I washed his hair. I know it is hard to believe but his hair is getting long! His lunch came in and he stayed sitting up while he ate it. After lunch he was pretty tired and wanted to nap. Karen and I went to Tracy's to sit poolside for a few hours, it was delightful! We went back to Mark's room around dinnertime and watched his new favorite show on Sundays, "Ice Truckers". I just keep telling myself "in sickness and in health" I hope he does not get any bright ideas and want to move to Alaska!?! Tomorrow Mark will have a dressing change. We are anxious to see how the skin grafts and burns are healing. His stomach and back are looking great, especially where they took the skin grafts 10 days ago! I am grateful for all of you out there praying for Mark and myself. KKLL, Paula

Paula & Mark.

Glad to hear u all were able to be outside so much. We missed all three of you at our annual 4 of July at Troy and Donna's. At least your kids were there and we were all with you in spirit. The food was great as always and Hope and I tried a new cocktail...I have to admit it was a little quiet without you and Karen!!!!!!

It sure sounds like Mark is very close to the end of his stay in Fresno. That would be so great to be home soon. For both of of you. I am still trying to take Grace to lunch. We might just end up at Starbucks if lunch doesn't work out.

I know Rachel will be happy to celebrate with you!!! She had a wild time with her friends. They made sure she did and took very good care of her. It was a little hard seeing her brushing her teeth at 2 a.m.. Kelsey came up also and she spent the night. Then celebrated Mike's birthday on Friday. Happy birthday to Mike and to your sissy Ann and to Erin also. Talk to you soon. KKLL. Leslie


Hi Paula and Mark

Glad you had a good 4th—pretty quiet here. Sounds like Mark is getting back on his feet. That is good. I bet the folks at the hospital look forward to having their lounge back when you are able to return to R/C. All the Hannons send their best. Love, Margie

Can Karen forward the journals to the choir members for a few weeks?


Dear MARK & Paula, Hello from a little bar in Grayland. They have free wi fi, so Janet and mom and I are having lunch and checking our emails and reading your journal to mom. She loved it and said you are a great writer. No I am not drinking. My one day sabbatical is over. I need to think and pray for you, Mark. It sounds like you are in a hurry to get out of there. YOU GO MARK! All the best. Love and prayers, Claire B

Mark and Paula,

Good day to you and your hospital staff (Paula you do have janitorial service in your office right?).

Glad to hear things are moving at the speed of light (well at least faster and more efficient than before). Happy Birthday month to all the great July babies. Keep Smiling—Peace-Love-Cheers—Rose and Gang

*Reflection*

*Mark was becoming more independent each day. It's funny as I have been writing this book. I have followed my ups and downs along the way and little did I know at July 5th we only had 5 more days to go. Reading about it gets me excited all over again.*

Moments play a powerful role in teaching
us how to make and celebrate progress.
—Matthew Kelly, *Perfectly Yourself*

# Endless Miracles and Homeward Bound

July 6, 2009

Hi. It took forever for Mark to get his dressing change today. But good things come to those who wait! no more surgeries! We are so excited. I put my big girl panties on today and I was in on the dressing change. I was anxious when it began but by the end I was helping and I know now I can do this when we leave. Of course I will need help from my nurse friends back at home. Mark will have a dressing change on Wednesday and Friday. And most likely Friday afternoon he will get a shower here and then he should be discharged and we will stay that night in Kingsburg. I cannot believe how his body has healed, just from last Wed. The Lourdes water does amazing healing. I am seeing the daily miracles from St. Bernadette. Also, Occupational Therapy came in and showed Mark how to put on his socks and pants. He gets to use a grabber, so he was excited to have a tool! Ace also took Mark to the stairs and Mark climbed 15 stairs and then back down! He said it caused him no pain. He is excited about getting out of here. I am a little anxious—this hospital is my comfort zone.

**They take such good care of him. God Bless you all! KKLL, Paula**
**July 7, 2009**
**Good afternoon, I forgot 2 important things. First, Monsignor came for a visit yesterday and we shared a few laughs. The second thing is that my niece turns 22 today. Happy Birthday Lauren! KKLL, Paula**

Uncle Mark and Aunt Paula,
YEAH!! God is good. I'm so glad you are going home soon. I'm so glad that UNCLE Mark is headed home soon. I'm sure it will bring challenges but those kiddos are missin' ya! Mark keep up your courageous fight! You are amazing. Love you both! Erin

HALLELUJAH!!! I am so happy to read your latest journal entry! Claire

We spent the last two days with family. First, up at Vince and Cindi's for 4th of July—AWESOME DINNER!!! We had the best seat in Ridgecrest for the legal show and all the illegal ones—so thank you Ridgecrest! Genevieve loved the special fireworks that Ann and Doug put on afterwards. She sat on Uncle Vince's lap and every time there was noise and fire and lights she would make this sound "ga ga ga ga ga" and laugh her head off and clap her hands. Vince was loving it because I believe he thinks he has a kindred pyro.
Then yesterday we had a BBQ and all the family was here to celebrate Ann and Mike's birthday. Mike did three Tri-Tips on the rotties-serie and it was divine. Genevieve swam even with all her cousins bombing the pool until there

were waves going over her head—she started making that same sound "ga ga ga ga ga" and it never phased her—though Grandma got up and moved away. I think I could get her swimming by the end of the summer—she just loves the water. She and Mike played with the toys and she would go under and get them off of the baja step.

We are all relieved by Mark's continuing upturn and his healing—we prayed both days for his ability to come home soon—the kids are all missing you! We love you, Ruth, Mike and family

Dear Mark and Paula,

We continue to think about you and pray for you each day in addition to reading all of the good news in your entries, Paula. Wonderful that your friends and family can be with you so often. Ridgecrest misses you both. Best wishes with each day and the activities and procedures. Love, Ruth and Larry

Paula and Mark,

I hope that today's dressing change brings good news. As everyday, I will keep Mark, you and your family in my thoughts and prayers. The faith, love, support and patience in California seems overflowing. I hope that you can get home soon. Sheri

Hi Mark and Paula,

Just wanted to let you know you are in our prayers everyday. God is wonderful! He is taking real good care of you. I love the pictures you posted. You all look wonderful especially you Mark! How did Paula get so lucky and blessed to find you. Keep the smiles coming :-)

Can't wait to come visit all of you at home! We love you. Tonia, Robert, Rashel, Andrew, Emily and Anthony

Paula and Mark,

The words we have all been waiting for… home…Thank you God!!! The words sure leapt off the page and I had to read your entry twice. Congratulations!!! Love, Russ, Hope and Katy

P.S. The textures are moving around Ridgecrest, Paula.

Yahoo!!! What wonderful news! Chandler was over here playing with Chris and he was excited to hear what your news would be! I'm so very happy for you. Vic's in adoration, I gotta call him and tell him the good news! Just told him. He and Theresa, his prayer pal, will remember you all tonight again. Love ya, Missy

YEAH!!!!! So glad to hear Mark is surgery free!!! What a blessing. Home is in sight!!! I am thrilled for you all!!! Katie H.

Paula and Mark,

We are all elated in Lawton that Mark gets to go home. What fantastic news for the both of you! When you called me that Saturday morning some five weeks ago—I thought my heart would be broken forever for what Mark and you would have to face. God has proven to me through both of your experiences how incredible He is even when times are difficult. I really will never know what you both had to go through because it didn't happen to me, but you made it seem manageable and you did it with faith. I am grateful that you felt blessed throughout the whole process. It helped me to feel reassured that Mark would recover himself again and your family could go on. I will continue to pray for his continued progress at home. Mark is a hero by his own right and so are you. With Love, Sheri

Hi Paula,

I love to get your updates, especially since the news just gets better each time I read it. Congrats on Mark's amazing progress (yours too, being in on the dressing change!), and how exciting that you both will be home soon. You're both in our family's daily prayers. XOXO! Gina and family

Oh my gosh…I am so excited for you both. That is amazing!!!! God is truly gooood. Paula you will be fine. You put it into gear and go. Plus you will have all of us here to do what ever we can to make it easy. I'm sure Mark will thrive even more when he is home.

Can't wait to see you both. KKLL. Leslie

Mark and Paula,

What wonderful news. No more surgeries and possibly going home on Friday. We are so happy for both of you and for your children. Love & hugs, Hank & Linda

Mark and Paula,

We are so happy to hear that you will probably be going home to your children very soon! You must be so excited!!! Hope the rest of this week goes by quickly. What a wonderful homecoming you will have with your family there offering love and support.

Marcia and Bill

Paula and Mark...Great news!! We'll be welcoming you back to Ridgecrest very soon it seems!!! We continue to keep you in our prayers. Sally and Gary

:0) Happy Face Time!

Prayers that the next couple of dressing changes go as well as planned & that Mark can continue taking on each new task towards independence & strength! Tracy

Mark and Paula,

We were so happy to read your journal entry today. We hope the rest of the week goes well and you will soon be on your way home.

Kim, Chuck, and Kate left our place just a few minutes ago. They are going to Uncle Mike's for the night and will then head home. It is sure quiet here! We'll be thinking about you this week (just like every other week!). Love, Pat and Joe

Good Morning Mark and Paula,

What wonderful news! We will continue to pray for an easy and smooth transition for all of you. Looking forward to your homecoming. Love and Miss you. Ann and Jerry (Doug)

Woo Hoo, great news!! wow he gets to go home now...That is so exciting and I am excited for all of you. Keep up the great healing and support and you will be all better in no time!

Awesome News Paula, and you will have plenty of help at home to help change his dressings and keep Mark well.

We continue in prayer for your whole family and that You will find it within yourselves to use this tragedy to help others in the same situation. God has a plan for all of us and I beleive Mark has been chosen.

Love to you all, Thanks for the great updates and news...Jill

It's great to hear Mark might be coming home this weekend. Paula you said there would be new pictures...The last ones showed us so much improvement I can hardly wait. Anyway good to hear the good news see you soon.

Lynn

Mark and Paula,

Thought a little humor might brighten your day...

With all the sadness going on in the world at the moment, it is worth reflecting on the death of a very important person, which went unnoticed. Larry LaPrise, the man who wrote "The Hokey Pokey", dies peacefully at the age of 93. The most traumatic part for his family was getting him into the coffin. They put his left leg in. And thats when the trouble started... We're still praying you here in Virginia! Pete and Loren

Wow!!! He looks fabulous! Susie

Paula, Mark and family,

What a blessing for Mark to be healing so wonderfully and to be surrounded by the loving support of your family and friends! You have been and continue to be in our prayers, and we can't wait to have you home!

Mom and Dad send their thoughts and prayers as well. Love you all! Antonette

Hi Paula and Mark,

It was great to be able to see you a bit on Monday. (Sorry, Mark, I will visit with you down the line in R/C. I wanted you to save your strength after having a few laughs with Monsignor)! I hope on my next visit to Fresno, you will NOT be there. We made a hospital tour that day and visited someone else over at St. Agnes Hospital.

Everyone is ready to have you end the "Hospital Chapter" and move on to the "Kingsburg Chapter"…you will handle each new chapter with the strength, dignity and faith that you have shared with all of us these many, long weeks. God bless you and your family and friends. Chris

AWESOME NEWS…I am soooo happy to hear how well Mark is doing. Best wishes on a sane trip home and easy transition! You keep the same spirit you've had all along and you will do fine! Though you will be leaving the hospital's hands…you will be at home, where I am sure a support system awaits you!!! BIG HUGS from the LEGLERS!

Sandy

Oh my gosh—we were so happy to see you get to go home Friday, Mark! That's so great. We were hoping it would be soon, of course, but hadn't heard any estimates as to when. No surgeries is fantastic, too. You had way too many already. We're so happy for you guys. Wish we were closer to help out when you're home, but will come visit whenever you give us the word. Until then, we'll be thinking about you all the time. I'm even more amazed with your bravery and strength, Mark, after hearing the story of what happened in more detail when Craig got home. It's unreal. Thankfully, the worst is behind you now and you can get home and hang with your family. Love, Wendy, Craig, Otto, and Kaysa

Paula,

It is great to hear about Mark's progress. That is wonderful to hear about his possibility of returning home this week-end. I read the journal to all in the I&E shop, and everyone is excited. Make sure to let Mark know that we're all so proud of him for his courage and his strength. I'll keep praying! Will

*Reflection*

*We were moving onward and upward to the next chapter. I remember feeling excited and scared at the same time. I was comfortable there, had my routine, knew what to expect. I had formed bonds of friendship with the staff, nurses and doctors.*

# Farewell to the Angels
# Disguised in Scrubs

July 8, 2009

Good Evening. I will catch you all up on the last two days. On Tuesday, Mark was able to have lunch on the patio with Karen and I. It was his idea! The OT worked with Mark again. He is now working with exercise bands to increase his strength. He is pretty weak from laying in bed for almost 6 weeks. Right after OT, Ace, his PT came and gave him a work out on the stairs. Mark is learning how to balance again so he did a lot of walking while closing his eyes. Today he was sitting up in the chair when we arrived. He looks so much more like himself when he is out of bed. His dressing change went well today and Doctor Dominic still believes Mark will be discharged Friday! He will have a shower and then a dressing change and then we are out of there! HAHA. I know it is never that easy. There is a lot of paperwork and acts of God that need to take place before we can leave the hospital. The whole staff knows we are planning on leaving on Friday so they have been cheering us on all week. We will miss them but are almost relieved it will not be our final goodbye since

**we will come back to them for check-ups. Love to you all, Paula**

Hooray, hooray! Mark's on his way! Working out with bands?? What is next? Pilates class? It's amazing to me how the therapists know to keep pushing from one level to the next. I love that Mark suggested that you do lunch out on your patio today…I have this image of you & him & Karen drinking tea & eating cucumber sandwiches under an umbrella! Good stuff, until somebody lights up a cigarette at the next table!

I'm sorry that we won't be in Ridgecrest for your grand homecoming—but we will certainly be there in spirit. Hang in there! Love, Katie N

We are so excited for you and Mark! Yeah! I shared your journals with Mom and Dad today and they said to send you their best wishes. I love the pictures too!

Have a safe trip home! Love, Lisa and James

Dear Ones,

I'm so happy to hear Mark's discharge will be very soon! The new pictures taken on the 4th are fabulous! If you ever feel discouragement, please take a moment to look at the pictures taken the weekend after Father's Day and those on the 4th. Mark's miraculous improvement is really visible! Blessings, Claire G

Paula and Mark,

We are still praying for Friday release. We are just so happy with the progress Mark has made. Even the stairs. That is fantastic. Love to you both, Linda & Hank

Paula and Mark

I am so excited for you both—FRIDAY!!!! Yippee!!! Home never sounded so good. We will pray all goes well in the next two day. We are thrilled for you both and Mark great job on all your hard work!! XOXO Katie H.

*Reflection*

*By this day he had improved so much he was getting back to his normal self and was anxious to get out of there and go home, so he was pushing himself and did everything the PT was telling him to do. We needed to make the departure on Friday as smooth as possible.*

# Packing

**July 9, 2009**

**Hi! Can you believe the time? I am writing early tonight because Karen and I will be busy packing the condo up and cleaning a few things. Mark is still scheduled for a shower and dressing change tomorrow. The OT gave Mark a thumbs up and so did the PT. Ace showed me all the exercises Mark needs to do. I will train our kids and our house will become Welsh's Rehab! Mark ate outside with us today. I still cannot believe we will leave tomorrow, God willing! Karen and I will go say good-night to Mark now and head to Kingsburg. KKLL, Paula**

Mark and Paula,

What??? Mark coming home???? What amazing news!!!!! I know this has been such a long journey for you both. I cannot believe how fast Mark has healed enough to be able to come home…God is good!!! His healing process will most likely accelerate even more when he gets home…There is nothing like home Toto!!! Please let Jeff and I know if there is anything we can do to help you guys…mow the lawn, cook a meal etc. It would be a blessing to us if we could help. Lisa H

Mark & Paula:

It's been few days since I have checked in, Praise God! We are so happy you are headed home. We will continue to pray for a safe trip home, both of you keep up the great work. We will be sure to say a few extra rosaries for you both. Ridgecrest here you come!!! Love, Denise and family

Hooray!!!!!!! Good to hear your cleared to go home! Keep up the good work and keep this site updated so we can keep up on all the good news you guys will experience. Love, Edie

BIG BIG SMILES TO YOU BOTH, Paula & Mark!!! Tracy

I don't know what date or time will come up (but really it's Thurs at 6:32). I am so happy you both get to come home—together—and this weekend ! You have both been so determined to meet this challenge—without losing sight of the goal—no matter what the bumps in the road to recovery have been. I'll bet the sunrise you see tomorrow will be like none you've ever seen before! Thank you both so much for sharing your faith and your personal strength with the rest of us poor saps. Continue with the forward motion and healing process Mark! Molto Bravo! Fantistico! "Like, totally awesome dude!"

Tammy

Yeah!! Praise the Lord! I'm soo happy that Mark can finally go home!! I am soo happy for you guys! Drive safe!! God bless the wonderful

Docs that the Lord provided Mark with!! Hope to see you soon!! Justin & LaRay

Dear Paula and Mark,

I've been under the weather the last few days…but I am so happy to read that you all are going to be going home soon!!!!!!

How exciting and I can't believe it's been only 6 weeks and Mark is doing remarkably well (insane in the membrane)!!! Mark, congrats for all the hard work you have put in to get better… It really is unbelievable. Take care and have a safe trip. Tami

Hi Mark and Paula,

I'm still keeping you in my prayers. I hope it all works out for you and you will get to go home on Friday. Hugs, Jo Elaine

Way to go Mark! God is good isn't He! Bless all those who have helped you get this far on this journey. You are amazing! So is Paula and your friends and family who have been there for you. I have seen faith, hope and charity working in these past 6 weeks and have learned a lot with everyone sharing themselves on CaringBridge. Hope we can keep up with the journal on this site so we can find out how you are doing at home too. Much love to you and all our family. Edie

Such good news and great expectations for tomorrow! Prayers continue with a special one that tonight will be Mark's last night in the hospital. Try to get some rest tonight, Paula; you will be so excited tomorrow. Have a safe trip home to RC on Saturday! Marcia

SO HAPPY TO HEAR YOU ARE SOOOO CLOSE TO GETTING HOME! Great job both of you!!!! Keeping you all in our prayers! Toby

*Reflection*

*We had one day to go and we were so excited to be leaving. Mark was improving throughout the days. We were skipping a rehabilitation center altogether. Mark had exceeded the doctors and PT's expectations. I was so proud of him and God was still letting us know His presence by His endless miracles.*

# So Close to Home

July 10, 2009

Hello. The eagle has landed! We are safe at the condo in Kingsburg. Mark is seeing for the first time where I have been staying for the last 6 weeks. He handled the car ride just fine. We are so happy to be out of the hospital. It was bitter sweet leaving the nurses. Karen went off to Tracy's for the night. I am forever grateful to her and the rest of all my family and friends, I was never alone! We will head home in the morning! Love you all! Paula

Hey! I should've missed reading your daily messages earlier (since the only days I missed have culminated in Mark's release!). That's some of the best news I've had since I don't know when. Welcome home. Hope to see you soon. Hugs & prayers, Mary G.

As we pack to go and meet Mom and Dad, we just wanted to say that we are so happy that you are on your way back home! We will keep praying that the Welsh Rehab Center will continue to make you strong! Have a safe trip home and enjoy your kids! I'm sure they will be so happy to see you...maybe you should video tape the moment so when they are not so happy to see you they can watch it! :-) God bless! Love, Lisa and James

Yeah! I just read the news that you are in Kingsburg! Who would ever think that little ol' Kingsburg would be the cause of bringing such joy and celebration all over this country as people read that "the eagle has landed" there! God bless you both. Thank you both for being such great teachers to the masses who have been reading this. Chris

**WAY TO GO MARK!** YOU ROCK. See you soon. Life is full of surprises. Claire B

Well, here we go from the Welsh Compound...looks like my last time from the Welsh Compound...which is a GREAT thing! Wonder whose compound I can write from next?? LOL!

Let's back up the truck here...4th of July weekend was fabulous! We had an awesome dinner at Vince's house. Filet Mignon and Salmon and Mojitos...I was ready to just stay there and not leave! We had just GiGi with us...so it was weird not to have the other kids doing wacky things to make us laugh! Ann and I bought some fireworks and the Honorable Jerry lit them off for us after the Fairground show. It was the best! Of course, a full tummy and a few mojitos and you could have lit a piece of grass on fire and it would have been an Ohh Ahh moment LOL! Thank you so much to he and Cindi...it was fabulous!

On to Ruth's the next day for Mike/Ann birthday celebration! Gord brought the kids over and I don't know who was missing who most... GiGi or her siblings! The food was awesome and another swim was right up our alley. The best part was when all the kids were cannonballing, bellyflopping and frog diving to get white caps in the pool! LOL! It was hilarious but GiGi just loved it...Ruth was right, Gram had to scoot back about 10 feet...LOL! I have never seen a pool have a white squall before!! HA HA!

We have had many trailer trash evenings... Grace decided to add to it one night and came and sat out in her bikini...she said all she was missing was a beer! Mitch has been in soccer camp all week and has learned some cool moves! Mitch, Chan and I went to Wal Mart and got him a new soccer ball and then of course diapers and wipes for Miss High Maintenance herself :) Chandler noticed Wal Mart has new shopping carts. LOL!

GiGi is learning "please" and "thank you" and her most favorite is "car" and she points to the garage in hopes someone is going somewhere. Usually none of us are going anywhere. LOL! Grandpa has now learned how to get the BackYardigan's on for her Highness and we all know all the songs now. Ne Hai Kai Lo (sp?)is her other favorite but their voices get on Grandma's nerves...they are a little high pitched and may cause need for a double scotch. LOL!

We are all so excited for your homecoming. I won't know how to act not driving around with a carseat in my car...and the kids singing in the background to Gwen Stefani's "Escape"... they learn the words quick and bust out...it's hilarious! Chan serenaded me with Genevieve's song off of her "Genevieve" CD...he imitates the chick pretty good. LOL!

We sent Grace to the market one night to get 2 gallons of milk. She said it was ridiculous to go to the market for just 2 gallons of milk. She wanted to buy something else with it so it wasn't just the milk alone. No one goes to the store to just get milk...but off she went. And lo and behold, the person in line in front of her bought EIGHT gallons of milk! LOL Oh and the neighbor down the street took 4 gallons out of his car the other night too...so she is over that now... PHEW...but she still will not go to the store in spandex...that is where she draws the line!!! LOL (Doug thinks we have all been sitting in the front yard a little TOO much...since we know about the neighbors grocery habits.)

They have been great troopers during all of this...and are so ready to see you both!

Much much love and prayers of safe travel! Dad, Mom, Ann, Amy, Grace, Mitch, Chan, GiGi & Eb!

P.S. Grace put gas in the truck all by herself! Go Big G Go! Oh and I got a for realsies hug last night...TWO arms...from the Big G herself!! Woot!

Yeah! what a relief welcome home. I am probably echoing what everyone else is saying let us know what you need when you get back. Perry & family.

Mark and Paula,

We wish you the Happiest of Homecomings and a safe journey back. You will continue to be in our prayers as you readjust to civilian life and continue your recovery and recuperation at home. If we can help with anything at all we are here. Thanks be to God!! Love to all and God Bless. Eddie and Coleen

Wonder Welshs—way to go! Home Sweet Home. So Happy for you! Rose

Uncel Mark and Aunt Paula,
Have a great homecoming. I will pray for safe and comfortable travels this weekend. I will also continue to pray for your continued progress and strength. Love you both. I'm sure the kids can not wait to see you. Erin

Great News!!!! You all have had such great strength getting to this point. God is good. Thank you for keeping us all updated. Have a safe trip home. Colleen B.

*Reflection*
*So many cheering us on. We had so many prayers and good thoughts lifting us up. I found strength, hope and comfort from everyone's words. I was venting and informing, it kept me sane through that time.*

*I had learned a long time ago at the Los Angeles Religious Education Congress (a four day event held by the Roman Catholic Archidiocese of Los Angeles in Anaheim) while sitting in bereavement class, when someone experiences a tragedy or loss of some kind, the need to tell their story is prevalent. It helps the healing process.*

*The trip did seem to take forever. I remember pulling up to the house, the kids had made welcome banners. It was very emotional to see our children, especially Genevieve. She was not too sure of Mark and his pressure garments—they were sticking out from under his clothes.*

# Home Sweet Blessed Home

July 12, 2009

Good Evening! Wow! We are back to reality! We have taken over the Welsh compound! Actually the children have been great! They were so loved and cared for by my folks and Auntie Amy and Auntie Ann. Although, Genevieve has been a little leery around Mark, we cut his hair today and she is warming up. He has pressure garments on his arms so, I think she just isn't too sure and wonders "what the heck is going on". Our days consist of all of us sitting in the living room, looking at each other, then watching Mark sleep, then Genevieve tells us "SHHH!" We had dinner last night together at our table. Genevieve acts up and shows off, so very entertaining. She tried to be serious at prayer time but she just cannot help herself. We have so much to be thankful for, even though Mark still has some healing to do. He prayed for all the burn victims still in the hospital. He is so grateful he is out. Some will be in for a few more months. We travel to Fresno in the morning for a dressing change. We will travel there once a week until his wounds are healed. I will do dressing changes Wednesdays and Fridays.

**Mark and I welcome visitors, please call first to make sure it is a good time. Some people have offered to do meals. We also welcome those. My sister, Karen will coordinate that for us. We think Tuesdays, Thursday, and Sundays would be good. This Tuesday and Thursday are spoken for. Karen will be out of town until Thursday so, you can get a hold of her starting Friday 8/1. We appreciate all of you! We are blessed! KKLL, Paula, Mark and family**

Bienveidos! Amigos Welsh, Our God is an AWESOME GOD, With Mark's help God is keeping his end of the stick. How wonderful is that. Prayers of thanksgiving are going out. I'll be seeing you soon my friends. amor y besos. Sara

Great to talk with you the other night Mark! You guys should be getting ready for your trip home now. Enjoy your own bed tonight!—Mike

*Reflection*
*We settled right back into our home. All of us spent a lot of time in our living room, and those of you that have been in our home know it is about 2×2 space. (hahaha). The Welshes were making up for a lack of togetherness. We couldn't think of anywhere else we wanted to be.*

# Family Road Trip to Fresno

July 14, 2009

Hello. Our trip to Fresno went well yesterday. The whole family went—lots of togetherness! Mark was done in two hours! Dr. Dominic said he is doing great. Mark's right leg has completely healed except around his ankle. His left leg is still healing where they took his skin, but should be healed by next week. His skin is just raw and peeling now so showers and moisturizer/sunblock will help. He will have dressing changes three times a week so Home Health will come Wednesday and Friday to help me. We will travel to Fresno next Tuesday so his PT can check him out plus he will have a dressing change. Mark has only taken his pain pills twice since we left the hospital, (before we came home in case Genevieve wanted to crawl all over him) and yesterday for his dressing change. That is such a huge MIRACLE that he has no pain. He is sleeping well too! We are so happy to be home! KKLL, Paula

Hi Paula and Mark,

Your note on Tuesday just made me (and everyone else reading this) just smile and smile and pray additional prayers of thanks! It was great to picture all of you together in your car as you went to Fresno...even the guardian angels, especially Mark's, didn't mind being squished! Chris

Well good afternoon! I just finished Karen's Hour of Adoration...and that was just what the Dr. ordered. Lots of prayers of gratitude and healing for so many people.

I can't begin to tell you how surreal it was to sit around your dinner table...this time with you and Mark as well. What a huge blessing that was...and of course the cold beer was just the icing on the cake! LOL! The tri-tip dinner was scrumptious Jim & Susan! Loved it!

It will be hard to leave tomorrow morning...but I will be in touch! My good friend Annette promises me a good time, starting off with a shot of Patron. LOL! After answering 911 together, we know how to chill in the right way! HA! Then on to Jolie's for some girl time! Woot Woot! Loving all of you, Amy

Finally Full Family Fresno Fun! Super Duper you all are troopers. Keep plugging away. We are cheering you all on. Xoxo Rose

Paula and Mark,

So happy that you are healing and adjusting well at home. I am very grateful that you are painfree alot of the time now. We ordered two months of Netflix for you. They are supposed to be notifying you by mail. I had them email the gift to your email address. If there are any problems, please let us know. Sheri

We are so glad to read that you are home and back in the loving arms of your family. We have been praying for you and continue to do so. Thank you so much for taking the time to keep us updated. This website is awesome. Diana, and family

Miracles, Miracles and more miracles. So glad he is not in pain—what a relief. Keep up the family time and healthy healing!!! Love all the good news. Katie H

So glad to hear your day trip to Fresno was full of family togetherness & that the medical business all went smoothly! Our continued prayers for you daily, dear Welsh family. Tracy

Mark and Paula—
WELCOME HOME! Debby and Family

Okay today was a day of complete leisure but I kept feeling like there was something I should be doing...changing poopy diapers, watching Backyardigans...getting lunch for your muffins or dinner...playing Phase 10 with the boys...or SOMETHING. LOL! It is very quiet here at the Taylor Compound!

I am so very glad you are both home...safe and sound :). God is so very good to all of us! I am taking Karen's hour of Adoration for her...I feel like I have alot to pray for and let God know how grateful I am...right? Right!

I hope today went well...thought about all of you...all day. Take good care and much love, Amy

P.S. I might have to sneak over at bedtime…I am missing the boys hugs at night before bed…and GiGi's kisses because she thinks she is going somewhere other than bed…and even Grace's half pat/dead arm hugs. LOL! Ann and Doug aren't kissing me and hugging me before bed so I am having some withdrawals. ha ha ha!!

Great news and we are glad he is back home! Charlie L.

Hi Mark and Paula,

We all are so happy that you made it home to your beautiful children. Enjoy the time with them and also some relaxation as much as possible. Hope your drive to Fresno goes good and we are always thinking and praying for you and your family. God is with you each step of the way. Take Care and We love you! Love, Tonia, Robert and Family

Glad to see that you are all home and safe. Healing will be faster in your own home where Mark is comfortable and can do what he wants. Keep up the great updates and keep us informed on his progress. Get some rest in between craziness and we will continue to pray for all of you. Hugs and Kisses to Aunt Weezer too…Jill

Dear Paula and Mark,

I can only imagine how wonderful it was for you to return to your children and your own home. Prayers continue for Mark's healing and your safe journey back to Fresno for the dressing change. Hopefully, you will both get some much needed rest this week after this trip is completed. Take care of yourselves!—Marcia

So glad to hear you both are home, safe and sound. Praise God for all the miracles you've had and the many more to come. We continually pray for you both. Thank you for all the updates. It is great to hear how you are doing. Jamie in Big Bear

Mark and Paula,

We just returned from two days of camping in the Washington mountains with our daughter and her family. As we left early Friday morning are prayer was that when we returned we would know for sure of your departure from the hospital and there it was when we got home this afternoon. We are so HAPPY for both of you and your family. And now you are in your own home.

We leave for California tomorrow (Monday). You be safe on your drive to Fresno for dressing changes. Love to all, Linda & Hank

*Reflection*

*I missed our children a lot because we were apart for so many days. I had to constantly redirect my focus on Mark's recovery. I knew we would be altogether again; I just didn't know when. It was so wonderful to reconnect emotionally and physically with them. I know Mark's healing started to take on a faster momentum because he felt stronger now that our family was whole again.*

# Life Goes On

July 19, 2009

Good Evening! Mark has made it through three showers and three dressing changes at home! His stomach is healed—just raw, peeling and itchy and his back is almost free of open sores. His upper legs are looking good but those lower legs are still a little bit swollen and have scattered sores. He will now be prone to blisters; anything rubbing like, pressure garments or clothes can cause them. We always have new ones to put Xeroform (a sterile petrolatum gauze dressing) on. He still is PAIN FREE! He walks the cul-de-sac at night and is keeping up on his exercises. I am still wandering aimless around the house at times. The hospital was a very controlled environment for me and I only had to care for myself. I have been home a week and it still feels a little overwhelming and awkward. I am able to leave Mark, but worry about him while I am away. He is fine and tells me not worry. Thanks for the continued prayers. We all need them. We will travel to Fresno on Tuesday and then hopefully we will have a two-week break. We hope to visit some of his nurses so the children will stay here and avoid the long day. KKLL, Paula

**July 22, 2009**

**Good Afternoon! I have been trying to get to this computer all morning. We do not have to go to Fresno for THREE WEEKS! Mark was measured for his pressure garments and when they come in we travel back for a fitting. He will have to wear a shirt and pants. The pants will be worn until the anniversary date of his burn, May 30th. The shirt will most likely be worn less time. These pressure garments will keep Mark's skin flat and hopefully free from scarring. They also helps with all the healing of his nerves and God-willing—avoid chronic pain down the road. Mark is able to do a lot more around the house now so he feels good about being able to contribute especially with poopy diapers! Thanks for all your continuing support, meals, prayers and love. KKLL, Paula**

Paula, Mark, Grace, Mitchell, Chandler, & little Miss G,

We are finally back in civilization…limited cell service, no internet & no phone for the last week or so. The first thing this morning I wanted to check on how everything was going with you guys…tried to send an email but the hotel email wouldn't work so here I am. You've been in our prayers & thoughts even if we couldn't communicate!

We're so glad to hear that you don't have to make the long drive to Fresno for 3 weeks! As nice (in a weird way) as that hospital was, it's great that you don't have to see it for awhile. And we're so thankful that Mark's making such great progress. I'm sure it is quite an adjustment for everyone to be at home again—a good adjustment but still takes some getting used to. Hang in there. The light at the end of the tunnel is getting brighter & brighter every day.

Our vacation has been fun except that I've spent the whole time being sick with bronchitis. Have had to go to the doctors' twice (in two different towns). But it was really nice to spend time with all our family. We're on the road back to Ridgecrest & are hoping that the triple digit heat you've all been suffering through will have eased before we get there! May God continue to bless all of you. Love, Katie N and family

Bravo!!! Everything sounds like it is right on schedule. What a Blessed family you have Mark and Paula. Love and prayers, Edie

Hi, Paula, Mark & Kids!

Mark, welcome home. We're still praying for you (now it's complete healing, no scarring/pain). Paula, if no one gives you an award/medal/prize for your marvellous job during Mark's ordeal, God will hopefully shorten any time you owe in Purgatory. Kids, you were wonderful: keep up the good work.

I should have thought of you while I was being dragged hither and yon (Ron and Anna wanted to go hiking, so we went to Yosemite [Bishop having forest fires: that had been our first destination.]). The scenery was magnificent, but they were in the throes of a heat wave (90's and above daytime). I refuse to tramp for miles where there are no bathrooms (I don't know how many we logged before A. was born; I did my share!) so I got in a lot of reading this trip. It's wonderful to be back in civilization, no matter what our outdoor temperature is!

Hope you all can relax and enjoy the rest of the summer. Hugs & prayers, Mary G.

Hidy Ho from the Boggs Compound!

I am so loving the good news about Mark... three weeks will be a nice break from there. I can understand the awkwardness...and I know it will slowly pass in time..."This too shall pass" has always gotten on my nerves...but it's so true.

Here we are on Operation Cleanout! Three full days of garage cleaning and have a few more to go. We have donated alot to a local hospice thrift shop here and they are glad to get it :). Jace helps us in the garage...nothing like a 4 yr old pulling out his toys that we are trying to stash to give away...you gotta love it!

Jace is in swim lessons this week, so that has been hilarious...he hates it, he loves it...he is going to drown...the water is burning him... he is going to drown...he can't do it...he loves it. LOL! He is too much. His teacher is going straight to heaven...we all bow to Miss Kayla!

Zane is in a great camp that keeps him very busy! They swim and do all kinds of great activities :) He is pooped when he gets home! Jolie loves it...camp, dinner, reads and to bed... wahooo. LOL!

Dana is working graves babysitting all the nice peeps at Folsom Prison...he is entertained watching "The Inmate Channel"...it bothers Jolie that the inmates see more movies than she does. LOL!

I am so loving it here! BUT, I am missing the goings on of your kids...although I do see some of the same drama flair here…your kids and her kids could put on quite a theatrical performance!

Well I should head out…and go see what is the schedule for tonight :) Still keeping all of you in our prayers…and missing you! Take good care of yourselves…Much Love, Amy

Dear Paula and Mark,

So glad to read that you don't have to be back "on the road" for a few weeks. That must be such a relief! Helping out with chores shows Mark's determination to get family life back to normal for all of you. Take time to relax together, too. Prayers continued—Marcia

wow! 3 weeks until your next trip. I didn't think that was going to happen so soon… Fantastic News!

(I'm sure you are a bit sick of 'my town' by now, and happy to be able to settle in for a good chunk of time now)

Jared returned home this week (remember he left back on July 5th) and one of the very 1st things he asked about was Mark & Paula. He couldn't believe you had gone home so long ago & was thrilled to hear about your progress! Thanks for the update!! We'll keep you in our prayers. Tracy

Hi Paula and Mark,

Glad to hear that you are all at home and the Mark is doing so well. We continue to Pray for healing and strength as you are both in for a long haul. Glad that Mark is pain free and getting around the house. It will make him heal

faster now that he is in his own environment…
that is WONDERFUL news!

Keep up the updates and relax when you can. I am sure that the kids are all helping out and making sure that Dad's every need is taken care of. Make sure to take time for yourself, even if its just a bit at a time.

I will make sure and drink some Wine for you…Have a good one! Jill

Hi Paula and Mark,

Patsy and I are reading email at the rec room here at our place in Frisco. We are so happy to hear of your healing Mark and will continue to pray for you.

Paula, I wondered how it would be when you went home. I can't imagine coming back into the "other world" after such an experience. Don't expect too much of yourself!!!!!

I have 2 huge bags of clothes to deliver when we come home in September. Hope they fit at the right season for Genevieve. Hello to all you Weidenkopfs. Love, Pat and Patsy

Hi Paula,

This email is for you. I read that you still feel overwhelmed and awkward, so I am just writing to reassure you that just because you are home, the prayers have NOT decreased from any of the hundreds of people who have emailed since the end of May. So…slowly relax and adjust…just don't go out all night and party! We love you and because of that we pray for you A LOT! Chris

Hello Welsh Family,

Glad to hear that You are all together again and Mark is doing well. I'm sure you are doing a great job Paula. Hope things will feel more comfortable real soon. I've enjoyed reading your journal, especially when I've had a bad day. It keeps me in check that things could be worse. Your family is a real inspiration. Take care, Lorraine

Paula and Mark,

Our continued prayers as you transition from the hospital to home. Your email was a good reminder to me that Mark and you are still facing challenges in his recovery and need prayers. I can't imagine all of what you are facing because I have not been through it myself. But I believe, that both of you will come through these trying times with flying colors and lots of room to spare. I will do what I can do and continue to pray for Mark, you and your family. May the day come very soon when you won't have this to deal with. Sheri

**August 1, 2009**

Good Evening! Wow, time flies! Not necessarily having fun the whole time:) Mark is doing well. He is getting stronger each and every day. Six laps around the cul-de-sac now. He drove the other day and had no problems. Home Health comes Monday-Wednesday-Friday and we enjoy the visits and the help. Mark had a hemoglobin check on Friday and it was 11.8 (normal range for men is 13.5–17.5)! He was a 7.3 when we left three weeks ago. We have been enjoying all the company, the meals, the outings to restaurants and even to a barbecue (where Mark was able to play horse shoes with some friends and co-workers). The kiddos and I have been getting ready for our annual beach trip. Mark will not be going. We will leave in the morning and be back next Sunday. Mark will be alone and is looking forward to it. I am a little anxious to leave him alone but I know the children and I need to get away. Home health will check in on him three days and he will have dinner with my brother one night. And he has enough food in the freezer to feed an army. We are blessed by each and every one of you. So many friends and family still praying for us and thinking of us. It really means the world to my family and me. We would not be able to keep plugging along without all of your love and support! KKLL, Paula

Hi Mark, Paula and Family,

So glad to hear how well Mark is doing. I am still keeping you guys in my prayers.

Amy is here this week visiting, I am so excited about that, it's about time she came to see me. Paula, Happy Birthday! Hope you have a Great Day. Jo

Paula and Mark,

What great news! So glad you will be able to work soon! Also glad to hear your beach trip went well, Paula. That brings back lots of good memories! We're traveling now and just had a chance to check email for the first time— Thanks for keeping up the CaringBridge! Love, Joe and Pat

I am so HAPPY to hear such great news!!! God Bless you guys. Love to you and family, Edie

Hi Paula & Mark~

I was so HAPPY to hear your voice on the message machine on Tuesday! But, so sad that I missed getting to see you. I was in Dr. & Dentist appts. all that afternoon, getting the kids ready for school, and I didn't have my phone on. I hope we can coordinate a visit next time, in 4 weeks.

I am glad to know that Mark has been given the OK to do some light work, that's such a big step in recovery! My continued prayers as each of you return to more normal routines...such blessings are found in everyday life! Tracy

Mark and Paula,

Oh my gosh I can't believe he is already going back to work. I am so proud of you Uncle Mark!! Congratulations on getting back to work and feeling good! It truly is a miracle you have recovered so quickly and so well. We love and miss you, Ben Erin Charlie and Ella

So great to hear you are all doing so well. Mark you have great courage and fortitude that I admire so much. Keep up the great work. Love, Edie

Dear Paula and Mark,
Paula, I'm glad you and the kids will be able to get away from the summer heat for a bit and relax at the beach. Well, with kids along, you might not be able to really relax, but a change of pace will be good for you, too. Enjoy watching those darling kids have fun in the sand and waves!
So glad to hear how well Mark is progressing—what wonderful news! Quiet time, alone at home for a week, might be very relaxing before the kids gear up for school again. Hope to read about more progress for Mark very soon. Prayers continue! Marcia

Paula, you deserve this vacation like no other you've had before. Mark has certainly proved how incredibly stong he is and I imagine he will enjoy the feeling of independence this week. Our continued prayers for you & your family! Tracy

*Reflection*
*I still tear up while reading the guestbook. After all these years I am still moved by peoples' words of comfort, prayer and consolation. I couldn't have gotten through this ordeal without them. I am eternally grateful to all those who prayed, reached out to us, sent well wishes and good thoughts our way. They truly sustained me. Our life did consist*

*of appointments and we were very aware of the cal-
endar and getting through that first year of visits to
Fresno. We knew the pressure garments were a big
stepping stone and we were eager to get Mark wearing them. I remember going to the beach. It was a
much needed vacation, the kids needed normalcy. I
was anxious about Mark being home by himself and
anxious about him going back to work.*

# Back to Work and Back to School

August 13, 2009

Hello. My beach trip was fun and, of course, I had such good company around! Mark survived his bachelor week and even visited work on Friday. He said it felt good to see everyone and their reactions. We traveled to Fresno on Tuesday (11th) and he received his pressure garments. We saw Ace (his PT) and a few other nurses. We miss them in a weird way. He also got released to go back to work, light duty only. He will start on Monday the 17th of September. He is looking forward to getting out of the house. Grace starts Burros on the 18th and the boys start Wednesday. I will be doing a jig around 7:15 a.m. Wednesday after they leave. Genevieve and I will be in charge again real soon! We will travel back to Fresno in four weeks so his scars can be looked at, and also see how he is handling work. If anyone told me in early June he would be able to go to work 79 days after his accident I wouldn't have believed it. Miracles are still happening, thanks to the Good Lord and all of your thoughts and prayers. KKLL, Paula

So happy to hear that things are going well for you. Hope you all have wonderful holidays to come. enjoy each other and God bless…Debbie B.

What a pleasure to see the new pictures (add pictures here)…and thank you for the update too.

Sending our love & continued prayers, throughout this year of healing, to Mark & your whole family, dear Paula. :o) Tracy

Dear Paula, Mark and family. We are so happy to hear such great news. Miracles do happen and God does listen!! Love you all, Bud and Connie

Paula & Mark,

It's great to hear the healing's going so well. We could see Mark must be doing better (he's been sighted at Mass of late). We'll keep you all in our prayers. Don't get negligent & rest on your laurels, though: keep up the exercise and other protocols you've been following (no relapses allowed!!):) Mary G.

Hi Mark and Family,

That is wonderful news. God is Good!! Hugs to everyone. Jo Elaine

So glad to hear things are getting back to normal for the Welsh clan! (Well, as normal as things can be in that house:) Your faith and determination are inspiration for us all and proof that God is good! We miss all of you…sending lots of love! Emily and family

P.S. Paula, how does it feel to be the big 4-0!!!!!!!!!!

Are the garments stretching or is Mark? Anyway, Glad you are all doing well. I will try to get over to see you when I can. Love you. Kirk

Hi Mark, Paula & kiddles—I am so glad to hear your great news—what a miracle—you must all be so very happy. It has taught us all a great lesson—to believe and to live each day to the fullest. Hugs to all of you—you are in our thoughts & prayers every day—Take care & God bless. Much love—Dorothy & Tom

### September 9, 2009

**Good afternoon. Mark, Karen, Genevieve and I went to Fresno yesterday for Mark's check-up. He has no limitations now. The sky is the limit! Some of his burn areas are healing quicker than others. The pressure garments help a lot with this. He actually had to be measured for new ones because the old ones have stretched a bit. We visited with some of the nurses and waved to Ace from afar. He was busy with a patient. We spent the afternoon with Tracy and her kiddos. Genevieve misses Audra already! Mark is back to riding bikes with the boys and he even danced with me at my nephew's wedding at the end of August. Most importantly he was able to help me dye my hair a few weeks ago! So, see, everything is getting back to our "new" normal. He even traveled to Reno for work. That was weird having him gone, but he had no problems leaving us:). We will all go camping in Big Pine this weekend to get away from the heat. Miracles are still happening! God bless you all. Paula**

I'm so excited to hear such fabulously good news!!!! God takes care of us all, Doesn't He! Love, Edie

Dear Paula and Mark,

So glad life is getting back into a normal routine, but I am sure it will never be quite the same. We all learned so much through your ordeal. Mark you were an amazing fighter. Paula was always upbeat and praising the Lord for every improvement along the way. I always love how family and friends come out of the wood-work to help in an emergency. What would we all do with out family and friends—even those we don't get to see very often. The power of prayer was amazing. May we all realize how precious life is and try not to take it for granted. Continue to heal and enjoy the cooler weather camping. Love, Katie H. and family

Paula and Mark,

Thanks for taking the time to send this GREAT report! Have fun in Big Pine. I'll see you in a couple of weeks to make a delivery :). Love, Pat and Joe

*Reflection*

*We were still witnessing miracles along the road to recovery. I have learned through all of this that miracles are a constant if you pay attention to detail. We were grateful for any tiny wound that had healed from a few weeks prior. That meant no infections. We did look at everything as a baby step-type progression because Mark was exceeding the doctors expectations based on other burn patients. Mark was an inspiration to me, most of all, but to so many others too. His goal was to get back to work and get into some kind of routine. He traveled to Reno with his boss and some others and was able to share about his incident. He was going to be okay. I probably felt it the strongest when he started back at work.*

# Thanksgiving Taking on a Whole New Meaning

November 4, 2009

Hello all. Here's the latest…Mark went back to his supervisor position last Tuesday (what he was doing before he got hurt). He is now on his seven days off…doing lots of honey-dos. He did not see that coming, poor guy. A few weeks back Mark took me up to his work and showed me where he got hurt, the hike up to the shower and then we drove to where he waited for the ambulance, which seemed like 30 miles. It was very therapeutic to actually see what I have been trying to visualize all these months. We have been closing all the chapters and the final one would be to meet the Mercy Air Angels that flew him to Fresno. We travel to Fresno December 3rd for a check up. Back on our Oct 19 appointment, we saw Dr. Dominic and he said Mark is still making him look good. May all of you have a blessed Thanksgiving. We are truly thankful for all of our friends, family and many strangers for all their prayers and support. God Bless. Mark, Paula, Grace, Mitchell, Chandler & Genevieve.

Love you & glad to hear all is going well. Need more pictures though! Just love to see you when they are posted. "Worth a Thousand Words". Carol

Your post keeps the rest of our lives in perspective. We all have so many blessings and your family is helping us to remember that! Great news that your family is moving through steps of closure and Great news that your lives are returning to a normal routine. Congrats on ALL the accomplishments you have ALL achieved since May! Tammy

SO HAPPY to hear Mark's positive recovery is still chugging along & amazing his Dr.

I miss having you here, dear Paula! (although I bet you are relieved that the year of therapy, etc. has been able to be done mostly from your home rather than here in Fresno, as was originally predicted).

It has undoubtedly been my honor to pray along side your wonderful family throughout this entire ordeal...please know that I think of you often & am sending wishes for a magical & blessed Holiday Season as you bring 2009 to a close. Love to you & yours, Tracy & family

Just wanted to "check in" on you all. I received your Thanksgiving Card...it brought tears to my eyes and goosebumps at the same time. I am so glad to hear how well you all are doing. You just had a fun girls trip, yes? Anyhow, I have been thinking of your family, so I thought I would post a little "hello" to you all. I hope you had a wonderful Christmas...I know it was for sure a special one...With Love, Toby

*Reflection*
  *We felt thankful, blissful, delighted, glad, happy, joyful, tickled and pleased!*

It is not difficult to live a full and abundant life when your soul is fed by faith.
— Marie Chapian, *Walk with Me Jesus*

# Spring is in the Air

March 24, 2010

Happy Spring! I cannot believe I have not updated this since November. Christmas came and went, and now it is March 24, 2010! Mark's brother Craig, wife Wendy and 2 children, Otto and Kaysa, came in early December from Minneapolis. Aunt Judy and Uncle Duane came in January from Iowa, his folks also traveled from Iowa in February. His sister, Sheri and husband John and daughter Jessica were here last week all the way from Oklahoma. We have been feeling the Welsh family love! They had not seen Mark since he was in the burn center so we really enjoyed our visits. Mark saw the doctor in December and got approval for a three month checkup. We went at the end of February and he only had to be measured for his pants and booties. His upper body has healed and has little to no scarring. We traveled to Fresno yesterday to pick up his new garments and we do not have to go back until June 15th, YEAH! We are hoping he will not need his leg garments after that appointment since that will be a little more than year from his accident. His booties will most likely stay on longer than a year due to the skin grafts and active scarring. He is still

**pain free and has no limitations, we know this to be another blessing and another miracle! Our children are doing well, the two-year old is running the household. Grace is enjoying being on the swim team and the boys are SPECIAL middle schoolers:) Easter Blessings to ALL! Love, Paula**

We are so glad to hear that everything is still going well for Mark! You are all still in our prayers. Thanks for the update! Love, Lisa and James

All good news! Miss you much! Happy Easter! Love, Emily

Great news paula......can we have lunch? Your mexican friend, Sara

Great News ! (the littlest one is always in charge.) Love and Prayers from Claire G

FANTASTIC NEWS! I love to hear about miracles! What a refreshing read! I am so happy for your family (and I just love that your middle schoolers are "SPECIAL"). Kudos to your entire family for sharing your experience and your strength! Tammy

Paula & Mark~
I am not really surprised to hear that Mark's healing has continued to defy the original prognosis given by the hospital staff. It seems the more they predicted his time & ability to heal, the more determined he was to do it faster & better.
YEAH for the Welsh Family!!!

On another note…I felt SO HAPPY the rest of the entire evening (last night) from getting that surprise visit & warm hugs from you both!

Thank you for taking the time to stop by & see me! Sending Lots of Love, Tracy

Mark and Paula,

We are so happy to hear that you are healing well and life is good in the busy Welsh household! Wishing you all God's blessings today, during this Easter season and continuing on and on! Ruth and Larry

*Reflection*

*The year was speeding by and we were almost to the one-year anniversary of Mark's accident. We could see the weather changing and we could see Mark's wounds changing and healing. The weather was warming up and smelling like Spring and we were still feeling the warmth of love and support from our community.*

# Our Miracles Runneth Over

June 29, 2010

Dear family & friends,

As I sit down at this computer, (of course with a glass of wine) I cannot believe another three months have gone by and I did not journal once. It is almost July 1st and I have to admit I have been procrastinating. I wish I had a few good excuses but I don't. We celebrated Mark's one-year anniversary of his accident (May 30th) with friends. He had to leave early to get to his night shift. I can honestly say I do not get anxious anymore when he is on the night shift, but phone calls before 7 a.m. make my heart jump. Sooo, let me catch you up on the children, Mitchell graduated 8th grade and is excited to be with his sister at the high school in the Fall:) She of course is so happy it will be only for one year. Chandler will be the lone Welsh at St. Ann's as a 7th grader. Genevieve will start pre-school in the fall—two mornings for her to play and learn with friends and two mornings to myself:) We are in the process of potty training her, good times! We will take our annual beach trip on July 10th, lounging on the beach, good food and drink and campfires:) It is hard to believe that it has been more than a year since Mark's injury. He has come so far. We saw Dr. Dominic on June 15th and received the best news—Mark would be pressure garment free! The doctor released him, which means no more doctor visits out of town. Of course we will still travel there to see friends. (Kirsten & Tracy that means you two.) He was amazed how much Mark healed since his March visit. Mark has some scarring but is pain free so he is satisfied with the results. We know his rapid healing is because of the abundance of prayers, visits, love, generosity, support, and more prayers. It still overwhelms Mark to know that people across the United States and beyond were praying for him. OK, I do not want any tears (HEEHEE) when I tell you this will be my last entry because for once I do not know what else to say...except that I love you all, we love you all and may God Bless each and everyone of you. Love the ones you are with, who knows what tomorrow brings!

KKLL, (Kiss, Kiss, Love, Love) Paula, Mark, Grace, Mitchell, Chandler & Genevieve.

**The End**

Dear Welsh Family,

Thanks for sharing the great news. It's been so nice reading your journal. Enjoy your vacation. Lorraine

What great news. May your life be smooth sailing from now on. All the best, Love and Prayers, Claire B and family

Writing in the guest book is a first for me. Better late than never. We are so happy for Mark that he doesn't need his pressure garments anymore. We continue to celebrate his successful recovery and thank God we still have him in our lives today. It has definitely been a year of miracles. Mark and Paula are such good examples of what a strong faith can do for you. Love, Karen, Gordy, Neal and Adam

Dear Paula and Mark,

We're thrilled that this is your last entry and wish you well in the future. Thanks for sharing your experiences in the past year. Have a great time at the beach! Love, Pat and Joe

P.S. Patsy and Susie are with us in Frisco and loved hearing your message at the breakfast table.

This chapter in your life has finally come to an end. It was a tough one but you have all come out stronger in faith and love than ever. Thanks for sharing. Sally

So happy to hear things are great with you guys. I won't stop my prayers though as the body may heal but our emotions and minds don't turn off with this kind of trauma. It affects everyone. I miss knowing that my Uncle Jim isn't here anymore. He was so much like my dad, your uncle Bud. God Bless to your whole family and our extended one also. Love to you guys. Edie

So Happy to hear how well Mark and the rest of the family is doing…God is Good! Hugs to all of you. Jo

Such wonderful news, Paula! Blessings for all of you. Marcia

*Reflection*

    *Miracles continually flowed from Heaven and healed Mark and blessed our family. The Holy Spirit guided me to point them all out for the world to see.*

# Mark's Decision to Share

*Mark's speech*

My name is Mark Welsh. I work for Coso Geothermal Plant in Ridgecrest, California. I'm a shift supervisor there. I started there in July of 1997.

We've been married 21 years pretty soon. We have four kids.

We're here today because of an incident that happened to me on May 30, 2009. I was on night shift. It was a typical day for me as normal. After midnight, control room operators finished up their paperwork and I started entering all the information into the database to generate a report and send it out. Around 4 a.m., I sent it out like I normally would do. From there I went to the gate. We have a gate that we have to enter, being that we are on (a military) base. During the day, there are solar panels that charge the batteries that at night are usually drained, so I went to check that. On my way back, getting ready for turnovers getting close to the end of the night shift, I decided I had a little more time so I went down to 51–16 pad ( an area where wells have been drilled). We were in the process of pigging a brine line that was plugged.

We had to get the sump full so they had water to do what they needed to do. So, like I

said, I had a little bit of time, so I went to check
to see how full the sump was. Of course they had
done a good job and it was. So, on the way I went
by EDP 3 (Emergency Dump Pond). As I turned
the corner, I saw all this water going down the
road. We rented water lines during this time. I
don't know if people know about Rain for Rents
(RFR). They're portable pumps that are diesel
driven that you can have a temporary line and
can take it wherever you want so we had a lot of
them going. Unfortunately, at that time, we had
a line blow out. So, I went to insulate it.

It was just before dawn, it was still dark, so I
pulled my truck up there and shined my light on
the RFR, got out of the truck and went over to the
RFR, ramped it down and shut it off. As I turned
around, I stepped into a hole—it was about four
feet deep and I fell into it. Water filled with hot
brine approximately 150 degrees filled to about
here (Mark pointed to his chest). Immediately I
knew that this was serious. I think I wasn't in a
lot of pain but I think my mind shut off at that
point at that part protecting myself. I knew I had
to get myself out of that hole. So, I tried my first
attempt. I remember the sides collapsing in on
me. I hopped over to the RFR pipe and I used
the pipe to pull myself out. From that point I ran
up to the shower we had up there and at the same
time I was calling the ERT (Emergency Response
Team) members to let them know what was happening and that I needed help.

So, I got myself into the shower, took off
my clothes and all that, and waited for them to
come. Of course then I started thinking about
infections and all these things and kinda entered
my mind and I started thinking I think I should

put my clothes back on, so I started unfortunately putting them back on. The first guy that got to me was Israel—he was one of the new ERT members. He decided, at that point, to take me up to the Navy 2 SWO where we had a little medical room with bandages and stuff like that and a bed so they took me there. Kirk and Tad and other people on the ERT met me there and worked on me while we waited for Olancha Fire Department to show up (approximately thirty miles away.). After they showed up, they took me down the hill to the Helipad at Coso Junction as they worked on me. They had the main guy there working on me on the way down. At the bottom of the hill, they already had a helicopter there waiting for me. They got me into the helicopter and from there I was flown to Fresno Hospital. They determined that I suffered 2nd /3rd degree burns over 73% of my body. I spent 42 days in the hospital. I had five surgeries and finally got back out. Luckily, I am here now.

Thinking about how serious the incident was, it could have been a lot worse. So I am fortunate about that. As I came back to work I got asked to go up to Reno to get trained on a new safety program the company was introducing called Safe Start. During the training we were asked to share an incident and apply one of the four states of mind that lead to it. I remember sitting there pretty much kinda telling them the same incident that I'm sharing with you today. As I was telling the story it really got me thinking about the incident a lot and it got me to place myself in all four categories. 1) Fatigue it was night shift and was at the end of the shift, so it was natural to feel tired. 2) Frustration we were dealing with several RFR and it consumed a lot time keeping them running. At the same time we had a lot of new people on the crew which added to the frustration because they didn't have the experience to deal with the situation. So there was a lot of frustration. 3) Rushing it's not like I physically got out of the truck and ran over to the RFR but I remember a lot of thoughts rushing through my head I got to get a hold of someone I got to stop this water I got to call the people, it's close to turnover, we're not going to get this done, there was actually a lot of thoughts going through my head although I wasn't physically rushing, mentally I was probably rushing through all that. 4) Complacency I believe was the biggest factor that lead to incident. The truth of the matter I was very comfortable in that situation I've seen it plenty of times and I really didn't think about what could happen because I never experienced the situation where a line blowing out causing a hole in the ground that deep. Had I stopped to think about it, you know it would of made sense. A hundred pounds discharge pressure breaking out into ground could easily dig a hole; but, because I never experienced it before I never really thought about it. So I really blame complacency the most. I was just too comfortable in what I was doing and I didn't think about what I was getting myself into and I put myself in the line of fire. And when I think about complacency, it really makes you forget about the hazards that surround you, or makes you numb to them. So I think that's the biggest challenge. You always got to be mindful of the hazards that surround you because simply put had I thought about the hazard there's no way I would have ever fallen into that hole. So you really have to be aware of the state of mind you are in while working, especially complacency.

There's basically two things I really want people to get out of this incident. As I apply "Safe Start" to this incident it is obvious why this incident happened. Like most of you, I never expected something like this would ever happen to me; but, unfortunately, it did. When it came to safety, I wouldn't say I was perfect; but, I also, prior to that, wouldn't say people were afraid to work with me because I was unsafe. You know, I don't think I had a reputation like that, so I think to myself why me? Why didn't it happen to someone who had worst habits than me? The biggest thing I get out of that is it could really happen to any of us. You know you can be, you could do things right 99 times out of 100 and it just takes that one time for you to let down your guard and for your mind to wander. You know I thought about everything else that morning except what I really should've been thinking about. I say it cost, not only myself, but my family a lot of heartache. And had I thought about it, this would have never happened. So that's one thing I really want people to think about; but, the other thing, and more importantly, the actions you take not only affect you, it also affects your loved ones. You know, I made decisions; I ran in there—I wouldn't say I ran, I went in there and I suffered the consequences of my actions. Consequences don't just affect ourselves, it affects the family too. You know I had a lot of people since then come up to me and say, "I couldn't imagine what you went through!" and all that and the thing is, I went through it and so I can

imagine it. The thing I can't imagine is the emotion my family went through hearing what happened to me. You know it happened about 4:45
a.m. I can't remember the exact time, my wife
had to take that phone call. She was in a sound
sleep, had to get that phone call saying you know
your husband just got burned, which at that
time Olancha Fire was saying 80% of my body.
I couldn't imagine taking that kind of phone call
and how upsetting that must have been. It had to
have been very difficult. Because of the decisions
I made, other people were affected by it.

My wife had plans. Actually she was supposed to go to a wedding that weekend. Her
cousin she used to live with, hadn't seen for a
long time, and she had really good plans for that
weekend; she was really looking forward to getting away from the kids. I guess I changed that
for her. I did get her away from the kids. Not the
exact way that she wanted to. I can't imagine hur-
rying around and trying to gain her composure.
I know how the family works, you have to start
making all the phone calls, and having to wake
up everybody and taking those phone calls and
actually having to get those phone calls out until
all the family, including my family who all live a
ways away: Parents who live in Quad Cities, Iowa;
my brother lived in Minneapolis, Minnesota;
and my sister lived in Lawton Oklahoma. So
nobody was near and she had to break that news
to everybody else. But like I say, I couldn't have
imagined that. Then, of course, it was four hours
away, actually, nobody knew where I was going at
the time. It took awhile. I don't know how long it
took, but it took awhile, to figure out where I was
going. So I couldn't imagine going through all

that. The thoughts that were going through my wife's mind, and the kids. Once they found out it was Fresno, that's a four hour drive for them. You know, having to make that drive, and all the thoughts I can imagine were going through their heads, wondering, how I was doing. As I was waiting for the ERT team, I analyzed the condition I was in. I mean I know had I not gotten myself out of that water, you know, it would have been all over. But once I got myself out of that water, and I started analyzing myself, I honestly thought, well, this is going to be a long road but I'm going to be okay. And I really believed that. But obviously she had different thoughts.

She had run that through her head. As you go through four hours of driving, getting there and having to wait for me to get out of surgery, the anticipation, you know wondering what's going on, how is he doing, is he going to survive. I couldn't imagine those things, just because of choices I made. She didn't make these choices, but I did. Also, like I said, I thought I was going to be all right, and I would have a long road, but I thought I would be okay. But she had to hear from the doctor that I had sustained life threatening injuries. I couldn't imagine hearing that from somebody but she had to go through that because of the decisions I made.

That's the tough things I have a hard time dealing with, or used to. I don't know, it's not as much any more but like I said I went through five surgeries. You know, she had to endure all those surgeries, wondering like I say, nothing is routine in a surgery. So for me, a different perspective for one surgery I had, I was having a bad day. I wanted out of the hospital and I had a surgery and the only thing I could think about is, hey, they're going to knock me out for eight hours. I'm not going to have a clue on what just happened. And I was really looking forward to it. I really needed that. But like I say, my wife didn't have that luxury, she had to sit there the whole time in the waiting room wondering what was going on. I didn't have to deal with any of that stuff. So I truly believe that my wife had it worse than I did.

I took the pain, the physical part of it but I think the emotional part that I caused, is worse. I truly believe that. And she also had to spend 42 days in the hospital just like I did and that was tough. I couldn't imagine being in that hospital, being in that situation, and worrying and watching everything. I would joke about being on good drugs but the truth of the matter is I was on good drugs. Which made it easier for me to cope with the situation. My wife didn't have that same luxury. They managed my pain well, luckily. So those are the two things I really want people to get out, like I say, this really could have happened regardless of how good you are safety wise—it only takes one time to let your guard down. And then secondly, these things just don't affect you. They affect everybody else including like the company. Like it didn't just affect my wife. You know my kids went through it, they really never talked much about it. I do remember Paula's parents had to come down during that time and watch our kids and her sisters were there too. And they used to complain on how they had several moms. I can just imagine. They complained about that too. But I'm sure they went through a lot of wondering and what was going on. Luckily, they were able to come see me a couple of times except for our youngest one, we thought she was too young but wondering how I was doing in that hospital and having to see me all bandaged up like that I can imagine that had to have been tough.

It also affected other people, well, not just my immediate family. Paula's sister, Karen, she was up there, she must have been there half the time. She just had a son, her oldest son graduated from high school that summer and he was going off to Chico college and I'm sure she would rather have spent more time with him that summer but she spent at least I would say 20 days up there in Fresno. I'm grateful she did that but it had to have been difficult for her. Paula's parents, who travel a lot, got stuck watching our kids for 42 days and that affected them. Her mom doesn't like the heat. She moved up to Big Bear (in the mountains) to get out of the heat. I got her back into the heat during that summer, so they suffered there too.

And I'd like to end on a positive note. Fortunately, I recovered from it and I would say I'm the same now as I was before this accident. So, I'm grateful for that. When I think about it, those are the kinds of painful things to think about. But actually, when I really think about it there's a lot more positive things that came out of it. Obviously, I would never wish this accident to ever happen, but it did. I really got a lot of more positive things out of it than negative things. And the reason why I can say that is I saw the best in people. Everybody was there supporting my family. Those are the things I think about. And everybody was amazing, the company was amazing, my friends, her family, we had so much support it was unbelievable. Those are the things I think about, not always the bad stuff. So many people gave so much to us, with gift cards and stuff like that you never can repay that kind of stuff. So some of the things we have done since the past it has changed and now every Christmas we try to do something for somebody else because of it. First couple of years, we sponsored a family and bought presents for the kids who couldn't afford it. One year we bought uniforms for kids at the school. One Christmas, this last Christmas, we ended up giving to Hurricane Sandy. A lot of that came because so many people were there for us that we felt we had to. I don't know if everybody saw that movie *Pay It Forward*, it does affect you. So I will end with that.

## *Paula's Speech Continued*

I read a book prior to Mark's injury called *Love, Greg and Lauren*. It's a true story about Lauren Manning. She had been burned by a blast of jet fuel at the World Trade Center on September 11, 2001. She was burned over 82.5% of her body, mostly third degree burns. She lay in a coma for months. Reading about the baths of debriding she would endure would bring me to tears. So you can imagine, while sitting in the car for four hours on my way up there, I started to fret and worry about what Mark would have to go through. That was one of my first questions I asked the nurse when I got her on the phone. She said they don't do that anymore, so I was already feeling a relief by the time I reached Bakersfield.

Okay, he didn't have to go through this debriding, and the scraping. It is no coincidence that I read that book prior to Mark's accident. I compared a lot of what Mark went through to her story and hers was way, way worse. But, I was still bothered by the fact that he was flown four hours away and why was he going so far away? You can have a million thoughts in your head, when something like this happens. What would I do with my four children? (I knew I would not leave Mark's side for this.) Where would I stay? Well, by Saturday night my parents, who lived in Big Bear, moved in with my four children. Mark only saw our three older children twice during this ordeal. He never saw Genevieve, our youngest, until we got home. We decided it would be too hard for him to see her and say good-bye (she was only one and a half at the time).

Within three days, a former boss of mine at Saint Ann's sent me the keys to her condo in Kingsburg which is about 20 minutes away from Fresno. It's a quaint little town where I lived until Mark got released from the hospital. It would be the haven where I had many slumber parties with friends and family that came and visited Mark. When my girlfriends and I would have to say good-bye to each other we would say "Well this has been fun in a weird way". We had no idea that this world renown physician, Dr. Dominic, happened to be on-call that Saturday and took care of Mark. Another thing too, when the ambulance took Mark down from Coso that the helicopter was onsite, waiting for the ambulance. That never happens. So there were miracles that happened along the way.

The four hour drive did not keep the visitors away. More than 60 people visited us. Some more than once. I was never alone. These visits, some shorter than others, distracted me and got my mind off of what was really going on. While the nurses had their shift change, I would go out to dinner with whomever was visiting and I was able to laugh and forget about where I was for a couple of hours. About the sixth night, I started feeling a little guilty about that. I called my friend, who had been checking on me and she explained "Paula that is a gift from God that you can escape for two hours and forget what is going on at the hospital." She put my mind at ease.

Mark's coworkers also played an instrumental part in helping me cope. When April called me that morning, her voice was so calm and reassuring—she was a huge comfort to me. I spoke with her a few times that morning, and, even though I was starting to get freaked out, her voice never waivered. Mark's boss, Chris "sitting over there in the corner wearing a red shirt". He listened to me vent almost on a daily basis. Sometimes I cried, sometimes I laughed. I am eternally grateful for his patience and compassion. He also traveled several times to visit Mark. He drove up there on Sunday, the day after it happened. I received many phone calls from Mark's coworkers and was able to get a different perspective from the fellow employees. Mark was such a dedicated employee. They never doubted that he would fully recover. But I had my doubts.

As a wife, I was so emotional about him. He was the father of our children. I did not see him like they saw him. I think it was the third or fourth night I was talking to one of Mark's coworkers, Tony. I do not remember exactly what he said, but it was something along these lines. "Mark is going to be fine. He's a stubborn son of a bit#%." I was to "Tell him to get better because I'm having to pray for his sorry ass, and I don't pray." Tony's little pep talk, or whatever you want to call it, helped me get a grip. I believed Tony when he said Mark was going to be fine. When my sister, Karen, and I met with the nurse for the first time, she told us that when Mark came out of surgery he would have a breathing tube in. When Karen and I met with the doctor for the first time, he told us he didn't have to put a tube in. He told us Mark's lungs were clear—there was no fluid in them. This perplexed the doctor. But I believe God had His hand in this too. It is a balancing act for the nurses when someone gets burned. They are pumping you full of fluids because your capillaries leak which means you are bleeding. Then they pump you full of Vitamin C concentrate, but then you run the risk of ballooning up. Then the allograft they have stapled on is in jeopardy of tearing.

The wounds were terrible to see, but he never rejected the tissue. Soon his coworkers and friends started listing funny comments about him and his cadaver tissue. Here are a few: "Dead man walking." "Are you comfortable in your own skin or someone else's?" "You need to get some dark skin so you can get a tan." All joking aside though, please think about donating your skin and tissue. It saved my husband's life. You can imagine when you burn yourself just a little bit the first thing you want to do is cover it with something. Well all that donated skin covered all of his burns. It lessened the pain. This was the only doctor doing this treatment at that time. They weren't even using that treatment at the Sherman Oaks Burn Center because I called. I started investigating. Did they do this? Dr. Dominic started it. The nurse that took care of him on his second night when she walked in she was so vivacious and said is that my 73 percent guy? This is unbelievable. She could not believe his swelling was down and his eyes were not bulging. Now I'll tell you something about his eyes bulging. His body had retained so much fluid the morning following his accident, his eyes were bulging out of his eye sockets. It was the grossest thing I had ever seen. He looked like a dead goldfish. Needless to say, I told him close his eyes. I could not stay in there very long. The next morning, I told my siblings that I couldn't handle looking at him. By that afternoon, his eyes were better. It was a miracle, I'm guessing. The nurse agreed it was incredible. She had never seen this kind of progress in the nine years she has worked there.

We were also told by her the physical therapist would start walking him in the morning. That is so unheard of in a 73-percent burn victim. His feeding tube was removed on the fourth day. He did so well in the beginning that 20 days later he was able to go outside. We were told there would be ups and downs. On the 21st day he started bleeding internally and needed several units of blood. I soon realized that the time line was not in our hands but in God's. He endured so many dressing changes and five surgeries. When I said at the beginning that he didn't have any third degree burns, he actually did, only they didn't know it. Apparently, the skin can keep on burning for several days afterward. A week later, we found out that from his knees to his ankles he did have third degree burns. He endured a lot of skin grafts down there. They were able to take skin from other parts of his body that had healed within the first three weeks.

After a few days, Mark and I also realized that there were worse patients than him. Someday, he would walk out of there. Some of the others would not be so lucky. Mark could have died that day and I do not take that for granted. He went to hell and back to recover, but this experience is not one that I will look back on and feel angry or mad. How could I? He was pain -free when we left the hospital after 42 days. He never needed pain medication.

By September (only 3 months later) he was back at work with no physical limitations. We were really blessed. Our kids were back at school and everything was back to normal. But, I have to tell you, I wasn't. I had a little breakdown. I had crying spells in the middle of the night, and a feeling of sheer panic. Then a friend told me I was experiencing Post Traumatic Stress Disorder. When you experience something traumatic in your life, your body kicks into survival mode— adrenaline pumping and you always have your shields up. Real emotions do not surface until your body can relax and you are ready to handle them. I made a few visits to a counselor. I later took the children too because I was worried about them; how they were processing everything and if they were holding back emotions too. Some children are more resilient. Ours were, thank God.

We had a family visit with the therapist. She asked how they were doing. They said they were doing great. The counselor said they may never feel raw emotions about their dad's accident until they were married and had children of their own. It was simple for them. They were just glad their dad was back at home. So some might say all these miracles are just coincidences; but I believe Mark, surviving the 73 percent burn; walking out of the hospital in 42 days; working back at his job at Coso in 80 days, with no physical limitations, are not coincidences.

God heard our prayers from around the world and by His grace Mark was healed. Since his accident, I've read a few books on people surviving tragedies. I have searched to find the meaning and purpose to our story and there is one little line in particular that makes sense to me, "Out of messes, come miracles."

When Mark and I gave our speech in Las Vegas, I was amazed at the response from everyone in the room. I thought I would talk and, if they received it well, I would get a round of applause. I had no idea that grown men would be touched so deeply that they wanted to share their personal stories. They shared the parts of our speeches that moved them. Someone told me I should be a motivational speaker. What a huge compliment. They were all so warm and kind. One gentleman told me it was our job as children of God to share stories of miracles and faith. Another one told me about how when his friend was knocked unconscious from falling from a horse, he had to call his wife and how that was the hardest phone call he had to make—he had to stay calm. A few of the men told us that they thought we had a strong marriage. Sometimes when tragedy strikes, it is hard to keep the family intact.

We appreciated that because we don't always view our marriage as strong. We have our problems and struggles like most couples. But I will tell you, I felt closest to Mark when we were in Las Vegas and, of course, when he was in the hospital.

We moved people and got them thinking about safety. An incident at work can not only turn the injured individual's life upside down, it will definitely have an effect on coworkers, family members, friends, and those that surround them.

> *Reflection*
> *Sharing my feelings came somewhat easy for me. Unfortunately, it has never been easy for Mark. I think men, in general, struggle with expressing their thoughts and feelings. Mark was able to muster up even more courage to tell his side of the story. I know God lent His hand and brought him to that Las Vegas conference room.*

We have such a short time on earth we should seek to live our fleeting days with meaning, peace, compassion, and contentment.
—Robert J. Wicks, *Streams of Contentment*

# Epilogue

After Mark left the hospital, the love, support, and prayers continued on Caring Bridge. People still read my entries even though they were few and far between. People cheered us on through all the slow improvements and also through the big milestones like no longer needing pressure garments.

I never felt alone because so many of my family's and friends' genuine interest and concern for Mark's recovery never wavered. The prayers never stopped coming and uplifted me throughout that year of recovery. We were shown what faith can do when trials and tribulations come your way. Be ready folks, because NO ONE is immune to these challenges. Rest assured you will be comforted by the fact God is always there and listening.

My life has taken a lot of twists and turns since Mark's accident. Some twists I am very proud of how I handled while other turns took me by surprise, and these I handled with less strength and frankly, some regret. These twists and turns do not define the person I am today but were critical in my journey, and for that, I am humbly grateful. God has never left me alone even though I have chosen to turn away from Him at difficult times. He always forgave me, and His timing of answers, blessings, and miracles have been impeccable.

In 2015, He saved my daughter and me when we were run over by a boat while riding a jet ski. In 2016, He sent me to the ER on my forty-seventh birthday, and within a month, I was diagnosed with a rare cancer at a very early stage. In 2019, He sent me to the ER again, just a few weeks' shy of my fiftieth birthday where the doctors found some congenital heart defects. I am awaiting open heart surgery as I write this.

I know I am a child of God and He continues to bless me.

CPSIA information can be obtained
at www.ICGtesting.com
Printed in the USA
LVHW092307030521
686438LV00004B/37